D1561278

CISCO MULTICAST
ROUTING AND SWITCHING

MCGRAW-HILL CISCO TECHNICAL EXPERT TITLES

Fischer   *Configuring Cisco Routers for ISDN*   *0-07-02273-5*
Gai   *Internetworking IPv6 with Cisco Routers*   *0-07-022836-1*
Held and Huntley   *Cisco Security Architectures*   *0-07-134708-9*
Lewis   *Cisco TCP/IP Professional Reference*   *0-07-041140-1*
Parkhurst   *Cisco Router OSPF Design and Implementation*   *0-07-048626-3*
Rossi   *Cisco and IP Addressing*   *0-07-134925-1*
Rossi   *Cisco Catalyst LAN Switching*   *0-07-134982-0*
Sackett   *Cisco Router Handbook*   *0-07-058097-9*
Slattery/Burton   *Advanced IP Routing in Cisco Networks*   *0-07-058144-4*
Van Meter   *Cisco and Fore ATM Internetworking*   *0-07-134842-5*

To order or receive additional information on these or any other McGraw-Hill titles, in the United States please call 1-800-722-4726, or visit us at www.computing.mcgraw-hill.com. In other countries, contact your McGraw-Hill representative.

Cisco Multicast Routing and Switching

William R. Parkhurst, PH.D. CCIE #2969

McGraw-Hill

New York   San Francisco   Washington, D.C.   Auckland   Bogotá
Caracas   Lisbon   London   Madrid   Mexico City   Milan   Montreal
New Delhi   San Juan   Singapore   Sydney   Tokyo   Toronto

Library of Congress Cataloging-in-Publication Data

Parkhurst, William R.
    Cisco multicast routing and switching / William Parkhurst.
        p.   cm.
    ISBN 0-07-134647-3
    1. Multicasting (Computer networks) I. Title.
    TK5105.887.P37 1999
    004.6'6—dc21   99-22718
                                                  CIP

McGraw-Hill

A Division of The McGraw-Hill Companies

1 2 3 4 5 6 7 8 9 0 DOC/DOC 9 0 4 3 2 1 0 9

ISBN: 0–07–134647–3

The sponsoring editor for this book was Steven Elliot, and the production supervisor was Claire Stanley. It was set by D & G Limited, LLC.

Printed and bound by R. R. Donnelly & Sons Company.

McGraw-Hill books are available at special quantity discounts to use as premiums and sales promotions, or for use in corporate training programs. For more information, please write to the Director of Special Sales, McGraw-Hill, 11 West 19th Street, New York, NY 10011. Or contact your local bookstore.

Throughout this book, trademarked names are used. Rather than put a trademark symbol after every occurrence of a trademarked name, we use names in an editorial fashion only, and to the benefit of the trademark owner, with no intention of infringement of the trademark. Where such designations appear in this book, they have been printed with initial caps.

This book is printed on recycled, acid-free paper containing a minimum of 50% recycled de-inked fiber.

CONTENTS

Contents

ACKNOWLEDGMENTS

When a project on the order of writing a technical book begins to absorb all your free time it becomes essential to have helpful friends and an understanding family.

I would like to take the opportunity to thank Dennis Vaggalis, Kevin Hanahan, and Floyd Montgomery of Cisco Systems for allowing me access to their lab facilities in Kansas City and for helping me with the configuration scenarios.

I owe a great debt to my wife Debbie for understanding that the chores would get done tomorrow and for taking the time to carefully proofread the manuscript. I was amazed at how many mistakes I missed and how many she found.

And finally, for being my constant companion during all those many months when I was writing this book, I want to thank Elvis the Rocketdog.

CISCO MULTICAST
ROUTING AND SWITCHING

Introduction to IP Multicasting

Before we begin our exploration of IP multicasting and multicast routing protocols, we will examine the models of communication between two or more hosts in an intranet or over the Internet. Any book bearing resemblance to a networking book should include a review of the OSI layered communication model (see Figure 1-1). The communication protocols that exist at the various levels in the OSI layered model interoperate extremely well because of the adherence to a layered protocol model. The original model was developed by the OSI to provide a logical separation between the various functions of a network. This model allows for the interaction of software modules from different vendors to coexist and operate properly as long as the published standards are followed.

The lowest layer of the OSI model is the physical layer. The physical layer deals with the electrical and mechanical specifications of a particular transport medium and associated interfaces. Physical layer examples are 10 and 100 Mbit ethernet, synchronous and asynchronous serial links, and ATM, to name a few. The physical layer is concerned with getting bits, in an electrical or optical form, from point A to point B. The physical layer does not care about the structure or format of the data that is being transmitted or received; it is only concerned with delivering ones and zeros from the source to the destination.

The next level in the OSI model above the physical layer is the data link layer. This layer is responsibile for creating frames that contain source and destination addresses, adding error detection and possibly correction fields

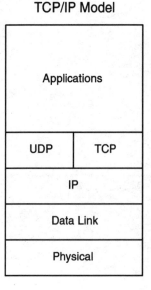

Figure 1-1
TCP/IP and OSI layered network models

TCP/IP Model

Applications	
UDP	TCP
IP	
Data Link	
Physical	

OSI Model

Application
Presentation
Session
Transport
Network
Data Link
Physical

to the frame, and, of course, incorporating a user's data into the frame. Protocols at the data link layer are not routable, and examples of such layers are ethernet and token ring.

The layer where a network designer spends the most time is the network layer. This layer handles routing across the Internet and is the most important layer as far as multicasting is concerned. For a protocol to be routable, the addressing scheme must include a network and a host address. The last statement is true for "normal" IP traffic, but not for multicast traffic. As we will see, multicast addresses are not in the form of network/host but represent a group address. Although a network/host address pair is not present in a multicast address, multicast traffic is routable. Examples of routable protocols are IP, IPX, AppleTalk, and DECNet.

The transport layer is used to multiplex and demultiplex data streams between upper layer application processes as seen in Figure 1-2. The three upper layers of the OSI model, application, presentation, and session, have been combined in the application layer in the TCP/IP layered model. Typically, it is more difficult to determine where a particular upper layer application should be logically placed. Networks can be designed without knowing which applications the users are going to be employing. Therefore, the specific application is not important, just the protocol that the application will be using. In fact, we will only concern ourselves with the lower four layers of the OSI and TCP/IP models.

Figure 1-2
Multiplexing and
demultiplexing in the
TCP/IP model

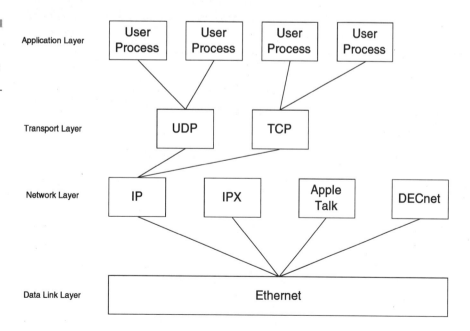

When an application such as telnet wants to send data, the data is sent to the TCP module at the transport layer and TCP then assigns a number to the local and remote telnet session, allowing TCP to determine the session where the data is to be delivered. IP either receives or delivers data to the UDP or TCP module, depending on the type of application.

Finally, an ethernet frame contains an identifier that identifies the network layer protocol it received the data from or the network layer protocol to which it should deliver the data.

To illustrate the interaction between the different layers in the OSI model, we will follow the flow of data from one host to another (see Figure 1-3). Assume we are running a telnet session between two hosts. User data is generated at the application layer and is then passed down the protocol stack to the TCP module in the transport layer. The TCP layer uses an identifier for the session, which is contained in the TCP header, and passes the TCP segment to the IP module at the network layer. IP then tags the packet as a TCP or UDP packet. When the packet is received at the data link layer, an ethernet frame is constructed with an ethernet header and trailer. The header, among other things, contains a field tagging the frame as one that carries the IP data. Finally, the frame is passed to the physical layer for transmission onto the network media.

When the ethernet frame is received by the remote host, the data link ethernet module strips off the ethernet header and trailer after determining that this frame carries IP data and passes the data to the IP module in the network layer. IP determines if the packet is a TCP or UDP packet and passes it to the appropriate module at the transport layer. Finally, TCP extracts the user data and sends it to the proper user process.

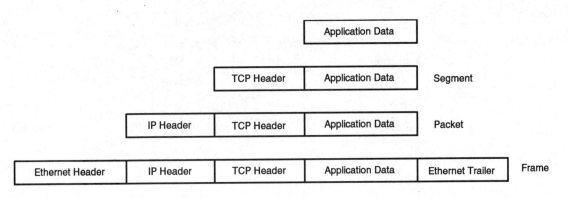

Figure 1-3 Data encapsulation

Unicast IP Communication Model

Three models exist for communication between hosts on a network whether or not the network is an intranet or the Internet. The first model is the unicast model, which is one-to-one communication. In Figures 1-4a through 1-4c, one host desires to send traffic to another specific host on the same IP subnet (IP addressing and subnets are covered in detail in Chapter 2, "Internet Protocol (IP), Unicast, Broadcast and Multicast Addresses"). For the ethernet *Local Area Network* (LAN), the hosts must contend with two different address schemes. The first scheme is the ethernet address that is burned into the *Network Interface Card* (NIC). The ethernet address is a

Figure 1-4a
Resolution of IP to ethernet address mapping

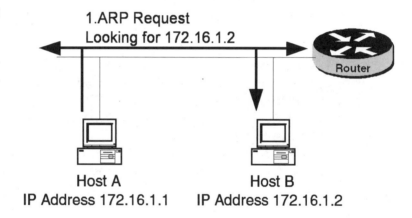

1. ARP Request Looking for 172.16.1.2

Host A
IP Address 172.16.1.1

Host B
IP Address 172.16.1.2

Figure 1-4b
Resolution of IP to ethernet address mapping, step two

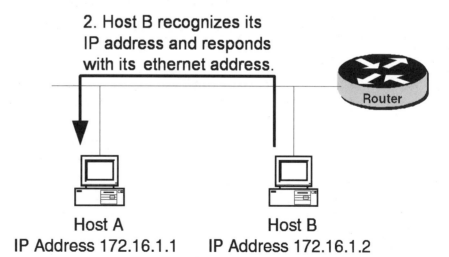

2. Host B recognizes its IP address and responds with its ethernet address.

Host A
IP Address 172.16.1.1

Host B
IP Address 172.16.1.2

Figure 1-4c
Resolution of IP to
ethernet address
mapping, step three

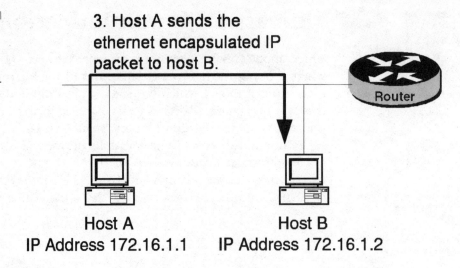

3. Host A sends the ethernet encapsulated IP packet to host B.

Router

Host A
IP Address 172.16.1.1

Host B
IP Address 172.16.1.2

six-byte (48-bit) link layer address that is globally unique and cannot be changed. Because the ethernet address is burned into the NIC, the ethernet address of the host changes if the NIC is changed. We have seen that on an ethernet LAN all data traffic is encapsulated in frames. Even though the host is sending to an IP address, the IP packet must be encapsulated in an ethernet frame. To accomplish the encapsulation, the sending host must resolve the receiving host's IP to ethernet address mapping. The mapping is accomplished using the *Address Resolution Protocol* (ARP).

In Figures 1-4a-c, host A wishes to send a packet to host B. Host A knows the IP address of host B but not the ethernet address of host B. The ARP process, illustrated in the figures, proceeds as follows:

1. Host A sends an ARP broadcast (see Figure 1-4a) that all hosts on the network receive, including the router.

2. Host B receives the ARP and recognizes that the IP address contained in the ARP request belongs to host B. Host B sends an ARP reply that contains the ethernet address for host B (see Figure 1-4b).

3. Host A can now encapsulate the IP packet in an ethernet frame and transmit the frame to host B (see Figure 1-4c).

   a. Host A sends an ARP request for IP address 172.16.1.2.

   b. Host B responds with its ethernet address.

   c. Host A can now send to host B.

If host A wants to send a packet to a host on another IP subnet, then the packet must be sent to the router. Host A will have a default gateway configured that points to the router interface attached to the LAN containing host A. Because the destination IP address is on a different subnet, host A knows to send the frame to the router and will send an ARP for the router's ethernet address. When the router receives the frame, the IP packet is extracted and the router determines from the destination IP address whether or not the destination is on a directly connected network. If it is on a directly connected network, the router sends an ARP onto that network to resolve the ethernet address of the destination. When the ARP reply is received from the destination, the router can build an ethernet frame containing the IP packet and then send the frame to the destination. If the destination is not on a directly connected network, the router consults the routing table and determines the next router where the frame should be sent. IP unicast routing protocols are not covered in this book, but references are listed at the end of the chapter for further study.

Broadcast Communication Model

The broadcast model is one in which a host sends to everyone on the subnet. ARP is not needed because the ethernet broadcast address is a well-known address with the value 0xFF FF FF FF FF FF (Broadcast IP addresses also exist and are covered in Chapter 2). In the unicast model, a host could send an IP packet to any host on any network (assuming we have a route to the destination host). In the broadcast model, the scope of the broadcast is the local subnet. Routers block broadcast traffic, so the scope of a broadcast is limited to the local subnet (see Figure 1-5).

Figure 1-5
Broadcast
communication
model

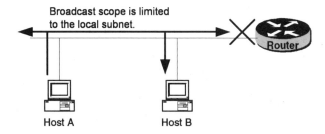

Broadcast scope is limited
to the local subnet.

Host A   Host B

Multicast Communication Model

Now the fun begins. The problem to solve here is the one-to-many communication scenario. If a host wants to send the same packet to more than one receiver, how can this be accomplished? We can try using the unicast communication model and would be successful, but problems occur. Assume host A wants to send a packet to five hosts using the unicast model. This implies that host A knows the IP address of each receiver. If this is the case, then host A would need to send the same packet to five different IP addresses, as shown in Figure 1-6.

As the number of receivers increases, the number of packets that needs to be sent increases linearly. In other words, for *n* receivers, the host would need to send *n* copies of each packet. If the host is sending a real-time audio or video presentation, this solution may be workable for very few receivers, but as the number of receivers increases, the load of replicating packets on the host would be such that the delay between distinct packets would be unacceptable. Also, the links on the source router, router E in Figure 1-6, would have the bandwidth severely depleted.

Another major problem with this scheme is the host not knowing where the receivers are. If the receivers that require the traffic don't change, then they could be entered, but this would be extremely restrictive because new receivers could not dynamically join or leave the group. And what about the broadcast model? Certainly every host on the local subnet would receive the traffic and each packet would only have to be sent

Figure 1-6
Using the unicast communication model to achieve multicasting capabilities

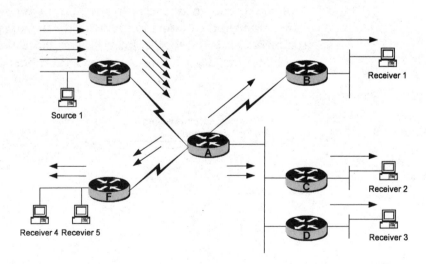

once. So what's the problem? Two come to mind. The first is that only receivers on the same subnet receive the traffic, while receivers on other subnets cannot receive it because the router blocks broadcasts. This is probably a good thing because we don't want a broadcast to be delivered to the whole world. Yes, some people would like to do this, but in general it is not a good idea.

The second problem with using a broadcast is that every host is required to process the ethernet broadcast in order to determine if the traffic is intended for the host. The IP packet would have to be extracted from the ethernet frame and, because the destination IP address is also a broadcast address, the UDP or TCP portion of the packet would need to be extracted and passed up the protocol stack. If there is a process expecting the data, it would be passed to the application layer. If there is not a process expecting the data, then the data would be discarded. For those hosts not expecting the data, this would be a waste of valuable processing time and a source of many user complaints. Looks like we need another model.

For the multicast communication model, we will need two new types of addresses, an IP multicast address and an ethernet multicast address. An IP multicast address identifies a group of receivers that want to receive traffic destined for the group. Because all IP packets are encapsulated in ethernet frames, a multicast ethernet address is also required. For the multicast model to function correctly, hosts should be able to receive both unicast and multicast traffic, which mandates that hosts need multiple IP and ethernet addresses. A unicast IP and ethernet address are used for unicast traffic and zero or more IP, and ethernet multicast addresses are used for multicast traffic. Zero multicast addresses are needed if the host will not be receiving multicast traffic. A pair of multicast addresses, IP and ethernet, are required for each multicast group that the receiver wishes to join. A major difference between the unicast and multicast addresses is that unicast addresses are unique on each host, while multicast addresses are not. If five hosts wish to receive multicast traffic destined for group A, for example, then the hosts would all listen for traffic destined for the same multicast address, both IP and ethernet. The amount of traffic from the unicast case would be greatly reduced, as shown in Figure 1-7.

Another characteristic that we would like to have with the multicasting model is the capability for dynamic group membership. A host should receive traffic for a particular multicast group only if there is an active application running that requires the data. Hosts should have the capability to join and leave multicast groups at will, eliminating the need for static group assignments. Efficient use of available bandwidth dictates that

Figure 1-7
Multicast
communication
model

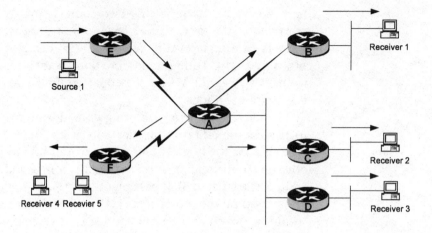

routers need to know whether or not the router needs to route multicast traffic to group members. The router must therefore be aware of the dynamic group membership information and must have routing protocols that can handle multicast traffic.

Outline of the Book

The presentations of the solutions to the requirements stated above comprise the remainder of this book. Chapter 2 presents the unicast and multicast IP addressing scheme in detail. Chapter 3, "Internet Group Management Protocol," deals with the *Internet Group Management Protocol* (IGMP), the protocol that is used between hosts and routers to report dynamic multicast group membership.

Chapter 4, "Cisco Group Management Protocol," discusses a proprietary Cisco protocol for determining group membership on a switch. The protocol, *Cisco Group Management Protocol* (CGMP) is used to limit multicast traffic on a *virtual LAN* (VLAN) to those hosts that wish to receive it.

Chapter 5, "Distance Vector Multicast Routing Protocol," begins the study of multicast routing protocols with the *Distance Vector Multicast Routing Protocol* (DVMRP), which is used on the *Internet Multicast Backbone* (MBONE). Cisco does not support a full DVMRP implementation but can interact with DVMRP for the exchange of routes from the MBONE into the local environment.

Chapter 6, "Protocol Independent Multicast—Dense Mode," and Chapter 7, "Protocol Independent Multicast—Sparse Mode," cover two flavors of the *Protocol Independent Multicast* (PIM) protocol. The first is referred to as *PIM Dense Mode* (PIM-DM). PIM-DM is typically used in a LAN environment, while the second flavor, *PIM Sparse Mode* (PIM-SM), is appropriate for *Wide Area Networks* (WAN). Both PIM-DM and PIM-SM have implementations on Cisco routers.

Connecting DVMRP and PIM networks is covered in Chapter 8, "PIM-DVMRP Networks." Because the MBONE runs DVMRP and Cisco implements PIM, a mechanism is needed for DVMRP-PIM interaction.

Multicast configuration commands that can be used with any of the Cisco-supported multicast routing protocols are discussed in Chapter 9, "Multicast Support Commands." Chapter 10, "Resource Reservation Protocol," takes us from multicast routing protocols to a protocol that is not used for routing but for reserving resources along the path from a multicast sender to a multicast receiver. The *Resource Reservation Protocol* (RSVP) is an Internet control protocol that can be used by multicast receivers to request a specific *quality of service* (QOS) for the data flow from a unicast or multicast source.

In each chapter that covers a Cisco-supported protocol, all Cisco router commands for configuring, monitoring, and debugging the protocol are presented with network scenarios to demonstrate their use. This is where I believe the value of this book becomes evident. Although the information for the specific routing protocols is contained in the appropriate *Request for Comment* (RFC) and extensive documentation exists from Cisco for multicast router configurations, I hope my explanations and examples will be used to supplement this information and fill in any gaps that may exist.

Recommended Reading List for IP Routing Protocols (RIP, IGRP, EIGRP, OSPF, and BGP)

Cisco Router OSPF Design and Implementation Guide, William R. Parkhurst, CCIE #2969, McGraw-Hill

Advanced IP Routing in Cisco Networks, Terry Slattery, CCIE #1026, and Bill Burton, CCIE #1119, McGraw-Hill

Cisco TCP/IP Routing Professional Reference, Chris Lewis, McGraw-Hill

Internet Routing Architectures, Bassam Halabi, Cisco Press. This book is an excellent presentation of the Border Gateway Protocol (BGP)

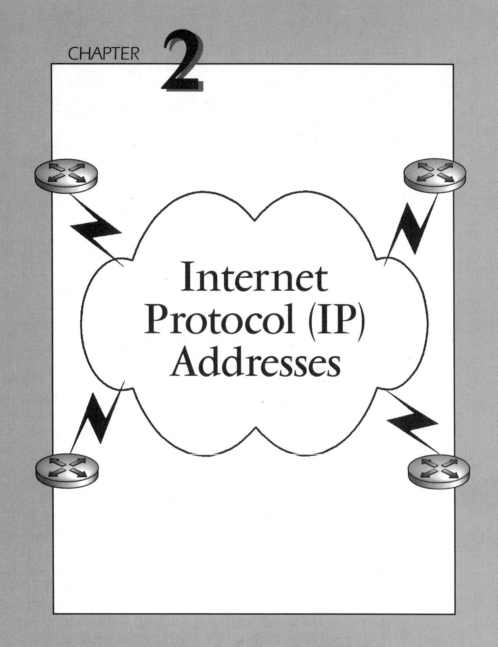

Internet
Protocol (IP)
Addresses

A complete understanding of unicast and multicast IP addressing is required in order to design and implement robust IP networks. Concepts such as subnetting and *Variable Length Subnet Masks* (VLSM) should be mastered so that IP addressing plans make efficient use of your assigned address space. The concept, operation, and configuration of IP unicast routing protocols, RIP, IGRP, EIGRP, and OSPF, also need to be mastered because most multicast routing protocols rely on the underlying unicast routing configuration.

IP Address Format

An IP address is a 32-bit number that can be represented in many formats. Routers and computers are designed to operate efficiently on binary numbers, so a binary representation is a natural way for them to store and manipulate IP addresses. A typical 32-bit IP address to a router would look something like this:

10011100000110100001111000111100

This may be a fine representation for routers, but for us it is not the most appealing method. So let's take a look at the binary representation and see if we can find a way to represent these numbers using a method that may be a bit more palatable. One way is to simply represent the IP address as a decimal number. The binary number used in the example above has a decimal value of

2,618,957,372

This may be easier to read, but the size of the number makes it cumbersome to work with. Another representation scheme is to break up the binary number into pieces and represent each piece as a decimal number. A natural size for binary pieces is 8 bits, which is the familiar "byte" or not-as-familiar "octet" (octet is the telecommunication term, but the two words can be used interchangeably). So let's take our binary number, write it using groups of 8 bits (four octets) and then represent each group as a decimal number.

10011100	00011010	00011110	00111100
156	26	30	60

	Low	High
TABLE 2-1		

	Low	High
Binary	00000000000000000000000000000000	11111111111111111111111111111111
Decimal	0	4,294,967,295
Dotted Decimal	0.0.0.0	255.255.255.255

TABLE 2-1

Range of IP
Addresses

We don't need all that space between the numbers, so let's use a period, or dot, as a separator. Now our IP address has the form

$$156.26.30.60$$

which is referred to as dotted decimal notation. How many IP addresses are there? The range of IP addresses in all our representation schemes is shown in Table 2-1.

Theoretically, there are 4,294,967,296 possible IP addresses, although we will discover in this chapter that the actual usable number of IP addresses is much smaller.

Classful IP Addressing

For a protocol to be routable, its address structure must be hierarchical, meaning that the address must contain at least two parts. For IP addresses, these parts are the network portion and the host portion. A host is an end station such as a computer workstation, router interface, or printer, while a network consists of one or more hosts. Figure 2-1 is a simple network consisting of two networks connected by a two-port router. The address of each host on this network, including the router interfaces, is given by its network and host numbers.

When the IP address scheme was designed, the decision was made to create five classes of IP addresses simply named Class A, B, C, D, and E. The

Figure 2-1

Hierarchical
addressing

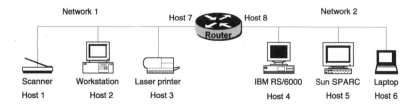

logic behind the first three network classes was that the IP addressing scheme would be used for a few networks with a large number of hosts (Class A), a moderate number of networks with a moderate number of hosts (Class B), and a large number of networks with a small number of hosts (Class C). Class D addresses would be used for multicasting and Class E addresses would be reserved for experimental use.

Having three classes of IP addresses to handle different size networks requires that the network part and the host part for each address class have unequal sizes. The breakdown for the allocation of bits for the network and host portion for the first four IP address classes is shown in Figure 2-2.

Class A addresses use 8 bits to identify the network and 24 bits to identify the host with the most significant bit of the first octet set to zero. Class B addresses use 16 bits to identify the network and 16 bits to identify the host with the first two bits of the first octet set to 1 0. Class C addresses use 24 bits to identify the network and 8 bits to identify the host with the first 3 bits of the first octet set to 1 1 0. Class D or multicast addresses differ from unicast addresses in their interpretation.

A Class A, B, or C address is used to identify a network and a host on that network. A Class D multicast address is used to identify a group of

Figure 2-2
Classful IP address structure

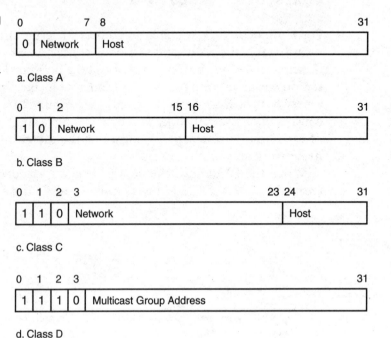

receivers and senders of multicast traffic. Additionally, multicast senders and receivers can be present on any network.

If we examine the first octet of each class, we can see that the range of values for the four classes is

$$00000001\ (1)–01111110\ (126) \qquad \text{for Class A}$$
$$10000000\ (128)–10111111\ (191) \qquad \text{for Class B}$$
$$11000000\ (192)–11011111\ (223) \qquad \text{for Class C}$$
$$11100000\ (224)–11101111\ (239) \qquad \text{for Class D}$$

Looking at the first octet of the IP address can easily identify the network class. For example, the address used previously, 156.26.30.60, is a Class B address because the first octet is between 128 and 191. Another (and more tedious) way to identify the class is to represent the first octet of the address in binary and see what the first couple of bits are set to. For example, 156 equals 10011100 in binary. The first two bits are 1 0, so according to Figure 2-1, this is a Class B address.

How many Class A, B, and C networks are there? Class A networks use 7 bits for the network ID, so 128 Class A networks are possible. Class B addresses use 6 bits from the first octet and all 8 bits of the second octet, so there are 16,384 networks (64 × 256), 64 from the first octet and 256 from the second octet. Class C addresses use 5 bits from the first octet, 8 bits from the second octet, and 8 bits from the third octet, so there are 2,097,152 possible Class C networks (32 × 256 × 256). Class D addresses are not associated with networks but with multicast groups.

Class A, B, and C addresses are unicast addresses. Each IP address in the first three classes is used to identify a particular and unique Internet host, while a Class D address is used to identify a group of hosts belonging to a particular IP multicast group. The multicast addresses are in the range 224.0.0.0 through 239.255.255.255 (currently assigned multicast addresses are listed in Appendix B). The range of addresses between 224.0.0.0 and 224.0.0.255, inclusive, is reserved for the use of routing protocols and other low-level topology discovery or maintenance protocols, such as gateway discovery and group membership reporting. Multicast routers should not forward any multicast datagram with destination addresses in this range, regardless of the TTL.

How many hosts can each network have? Class A networks have 24 bits to identify a host; this equals 1,677,216 possible hosts per network! Class B networks have 16 bits to identify a host, which equals 65,536 hosts, and Class C networks have 8 bits to identify a host, which equals 256 possible hosts. Table 2-2 lists the capabilities for Class A, B, and C addresses.

TABLE 2-2

IP Classful Address
Capabilities

Class	Networks	Hosts
A	126	16,777,214
B	16,384	65,534
C	2,097,152	254

You may have noticed that the number of hosts listed in Table 2-1 is always two less than the number calculated. The reason for this discrepancy is that two special addresses can't be assigned to a host. A host address of all ones is the broadcast address for a particular network, and a host address of all zeros is used by a host to temporarily identify itself ('this host') until it has been assigned an IP address. Only 126 Class A networks exist because network 0 cannot be used, and network 127 is reserved for the loopback address that is used for testing interprocess communication. When a host sends a packet to 127.0.0.1, the data is not sent on the network but is returned immediately to the sending host.

The IP address blocks listed below have been reserved for private Internets.

10.0.0.0 — 10.255.255.255
172.16.0.0 — 172.31.255.255
192.168.0.0 — 192.168.255.255

These private IP addresses should never be advertised on the Internet because they can be used by any private Internet. If these addresses are used, then a technique such as network address translation would need to be used in the private Internet to be connected to the public Internet.

Classful IP address assignments can be extremely inefficient as the following design problem demonstrates. Assume we are designing a network for a campus that has approximately 1500 nodes or end-stations. Also assume that the predicted future growth of the network over the next five years will be no more than 5000 nodes. At first glance, it would seem that a Class B network would suffice for the current network requirements and also leave plenty of room for future growth. Having 1500-plus nodes (5000-plus in the future) would be a very large ethernet collision domain. If we want to limit the number of nodes on an ethernet segment to no more than 100, then we need 50 networks to accomplish our design. Regardless of which class of IP network addresses we decide to use (assuming we could choose any addresses we want), there will be an enormous waste of IP addresses as shown in Table 2-3.

TABLE 2-3

IP Address Design
Inefficiencies

Network Class	Addresses Required	Addresses Available	Addresses Wasted
A	100	16,777,214	16,777,114
B	100	65,534	65,434
C	100	254	154

Now multiply each entry in Table 2-3 by the 50 networks that are required and you can easily see that regardless of which address class we choose, an enormous number of IP addresses will be wasted. Also, if we are to have connectivity to the Internet, then the network will have to advertise 50 networks to the Internet routers. Multiply that by the number of campuses in the world and you have a situation where the size of the Internet routing tables becomes unmanageable. How do we overcome these problems? In a word, subnetting.

IP Subnets

The solution to our design problem is to divide whatever class of IP address we are assigned into a number of smaller networks with fewer hosts per network. This is accomplished by "borrowing" bits from the host portion of our IP address and using them in the network portion. How do we and, more importantly, how does a router know how many bits to use for the network and how many to use for the host? The answer is by using a subnet mask.

A subnet mask is a 32-bit binary number that identifies which bits in the address are used for the host and which bits are used for the network. A one in the mask identifies the corresponding bit in the IP address as a network bit, and a zero in the mask identifies the corresponding bit in the IP address as a host bit. A router accomplishes this operation by performing a bitwise AND operation with the IP address and the subnet mask.

$$0 \text{ AND } 0 = 0 \quad 0 \text{ AND } 1 = 0$$
$$1 \text{ AND } 0 = 0 \quad 1 \text{ AND } 1 = 1$$

As an example, consider the IP address/subnet mask pair

156.26.30.60/255.255.240.0

which has the binary representations

Address	10111100	00011010	00011110	00111100
Mask	11111111	11111111	11110000	00000000

Performing the AND operation yields

    10111100   00011010   00010000   00000000

Converting the result to dotted decimal notation yields the network portion of the IP address

156.26.16.0

One subnet mask restriction is that the 1 bits in the mask must be contiguous. Because of this, an alternative representation for the mask is just to indicate how many 1 bits are in the mask. For example, the IP address/subnet mask pair in the previous example can be written as 156.26.30.60/20. The subnet masks for non-subnetted networks are shown in Figure 2-3.

Subnet masks never have fewer ones than the masks listed in Figure 2-3. A Class C address, for example, cannot have a subnet mask of 255.255.0.0. *Request for Comment* (RFC) 950 first defined the subnetting of IP addresses and does not allow the use of the all-zeros and all-ones subnet, so we will initially look at subnetting examples that obey these restrictions. In later examples, we will see how we can remove these restrictions with the use of an appropriate routing protocol, such as OSPF. The number of subnet bits cannot be one because of the restriction in RFC 950 (see Tables 2-4, 2-5, and 2-6). A 1-bit subnet mask would have a value of either zero (all zeros) or one (all ones) and this is not allowed.

Figure 2-3
Standard IP subnet masks

Class A

11111111.00000000.00000000.00000000
255.0.0.0

Class B

11111111.11111111.00000000.00000000
255.255.0.0

Class C

11111111.11111111.11111111.00000000
255.255.255.0

TABLE 2-4	Number of Subnet bits	Subnet Mask	Number of Subnetworks	Number of Hosts/Subnet	Total Number of Hosts
Class A Subnet Masks	1	—	—	—	—
	2	255.192.0.0	2	4194302	8388604
	3	255.224.0.0	6	2097150	12582900
	4	255.240.0.0	14	1048574	14680036
	5	255.248.0.0	30	524286	15728580
	6	255.252.0.0	62	262142	16252804
	7	255.254.0.0	126	131070	16514820
	8	255.255.0.0	254	65534	16645636
	9	255.255.128.0	510	32766	16710660
	10	255.255.192.0	1022	16382	16742404
	11	255.255.224.0	2046	8190	16756740
	12	255.255.240.0	4094	4094	16760836
	13	255.255.248.0	8190	2046	16756740
	14	255.255.252.0	16382	1022	16742404
	15	255.255.254.0	32766	510	16710660
	16	255.255.255.0	65534	254	16645636
	17	255.255.255.128	131070	126	16514820
	18	255.255.255.192	262142	62	16252804
	19	255.255.255.224	524286	30	15728580
	20	255.255.255.240	1048574	14	14680036
	21	255.255.255.248	2097150	6	12582900
	22	255.255.255.252	4194302	2	8388604
	23	—	—	—	—
	24	—	—	—	—

A 15-bit subnet mask for Class B and a 7-bit subnet mask for Class C is also illegal because it would leave only 1-bit for the host, which we have seen cannot be all zeros or all ones. A 16-bit subnet mask for Class B or an 8-bit subnet mask for Class C makes no sense because this would leave zero host bits.

TABLE 2-5

Class B
Subnet Masks

Number of Subnet Bits	Subnet Mask	Number of Subnetworks	Number of Hosts/Subnet	Total Number of Hosts
1	—	—	—	—
2	255.255.192.0	2	16382	32764
3	255.255.224.0	6	8190	49140
4	255.255.240.0	14	4094	57316
5	255.255.248.0	30	2046	61380
6	255.255.252.0	62	1022	63364
7	255.255.254.0	126	510	64260
8	255.255.255.0	254	254	64516
9	255.255.255.128	510	126	64260
10	255.255.255.192	1022	62	63364
11	255.255.255.224	2046	30	61380
12	255.255.255.240	4094	14	57316
13	255.255.255.248	8190	6	49140
14	255.255.255.252	16382	2	32764
15	—	—	—	—
16	—	—	—	—

TABLE 2-6

Class C
Subnet Masks

Number of Subnet Bits	Subnet Mask	Number of Subnetworks	Number of Hosts/Subnet	Total Number of Hosts
1	—	—	—	—
2	255.255.255.192	2	62	124
3	255.255.255.224	6	30	180
4	255.255.255.240	14	14	196
5	255.255.255.248	30	6	170
6	255.255.255.252	62	2	124
7	—	—	—	—
8	—	—	—	—

Subnet Examples

In the following examples, determine if the address/subnet pair is legal. If it is legal, determine the network number and the range of host addresses for that network. Also determine for the mask, the number of available networks and available hosts per network.

1. IP address = 193.144.233.130

   Subnet mask 5 255.255.255.192

   For a Class C address, we only need to look at the last octet of the address and the mask.

   130 = 1000 0010
   192 = 1100 0000

   This is a legal pair because neither the subnet nor the host is all zeros or all ones.

   Network equals 193.144.233.128 because the mask selects the upper two bits of the address (130) and the rest of the bits are set to zero to identify the network.

   Range of hosts = 193.144.233.129–193.144.233.190.

   The host portion (last six bits) can have values ranging from 000001 to 111110 (remember they can't be all zeros or all ones). Add in the subnet portion, which is the upper two bits of the address (in this case, 1 0), and you have 10 000001 to 10 111110 for the host addresses.

   From Table 2-6, the number of available networks is 2 and the number of hosts is 62.

2. IP address = 156.26.30.60

   Subnet Mask = 255.255.255.0

   This is relatively easy because the entire third octet is used for the subnet and the entire fourth octet is used for the host. This is a legal pair because neither the subnet nor the host is all zeros or all ones.

Network = 156.26.30.0

Range of hosts = 156.26.30.1–156.26.30.254

From Table 2-5, the number of networks is 254 and the number of hosts is 254.

3. IP address = 199.200.201.50

   Mask = 255.255.255.128

   This is illegal because the subnet mask only borrows 1 bit from the host and that bit has to be either zero or one.

4. IP address = 191.200.201.50

   Mask = 255.255.255.128

   This is a legal pair because the address is Class B and we are borrowing 9 bits from the host portion.

Network = 191.200.201.0

Range of hosts = 191.200.201.1–191.200.201.126

From Table 2-5, the number of networks is 510 and the number of hosts is 126.

Subnetting can be viewed as creating a three-part hierarchical address. The network portion of the address can be found by applying the standard subnet mask to the IP address (refer to Figure 2-3). The subnet is determined from the bits "borrowed" from the host portion and the host number is simply those bits that are left over. For an example, we will examine the Class B address/mask pair

144.223.0.0/255.255.255.0

and determine the network number, the subnetwork numbers, and the range of host numbers. The network number is found by applying the standard Class B 16-bit subnet mask, which yields the network

144.223.0.0

The subnet is the entire third octet, so the 254 subnets are

$$144.223.1.0$$
$$144.223.2.0$$

.
.
.

$$144.223.254.0$$

and the range of hosts for each subnet is 1 to 254. Now let's try a bit more complicated example. Consider the address/mask pair

$$144.223.0.0/255.255.255.224$$

The network number is still 144.223.0.0. The subnet mask borrows 11 bits from the host portion of the address. The first 8 bits borrowed include the entire third octet, which has a value of 0 to 255. The 3 bits borrowed from the third octet have the values

$$
\begin{aligned}
000\ 00000 &= 0 \\
001\ 00000 &= 32 \\
010\ 00000 &= 64 \\
011\ 00000 &= 96 \\
100\ 00000 &= 128 \\
101\ 00000 &= 160 \\
110\ 00000 &= 192 \\
111\ 00000 &= 224
\end{aligned}
$$

Why are the values 0 (all zeros) and 255 (all ones) for the third octet, and 0 (all zeros) and 224 (all ones) from the fourth octet included? The third octet can be 0 if the 3 bits in the fourth octet are not zero. The third octet can also be all ones if the 3 bits in the fourth octet are not all ones. The 3 bits in the fourth octet can be all zeros if the third octet is not all zeros, and the 3 bits from the fourth octet can be all ones if the third octet is not all ones. In other words, the 11 subnet bits cannot be all zeros or all ones. Therefore, the range of subnet numbers is

144.223.0.32
144.223.0.64
.
.
.

144.223.0.224
144.223.1.0
144.223.1.32
.
.

144.223.255.0
.
.

144.223.255.192

Determining the range of host addresses for each subnet requires more effort. The bit pattern for the fourth octet of network 144.223.0.32 is

001 hhhhh

where hhhhh represents the host number, which cannot be all zeros or all ones. Therefore, the first legal host number is 00001, making the fourth octet

00100001 = 33

so the first host address is

144.223.0.33

and the last legal host bit pattern for the fourth octet is

00111110 = 62

which gives the range of hosts' addresses for the first subnet as

144.223.0.33–144.223.0.62

The broadcast address for each subnet is found by setting all the bits in the host portion to 1. The broadcast address for subnet 144.223.0.32 is determined by setting the last 5 bits of the fourth octet to 1 yielding

$$00111111 = 63$$

Putting it all together gives us the broadcast address

$$144.223.0.63$$

5. Determine all the subnet numbers for the address/mask pair 193.128.55.0/255.255.255.240. Also determine the range of host addresses and the broadcast address for the fourth subnet.

Network	Hosts
193.128.55.0	1–14 (If IP subnet-zero is used)
193.128.55.16	17–30
193.128.55.32	33–46
193.128.55.48	49–62, Broadcast address = 193.128.55.63
193.128.55.64	65–78
193.128.55.80	81–94
193.128.55.96	97–110
193.128.55.112	113–126
193.128.55.128	129–142
193.128.55.144	145–158
193.128.55.160	161–174
193.128.55.176	177–190
193.128.55.192	193–206
193.128.55.208	209–222
193.128.55.224	225–238
193.128.55.240	241–254

IP Address Design Example 1

Assume your company has been assigned the Class C address 198.28.61.0 and you have determined that you require four networks with a maximum of 25 hosts per network. From Table 2-6, you will need three subnet bits, resulting in a subnet mask of 255.255.255.224. The subnet numbers for this design are any four of the following, as shown in Figure 2-4.

198.28.61.32
198.28.61.64
198.28.61.96
198.28.61.128
198.28.61.160
198.28.61.192

Although subnets solve some of the problems associated with the inefficient use of IP address space, situations occur when simple subnetting does not suffice. Consider the network in Figure 2-5 in which two routers are connected by a serial link. This serial link is a point-to-point connection, so there are only two hosts on the link, the two router interfaces. Each network must also be on a separate subnet, so no matter which subnet mask we choose, we will be wasting IP addresses. If we are using a Class B address with a 24-bit subnet mask, then the subnet assigned to the serial link will only use two out of a possible 254 host addresses.

If we could use different subnet masks for different subnetworks, then the limitations of Figure 2-5 could be solved. A subnet mask of 255.255.255.252 (or /30) can accommodate only two hosts, which is perfect for a point-to-point serial link. Unfortunately, this mask, if used throughout the network, would limit all subnets to two hosts. The ideal solution

Figure 2-4
IP address design
example 1

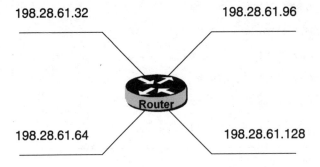

198.28.61.32   198.28.61.96

198.28.61.64   198.28.61.128

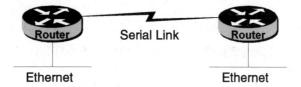

Figure 2-5
Limitations of simple
subnetting

would be to vary the length of the subnet mask and adjust it according to the needs of each individual network.

Variable Length Subnet Masks

RFC 1009, 1987, specifies the procedures for using multiple subnet masks. This technique is referred to as *variable length subnet masks* (VLSM). The term VLSM can be confusing because the subnet mask for a specific network does not vary but is fixed. VLSM means that the subnet masks for different subnets can have unequal lengths. As an example, it would allow a subnet mask of 255.255.255.252 to be assigned to a serial link and 255.255.255.0 to an ethernet network. Once the masks are assigned, however, they do not change, at least by themselves.

The VLSM technique is very useful for allocating IP addresses more efficiently (less waste) and for reducing the size of routing tables. However, VLSM can also cause a number of massive network headaches if not used properly.

VLSM EXAMPLE 1 Let's apply VLSM to the network in Figure 2-5. Assume we have been assigned the Class B network 156.26.0.0. The ethernet networks are assigned addresses using a /24 subnet mask; we will use the first two networks with this mask, 156.26.1.0 and 156.26.2.0. The third network, 156.26.3.0, will be sub-subnetted using a /30 subnet mask, which will give us a possible 62 sub-subnets we can use for serial connections. Notice that we are subnetting an already subnetted network, 156.26.3.0. Figure 2-6 illustrates this technique.

Figure 2-6 visually represents the technique that should be used when using VLSM. Start with the standard subnet mask (/8, /16, or /24 for Class A, B, or C). Determine the network with the required maximum number of hosts, in this case 254. Then subnet using a mask that will give you networks that can handle the largest number of hosts you need. For smaller networks, sub-subnet the large networks and keep going until you have satisfied your requirements.

Figure 2-6
VLSM example 1

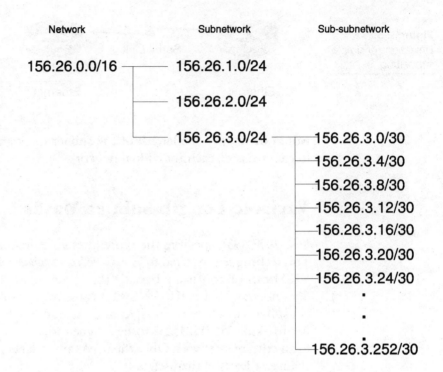

VLSM EXAMPLE 2 The best way to master a technique is practice, practice, practice, so here we go. Given the IP network 202.128.236.0, design a network with the following requirements:

■ Four networks with a maximum of 26 hosts

■ Three networks with a maximum of 10 hosts

■ Four point-to-point serial links

Starting with the greatest number of hosts per network, we can use a /27 subnet mask to satisfy the first requirement. From Table 2-6, this gives us six networks of 30 hosts each with two networks left over to sub-subnet. To satisfy the next requirement, we can sub-subnet the two leftover /27 networks using a /28 subnet mask to give us four networks with 14 hosts each. Finally, take one of the four sub-subnetted networks and sub-sub-subnet using a /30 subnet mask.

How did I arrive at the diagram in Figure 2-7? Let's take a closer look as to where these network numbers came from; then we'll look at another VLSM design problem to ensure that you have mastered the technique.

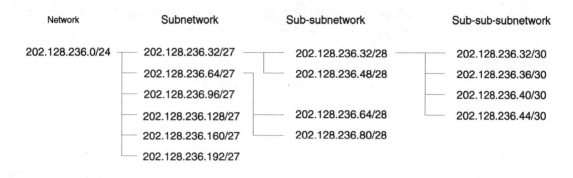

Figure 2-7 VLSM example 2

1. Determine the mask for the networks containing the greatest number of hosts.

   The first requirement is for four networks with a maximum of 26 hosts. Using Table 2-6, we need three subnet bits or a /27 subnet mask. The fourth octet of our IP network would be segmented as

$$S\ S\ S\ H\ H\ H\ H\ H$$

   where S S S indicates the subnet bits and H H H H H indicates the host bits. The subnets then are

$$
\begin{aligned}
0\ 0\ 1\ 0\ 0\ 0\ 0\ 0 &= \ 32 \\
0\ 1\ 0\ 0\ 0\ 0\ 0\ 0 &= \ 64 \\
0\ 1\ 1\ 0\ 0\ 0\ 0\ 0 &= \ 96 \\
1\ 0\ 0\ 0\ 0\ 0\ 0\ 0 &= 128 \\
1\ 0\ 1\ 0\ 0\ 0\ 0\ 0 &= 160 \\
1\ 1\ 0\ 0\ 0\ 0\ 0\ 0 &= 192
\end{aligned}
$$

   and we are using subnets 96 through 192 for the networks containing 26 hosts because these subnets can handle a maximum of 30 hosts.

2. Sub-subnet the subnetted networks as needed.

   The second requirement calls for three networks with a maximum of 10 hosts each. Again, we consult Table 2-6 and see that we need four subnet bits or a /28 subnet mask. We will subsubnet network 202.128.236.32 and 202.128.236.64. The first three subnet bits are fixed with the values 001 (subnet 32) and 010 (subnet 64), so now we have

$$0\ 0\ 1\ S\ H\ H\ H\ H$$
$$0\ 1\ 0\ S\ H\ H\ H\ H$$

Network 32 S can be 0 or 1, giving us

$$0\ 0\ 1\ 0\ H\ H\ H\ H$$
$$0\ 0\ 1\ 1\ H\ H\ H\ H$$

Setting the host bits to 0, the sub-subnets are

$$0\ 0\ 1\ 0\ 0\ 0\ 0\ 0 = 32$$
$$0\ 0\ 1\ 1\ 0\ 0\ 0\ 0 = 48$$

Applying the same procedure to subnet 64, we get

$$0\ 1\ 0\ 0\ 0\ 0\ 0\ 0 = 64$$
$$0\ 1\ 0\ 1\ 0\ 0\ 0\ 0 = 80$$

3. To satisfy the last requirement of four point-to-point serial links, we will sub-sub-subnet sub-subnet 32, which now is equal to

$$0\ 0\ 1\ 0\ S\ S\ H\ H$$

S S can be either 0 0, 0 1, 1 0 , or 1 1 yielding

$$0\ 0\ 1\ 0\ 0\ 0\ 0\ 0 = 32$$
$$0\ 0\ 1\ 0\ 0\ 1\ 0\ 0 = 36$$
$$0\ 0\ 1\ 0\ 1\ 0\ 0\ 0 = 40$$
$$0\ 0\ 1\ 0\ 1\ 1\ 0\ 0 = 44$$

As a final task for this exercise, determine the range of hosts and the broadcast addresses for networks 202.128.236.192, 202.128.236.80, and 202.128.236.40. The fourth octet of network 202.128.236.192 is

$$1\ 1\ H\ H\ H\ H\ H\ H$$

and the host bits can range from

$$0\ 0\ 0\ 0\ 0\ 1{-}1\ 1\ 1\ 1\ 1\ 0$$

which gives us a range of

$$1\ 1\ 0\ 0\ 0\ 0\ 0\ 1\ (193)–1\ 1\ 1\ 1\ 1\ 1\ 1\ 0\ (254)$$

The broadcast address is determined by setting the host bits to 1, which is

$$1\ 1\ 1\ 1\ 1\ 1\ 1\ 1 = 255$$

so the broadcast address is 202.128.236.255. For network 202.128.236.80, the fourth octet contains

$$0\ 1\ 0\ 1\ H\ H\ H\ H$$

so the range of host addresses is

$$0\ 1\ 0\ 1\ 0\ 0\ 0\ 1\ (81)–0\ 1\ 0\ 1\ 1\ 1\ 1\ 0\ (94)$$

and the broadcast address is

$$0\ 1\ 0\ 1\ 1\ 1\ 1\ 1\ (95)$$

For network 202.128.236.40, the fourth octet contains

$$0\ 0\ 1\ 0\ 1\ 0\ H\ H$$

Because H H cannot be 0 0 or 1 1, the host addresses for this network are 202.128.236.41 and 202.128.236.42 with a broadcast address of 202.128.236.243. The realization of this network design is shown in Figure 2-8.

For the final VLSM example, design a network using the Class C address 200.100.50.0 that satisfies the following requirements:

■ Nine serial point-to-point links

■ Four networks with a maximum of 30 hosts

■ Three networks with a maximum of five hosts

Determine the address host ranges and the broadcast address for each subnet.

From Table 2-6, a 3-bit subnet mask will give us six networks of 30 hosts each.

$$\text{Subnet mask} = 255.255.255.224$$

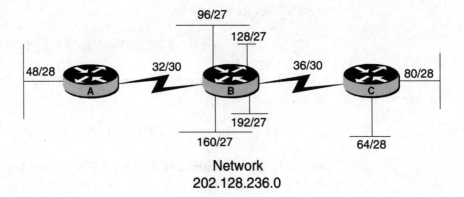

Figure 2-8
Realization of VLSM example 2

96/27
128/27
48/28 — A — 32/30 — B — 36/30 — C — 80/28
192/27
160/27
64/28

Network
202.128.236.0

Networks	Hosts	Broadcast Address
200.100.50.0	1–30	200.100.50.31 (if we use IP subnet-zero)
200.100.50.32	33–62	200.100.50.63
200.100.50.64	65–94	200.100.50.95
200.100.50.96	97–126	200.100.50.127
200.100.50.128	129–158	200.100.50.159
200.100.50.160	161–190	200.100.50.191
200.100.50.192	193–222	200.100.50.223

One solution is to use the first four networks to satisfy the requirement of four networks with 30 hosts each. For the requirement of three networks with five hosts each, we can sub-subnet network 200.100.50.160 using the 5-bit subnet mask 200.100.50.160/255.255.255.248, which gives us the networks listed below.

Network	Hosts	Broadcast Address
200.100.50.160	161–166	200.100.50.167
200.100.50.168	169–174	200.100.50.175
200.100.50.176	177–182	200.100.50.183
200.100.50.184	185–190	200.100.50.191

We can use any three of the four networks to satisfy the requirement of three networks with five hosts.

Finally we can sub-subnet the 200.100.50.192 network using a 30-bit subnet mask that gives us the networks listed below.

Network	Hosts	Broadcast Address
200.100.50.192	193–194	200.100.50.195
200.100.50.196	197—198	200.100.50.199
200.100.50.200	201—202	200.100.50.203
200.100.50.204	205—206	200.100.50.207
200.100.50.208	209–210	200.100.50.211
200.100.50.212	213–214	200.100.50.215
200.100.50.216	217–218	200.100.50.219
200.100.50.220	221—222	200.100.50.223
200.100.50.224	225–226	200.100.50.227
200.100.50.228	229–230	200.100.50.231
200.100.50.232	233–234	200.100.50.235
200.100.50.236	237–238	200.100.50.239
200.100.50.240	241–242	200.100.50.243
200.100.50.244	245–246	200.100.50.247
200.100.50.248	249–250	200.100.50.251

Choose any nine of the networks for the serial links.

Subnet masks can also be used with Class D multicast addresses. As an example, assume we have the following Class D address/mask pair.

$$225.250.250.0/255.255.255.0$$

This address mask/pair would then represent all the multicast groups from 225.250.250.0–225.250.250.255. The multicast address/mask pair can be used to summarize the range of groups that a router will allow or that a multicast entity will service. We will learn more about the use of a mask with a multicast address later in the book.

Internet
Group
Management
Protocol

When a multicast router receives traffic destined for a multicast group, the router needs to know on which interfaces the traffic should be forwarded. The decision to forward is based on whether or not any group members or forwarding routers are on the subnet. Forwarding multicast traffic onto a subnet that has no group members is a waste of bandwidth.

Figure 3-1 illustrates the situation where a multicast router is receiving traffic for the group 224.65.10.154. Subnet 1 has no group members, so there is no need for the router to forward the traffic to subnet 1. Subnet 2 has one host, host C, which is a member of the multicast group 224.65.10.154, so the multicast traffic will be forwarded to subnet 2. What if host D in Figure 3-1 joins the group? The router only needs to know that at least one group member is on the subnet and it does not matter to the router if there is one group member or if there are 100.

Figure 3-2 shows the scenario where subnet 1 has no group members, but a downstream multicast router on subnet 1 has group members attached to one of the router's interfaces. The multicast traffic would need to be forwarded onto subnet 1. As shown, the *Internet Group Management Protocol* (IGMP) is used between hosts and routers, and the multicast routing protocols, *Distance Vector Multicast Routing Protocol* (DVMRP) and *Protocol Independent Multicast* (PIM), are used between multicast routers.

IGMP is the mechanism used by hosts on a network to inform directly-attached routers which multicast group(s) the host wants to either join or leave. Multicast routers use IGMP to determine if any members of the multicast groups are located on any of their attached networks. If group members are present, multicast routers can then join a particular multicast group and forward multicast traffic to hosts that have joined the group(s). The original IGMP specification is detailed in RFC 1112, "Host Extensions for IP Multicasting." This specification is typically referred to

Figure 3-1
Forwarding of
multicast traffic

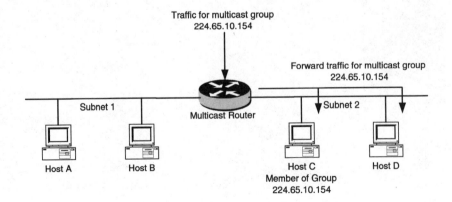

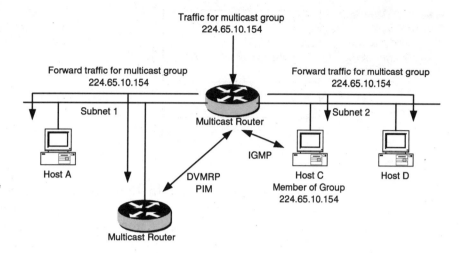

as IGMP version 1 and was written by S. Deering of Stanford University in August 1989. A subsequent RFC, written by W. Fenner of Xerox PARC, updated the original IGMP version 1 RFC. The update is RFC 2236, "Internet Group Management Protocol, Version 2." Both RFCs will be examined because a mix of IGMP version 1 and version 2 hosts and routers may be present in the network, and you need to be aware of interoperability issues between the versions. Following the discussion of IGMP version 1 and version 2, we will examine configuring, monitoring, and debugging IGMP on Cisco routers.

RFC 1112, Host Extensions for IP Multicasting (IGMP Version 1)

RFC 1112 obsoletes RFCs 988 and 1054 and details the requirements of a host in order for it to be able to support IP multicasting. The multicasting support needed is for hosts to be able to join and leave multicast groups with IP addresses in the range 224.0.0.0 to 239.255.255.255. Also specified are the mechanisms for hosts to be able to receive and send multicast traffic.

A host can have one out of three levels of multicasting capabilities. Level 0 defines a host that has no multicasting functionality beyond being able to detect and discard an IP Class D multicast packet. A level 1

Figure 3-3
IGMP resides at the
network layer of the
IP layered model.

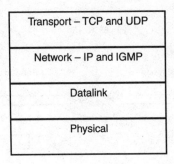

| Transport – TCP and UDP |
| Network – IP and IGMP |
| Datalink |
| Physical |

host can send but not receive IP multicast traffic, while a level 2 host is a fully capable multicast entity and can send and receive multicast traffic. Level 2 hosts are required to implement IGMP and we will assume that all hosts in the following discussion are level 2 hosts. The relationship between IGMP and IP layered models is shown in Figure 3-3.

Sending an IGMP packet is really no different than sending a broadcast or unicast IP packet, although additional functionality is required for a level 2 host. The first required function concerns the TTL field in the IGMP packet. If a TTL value is not explicitly set, then the default TTL value should be set to 1 to prevent the IGMP traffic from leaving the host's network. The second required function is for hosts that are connected to more than one network. The host should only transmit multicast traffic on one of the directly connected networks because, in the multicasting paradigm, routers have the responsibility of forwarding multicast traffic to other networks. The third and last function specifies what a host should do when sending a multicast packet to a group of which the host is also a member. The transmitted multicast packet should be looped back to the host and the received packet that the host just sent should be discarded.

Ethernet Multicast Addressing

The datalink layer also requires additional functionality for mapping Class D IP addresses to ethernet MAC addresses. The procedure outlined in the RFC also applies to FDDI, but a procedure is not specified for a token ring. The mapping from multicast to token ring layer 2 addresses presented here are the implementation on Cisco routers. The ethernet and FDDI layer 3 to layer 2 address mapping is relatively straightforward. The low-order 23 bits of the IP multicast address replace the low-order 23 bits of the ethernet multicast address 01:00:5E:00:00:00, as shown in Figure 3-4.

As you can see in Figure 3-4, nine bits in the group IP address do not take place in the mapping, the upper byte, and the most significant bit of the next-to-upper byte. The upper four bits of the upper byte are always 1110 because these are all Class D IP addresses. This means that in reality there are only five bits that are not involved in the mapping. Whatever the value of these bits, the multicast ethernet address is the same. Because there are 32 possible combinations of five bits, the mapping is not unique. In the example in Figure 3-2, 31 other Class D IP addresses map to the same multicast ethernet address.

Let's examine the most significant byte of the IP address, 225.65.10.154. The byte 225 is represented in binary as 1110 0001. The upper four bits do not change because they are always 1110 for a Class D IP multicast address.

Figure 3-4
Formation of the ethernet multicast address

225	65	10	154
E1	41	0A	9A
1110 0001	0 | 100 0001	0000 1010	1001 1010

a. Class D IP address represented in decimal, hexadecimal, and binary. The last 23 bits are used to form the multicast ethernet address.

01	00	5E	00	00	00
0000 0001	0000 0000	0101 1110	0 | 000 0000	0000 0000	0000 0000

b. Host multicast ethernet address template represented in hexadecimal and binary.

01	00	5E	41	0A	9A
0000 0001	0000 0000	0101 1110	0 | 100 0001	0000 1010	1001 1010

c. The final multicast ethernet address is formed by taking the last 23 bits of the IP address and substituting them for the last 23 bits of the ethernet address template.

TABLE 3-1

Class D multicast IP addresses that map to the multicast ethernet address 01:00:5E:41:0A:9A

224.65.10.154	225.65.10.154	226.65.10.154	227.65.10.154
228.65.10.154	229.65.10.154	230.65.10.154	231.65.10.154
232.65.10.154	223.65.10.154	234.65.10.154	235.65.10.154.
236.65.10.154	237.65.10.154	238.65.10.154	239.65.10.154
224.193.10.154	225.193.10.154	226.193.10.154	227.193.10.154
228.193.10.154	229.193.10.154	230.193.10.154	231.193.10.154
232.193.10.154	233.193.10.154	234.193.10.154	235.193.10.154
236.193.10.154	237.193.10.154	238.193.10.154	239.193.10.154

The lower four bits have a range of values from 0000 to 1111, so the decimal range of values for the upper byte is 224 (224 + 0) to 239 (224 + 15). The most significant bit of the next-to-upper byte can be either 0 or 1, so this byte can be either 65 (0 + 65) or 193 (65 + 128). The upper byte can take on 16 values and the next-to-upper byte can take on two values, so there is a total of 32 Class D IP multicast addresses (16 × 2) that map to the multicast ethernet address 01 00 5E 41 0A 9A, as listed in Table 3-1. A host implementation must not only examine the ethernet address of the received multicast ethernet frame at layer 2 but must also examine the multicast IP address at layer 3 to determine if the packet is destined for a group that the host has joined.

EXERCISE 3-1

Determine which Class D IP multicast addresses map to the multicast ethernet address 01:00:5E:5F:00:01.

Solution. We need to add the low-order 23 bits of the multicast ethernet address to the partial IP address 1110 xxxxx000 0000 0000 0000 0000, which gives us

1110 xxxxx101 1111 0000 0000 0000 0001

where xxxx x = 0000 0–1111 1.

With xxxx x = 0000 0, the IP address is 224.95.0.1.
With xxxx x = 1111 1, the IP address is 239.223.0.1.

The other 30 possible IP addresses are found by substituting xxxx x with 0000 1–1111 0.

Token Ring Multicast Addressing

The bit order of the transmitted bytes for token ring is the opposite of ethernet. For example, the token ring address C0:00:00:05:00:01 has the binary representation

1100 0000 0000 0000 0000 0000 0000 0101 0000 0000 0000 0001

When written in ethernet form, the order of the bits in each byte is reversed, so the ethernet binary representation would be

0000 0011 0000 0000 0000 0000 1010 0000 0000 0000 1000 0000

which has the hexadecimal form

03:00:00:A0:00:80.

The mapping of a multicast Class D IP address for token ring can be accomplished using one of two methods. The first method is to map all Class D multicast IP addresses to a single token ring functional address as shown:

224.x.x.x-> C0:00:00:04:00:00

The general form of a token ring functional address is C0:00:00:04:xx:xx. Functional addresses are used for token ring functions, such as Ring Error Monitor. The last two bytes usually have only one bit set to 1 and a bit in the third byte is used to determine if this address is a functional address. The third byte of an ethernet multicast address is 5E, which, if used in a token ring to multicast IP address mapping, would trick the token ring hosts into accepting that the multicast address is functional. This is the reason that the same mapping method used for ethernet cannot be used for token ring. Mapping all IP multicast addresses to the same token ring functional address means that token ring end stations cannot determine if the multicast traffic is destined for them until the packet is examined at layer three. If multicast traffic is present on the token ring, then every host must examine the packet at layer three (in software), instead of at layer two (by the network interface card). This can put a strain on end stations that are not listening for packets of that particular multicast group.

The other method of mapping multicast IP addresses to token ring addresses is to simply map every multicast IP address to the broadcast address:

$$224.x.x.x \rightarrow FF:FF:FF:FF:FF:FF$$

To force the token ring interface to use the functional address, use the following command in interface configuration mode:

```
interface Token-ring 0
ip multicast use-functional
```

Internet Group Management Protocol, IGMP Version 1

IGMP is used by hosts to inform the directly connected router of their choice to join a multicast group. IGMP messages have the format shown in Figure 3-5. IGMP messages are encapsulated in IP datagrams and use a protocol identifier of 2.

Figure 3-5
IGMP version 1
message format

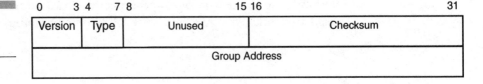

0   3 4   7 8   15 16   31
Version	Type	Unused	Checksum
Group Address		

Version Number = 1

Type	1 = Host Membership Query
	2 = Host Membership Report
Unused	Set to zero when sending
	Ignore when receiving
Checksum	16-bit complement of the complement sum of the 8-byte
	IGMP message
Group Address	Host Membership Query Message = 0
	Host Membership Report Message = IP multicast address
	of the group being reported

A router sends Host Membership Query messages to determine if any hosts are members of any multicast groups (see Figure 3-6). As long as one host responds to the query, then the router must continue to send multicast traffic for that group to the network. Queries are sent to the all-hosts group address (224.0.0.1) and have a TTL value of 1.

When a host receives a Host Membership Query message, the host responds with one or more Host Membership Report messages (see Figure 3-7). Each Host Membership Report message contains the multicast group of which the host is a member.

If multiple group members are on the network, a flood of report messages can be generated. Two techniques can be employed to avoid this possibility. The first is to have the host start a delay timer with a delay value randomly chosen between zero and some maximum value, usually 10 seconds. When the delay timer expires, the host sends the report. This spreads

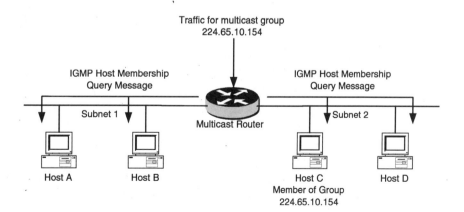

Figure 3-6

Multicast routers use IGMP Host Membership Query messages to determine if any hosts are members of any multicast group.

■■■ ■■■ ■■ ■■
Figure 3-7
Hosts report their
group memberships
with IGMP Host
Membership Reports.

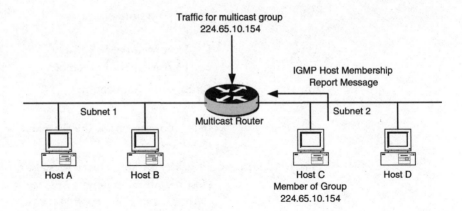

the Host Membership Reports over time. Because a router only needs to know if there is at least one group member on the network, it is not necessary for every host that is a member of a group to send a Host Membership Report message.

The second technique is to send the report to the host group address that is being reported. Hosts still use the delay timer, but if they receive a Host Membership Report for the group that they are waiting to report, the timer is canceled and no report is sent. This method is preferred because only one report is generated for each Host Membership Query (see Figures 3-8 and 3-9).

In Figure 3-8, when hosts A, C, and D receive a Host Membership Query message from the router, the hosts start a timer with a random value. When the first timer counts down to zero, an IGMP Host Membership Report is sent, as in the example by host A. When host A sends the report, the timer values for hosts C and D have decremented by one. Before the timers for host C and D expire, they receive the Host Membership Report that is sent by host A. Because this is a report for the group that they are waiting to report to, there is no need for hosts C and D to send their reports.

The various states that a host can be in are shown in Figure 3-10. Hosts can be in one of three states: Non-Member, Delaying Member, and Idle Member. In the Non-Member state, a host is simply not a member of the multicast group. The Delaying Member state indicates that the host is a member of the multicast group, has received a Host Membership Query message from the router, and has the report delay timer running. A host enters the idle state after it has sent a Host Membership Report message to the router or has heard a Host Membership Report from another host that is a member of the group. Hosts will make transition between states

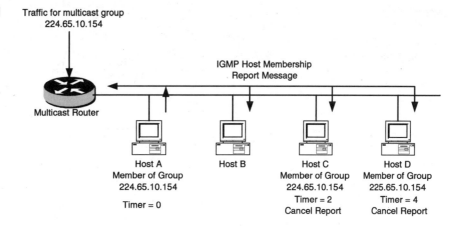

Figure 3-9
Host report group
memberships with
IGMP Host
Membership Reports.

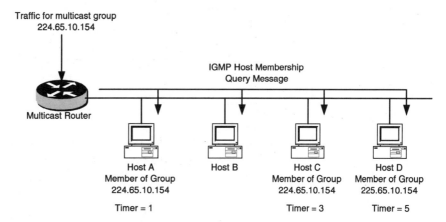

Figure 3-8
Routers determine
group membership
using IGMP Host
Membership Queries.

on the occurrence of the following events:

1. A host decides to join a multicast group.
2. A host decides to leave a multicast group.
3. A Host Membership Query message is received.
4. A Host Membership Report is received.
5. The host's delay timer has expired.

When a host decides to join a multicast group, it does not know if any other hosts are on the network that are members of the group. If this host is the first member and the host waits for a Host Membership Query from the router, the host will wait forever. Therefore, when a host decides to join a multicast group, it should immediately send a Host Membership Report. The possibility exists, however, that this initial report message will not

Figure 3-10
IGMP Version 1 host
state diagram

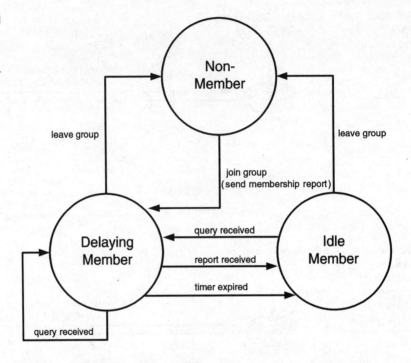

reach the router. The host should make a transition from the Non-Member state to the Delaying Member state, as though the host had received a Host Membership Query message. The host then starts the delay timer. If a Host Membership Report is received, the host stops the timer and makes a transition to the Idle Member state. If the timer expires, the host sends a Host Membership Report message to the router and then moves to the idle state. When a Host Membership query is received, the host could be in any of the three states. In the Non-Member state, the host simply ignores the message. In the idle state, the host will make a transition to the delaying state and start the report delay timer. If the report is received while the host is in the delaying state, the host does not reset the timer but continues to delay with the current timer value. Finally, when a host decides to leave the group, it does so silently because there is not a leave group message in IGMP version 1. If the host is the last host to leave the group, the router does not know this until there has been no response to the router's periodic Host Membership Query messages.

Internet Group Management Protocol, IGMP Version 2

IGMP version 2 is detailed in RFC 2236 (Copyright © The Internet Society 1997), written by W. Fenner of Xerox PARC in November 1997. IGMP version 2 messages have the format shown in Figure 3-11. The shaded parameters highlight the changes from the IGMP version 1 packet.

Type: 0×11 = Membership Query

   0×16 = Version 2 Membership Report

   0×17 = Leave Group

   0×12 = Version 1 Membership Report for backwards compatibility with IGMP version 1.

Membership Query messages, type 0×11, come in two flavors. The first is a General Query that is used to determine which groups on a network have active members. The second is a Group-Specific Query that is used to determine if a particular multicast group has active members. The type of Membership Query message can be determined by the group address. For a General Query, the group address is zero and, for a Membership Query, the group address contains the address of the multicast group that is being queried.

The *Maximum Response Time* field (Max. Rtime) applies only to Membership Query messages. This field specifies the maximum amount of time a host can wait before responding to a Membership Query report. Maximum Response Time is in units of 0.1 seconds.

Protocol Operation

One improvement that IGMP version 2 has over version 1 concerns multi-access networks, such as ethernet, that have more than one attached multicast router (see Figure 3-12). Only one router needs to send Membership Query

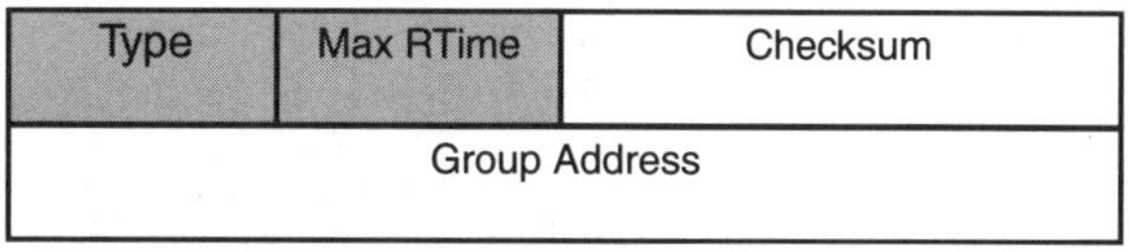

Figure 3-11
IGMP version 2
packet format

Type	Max RTime	Checksum
Group Address		

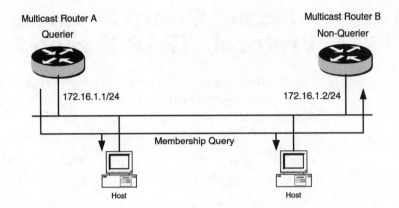

Figure 3-12
On a multi-access
network, the router
with the lowest IP
address becomes the
Querier.

messages because all attached routers running IGMP hear the Membership
Report messages from the hosts. IGMP version 2 adds a feature that enables
routers to determine which router is responsible for sending Membership
Query messages with the other routers becoming Non-Querier routers. In
Figure 3-12, assume that router A sends the first Membership Query message
onto the multi-access network. Router B receives this message and, because
router A has a lower IP address than router B, router A remains the Querier
for the network and router B the Non-Querier. If router B had sent the first
Membership Query message (all routers start in the role of Querier), this
would not suppress Membership Query messages from router A because
router A has the lower IP address. Router A would send a Membership Query
message and router B, upon receiving this message, would become a Non-
Querier for the network.

IGMP Version 2:
Timers and Counters

To account for the possibility of router A ceasing to send Query messages,
Non-Querier routers set a timer, the Other Querier Present Interval timer,
whenever a Query message is received. If this timer expires before receiving a Query message, the router assumes the role of Querier. Of course,
more than one Non-Querier router may be attached to the network and
they will all try to assume the role of Querier. As before, the router with
the lowest IP address on the network becomes Querier and the others
assume the Non-Querier role.

To prevent Non-Querier routers from mistakenly assuming the role of Querier, the Querier router must periodically send Membership Query messages using the Query Interval timer. Of course, the Query Interval Timer must be less than the Other Querier Present Interval timer. The timer values that are used in IGMP Version 2 are listed in Table 3-2.

When IGMP is first enabled on a multicast router, the router should send a number of General Query messages to determine if the hosts on the network are members of any multicast groups. The number of initial queries is given by the Startup Query Count and the initial queries are separated in time by the Startup Query Interval. When a host receives a General Query message from the router, the host sets a delay timer for each multicast group of which the host is a member. These delay values are chosen at random from the range 0 to Maximum Response Time (specified in the IGMP version 2 packet), and the value zero is not used. If any of these timers counts down to zero before the host has heard a Membership Report for a particular group, the host sends a Membership Report to the multicast group. If a host receives a Membership Report from another host for a group that the host is a member, the timer and report for that group is canceled. If a host receives a Membership Query for a group that the host already has a timer running, the timer is reset only if the remaining value of the timer is greater than the value of the Maximum Response Time contained in the IGMP packet.

TABLE 3-2

IGMP Version 2 timers, counters, and variables

Parameter	Default Value
Robustness Variable (RV)	2 (Must not be zero and should not be 1)
Query Interval (QI)	125 Seconds
Query Response Interval (QRI)	100 (10 seconds)
Startup Query Interval (SQI)	One-quarter of the Query Interval = 31
Startup Query Count (SQC)	Robustness Variable Value
Other Querier Present Interval (OQPI)	(RV $\cdot$ QI) + QRI/2 = 255
Group Membership Interval (GMI)	(RV $\cdot$ QI) + QRI = 260
Last Member Query Interval (LMQI)	10 (1 second)
Last Member Query Count (LMQC)	Robustness Variable Value
Unsolicited Report Interval (URI)	10 seconds
Version 1 Router Present Timeout	400 Seconds

When an IGMP-enabled multicast router receives a Membership Report from a host, the router checks the table of multicast groups for which the router is forwarding multicast traffic. If the group being reported by the host is not in the router's table, the router adds this group to the table. For each multicast group in the router's table, a periodic timer is set to the value Group Membership Interval. Whenever a router receives a Membership Report from a host for a multicast group, the timer associated with that group is reset to the value Group Membership Interval. When the Group Membership Interval timer counts down to zero, meaning that no Membership Reports have been received from a host during this time period, the router assumes that hosts on the network no longer want to receive multicast traffic for that particular group, and the router does not forward multicast traffic for it.

When a multicast application is enabled, the host should immediately send a Membership Report for the group that the application needs to join. Because the possibility exists that the report could be lost, the host should send a Membership Report at least one more time after delaying for the Unsolicited Report Interval.

Another addition to IGMP version 2 is the Leave Group message. In IGMP version 1, hosts left the group quietly and no message was sent. When a host decides to leave a group and if the host was the one that responded to the last Membership Query message, then the host should send a Leave Group message to the address 224.0.0.2, the all-routers multicast group. If the host was not the last one to respond to the Membership Query message, then a Leave Group message does not have to be sent, but it does no harm to send one, except for using a little bit of bandwidth. The RFC also allows the sending of the Leave Group message to the group address instead of the all-routers address. The benefit of sending the Leave Group message to the all-routers address is that hosts that are members of that group do not have to process the message.

When the Querier router receives the Leave Group message, the router does not know if this was the last host on the network for that group. The Querier router sends a number of Group-Specific Membership Queries, one in which the group address in the IGMP packet contains the address of the group being left. The number of Group-Specific Queries that are sent is given by the value Last Member Query Count, which is equal to the value of the *Robustness Variable* (RV) as shown in Table 3-2. The Group-Specific Queries are sent on an interval equal to the Last Member Query Interval. The Group-Specific Queries have the Maximum Response Interval in the IGMP packet set to the value of the Last Member Query Interval (see Figure 3-13). After sending the Group-Specific Queries, the router waits for a time given by the Last Member Query Interval for Group Membership reports. If none are received, then multicast traffic for the specific group is no longer forwarded by the router. The state diagram for a host running IGMP version 2 is shown in Figure 3-14.

As shown in Figure 3-14, an IGMP version 2 host can be in one of three states. The Non-Member state indicates that the host does not belong to the multicast group; the host will make a transition to the Delaying Member state when the host decides to join the multicast group. The host sends a Membership Report for the group and sets a timer as though the host received a Membership Query from the router.

There are four transitions from the Delaying Member state. If the host's timer counts down to zero, the host sends a Membership Report and makes a transition to the Idle Member state. If a Membership Report for

Figure 3-13
IGMP version 2
packet format for the
Group-Specific Query
in response to a
Leave Group
message

Type = 0x11	LMQ1	Checksum
Group Address = Address of group being left		

Figure 3-14
IGMP version 2 host
state diagram. Each
group a host belongs
to has its own state.

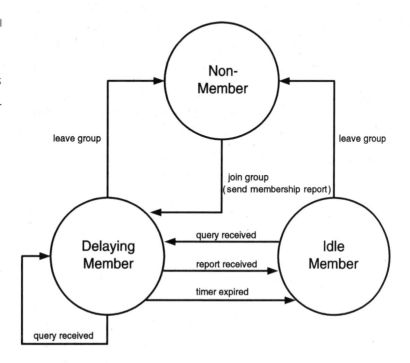

the group is received from another host, the host stops the delay timer and makes a transition to the Idle Member state. If a Membership Query is received from the router, the host resets the delay timer if the Maximum Response Time in the IGMP message is less than the time remaining on the delay timer. In this case, the host remains in the Delaying Member state. Finally, a host makes a transition from the Delaying Member state to the Non-Member state if the host decides to leave the group. The host sends a Leave Group message if it was the host that responded to the last Membership Query message. A host makes a transition from the Idle Member state on one of two events. If a Membership Query is received for the group, the host makes a transition to the Delaying Member state and starts the delay timer. If a host decides to leave the group while in the Idle Member state, the host sends a Leave Group message and makes a transition to the Non-Member state. The all-systems group (224.0.0.1) is a special case with respect to the host state diagram. Every host that is running IGMP version 2 is a member of the all-systems group, but no reports are ever sent for this group and the hosts are always in the Idle Member state with respect to this group.

If there is more than one router on the network, then the possibility exists that one or more routers are running IGMP version 1 and one or more routers are running IGMP version 2. A version 2 host can therefore be in one of two states with respect to the multicast routers that are present on the network, as shown in Figure 3-15.

Hosts will initially be in the state No IGMP Version 1 Router Present. If a host receives a version 1 IGMP Membership Query, one in which the Maximum Runtime field is zero, the host makes a transition to the state IGMP Version 1 Router Present and sets a timer equal to the value Version 1 Router Present Timeout. Whenever a version 1 Membership Query

Figure 3-15
IGMP version 1 and
version 2 interaction

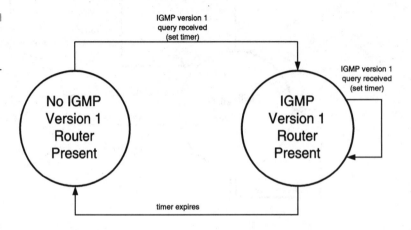

is received while in this state, the timer is reset to the Version 1 Router Present Timeout value. If this timer counts down to zero, then the host makes a transition to the No IGMP Version 1 Router Present state.

IGMP Router States

We have seen that a router can be in one of two states with respect to its query status on the network, being either the Querier or the Non-Querier, as shown in Figure 3-16. An IGMPv2-enabled router starts in the Initial state, sends a General Membership Query message, and sets the General Query timer. Whenever the General Query Timer expires, the timer is reset and a General Membership Query message is sent. If a router in the Querier state hears a General Membership Querier message from a router with a lower IP address, then the router makes a transition from the Query state to the Non-Querier state and sets the Other Querier Present Timer. While in the Non-Querier state, this Other Querier Present Timer is reset each time a General Membership Query is received from a router with a lower IP address. If the timer times out, then no General Membership Queries have been received during the Other Querier Present time and the router changes from the Non-Querier state to the Query state.

The state diagram for a router in the Query state is shown in Figure 3-17 and the Non-Query state in Figure 3-18. When IGMPv2 is initialized, the router enters the initial state and sends General Membership Queries on all interfaces and then makes a transition to the Querier state. If no members are present on an attached network, the state for that interface will be No Members Present. Because no members are present on the network, the router does not need to periodically transmit General Membership Queries out of the interface.

Routers will be notified by hosts that want to join a particular group. A host can either transmit a version 1 or version 2 IGMP Membership report. If only version 2 Membership Reports are received, the router will make a transition to the Members Present state. If a version 1 report is received, then the router will make a transition to the Version 1 Members Present state, even though there may be version 2 hosts present.

While in the Version 1 Members Present state, the router needs to track whether or not version 2 hosts are present on the attached network. When the version 1 host timer expires, the router will either move to the Members Present state if there are version 2 hosts present or to the No Members Present state. As long as version 1 Membership Reports are being received, the router will stay in the Version 1 Members Present state.

Figure 3-16
Query status state
diagram for IGMPv2-
enabled routers

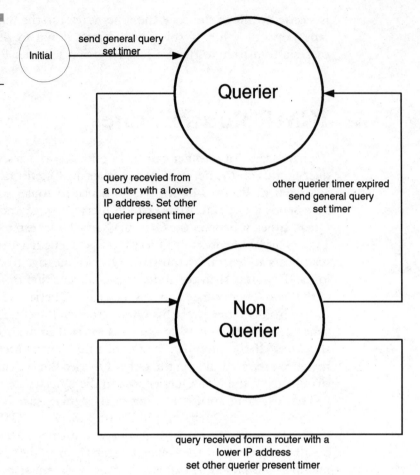

Figure 3-16
Query status state
diagram for IGMPv2-
enabled routers

In the Members Present State, the reception of version 2 Membership Reports refreshes the Group Membership Interval timer and the router stays in the Members Present state. If a version 1 Membership Report is received, a transition to the Version 1 Members Present state occurs. Recall that one enhancement to IGMP version 2 was the Leave Group Message. When a Leave Group Message is received, the router has no idea if this is the last host to leave the group because routers only need to track if there is at least one member of the group on the network and not the number of members. A Leave Group Message in the Members Present state causes a transition to the Checking Membership state, while a Leave Group message in the Version 1 Members Present state has no effect because there is at least one Version 1 host that is still a member of the group.

Figure 3-17
State diagram for an
IGMPv2 enabled
router in the Query
state

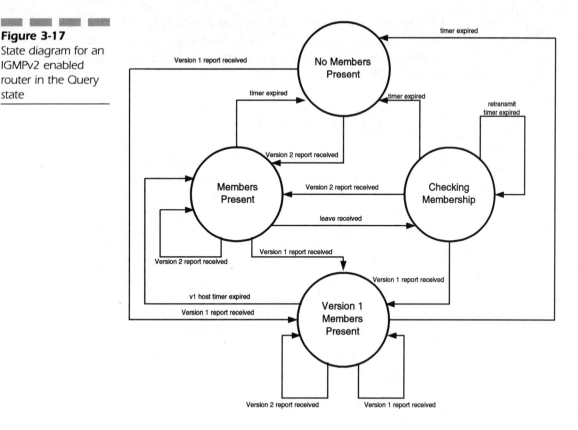

Figure 3-18
State diagram for an
IGMPv2-enabled
router in the Non-
Querier state

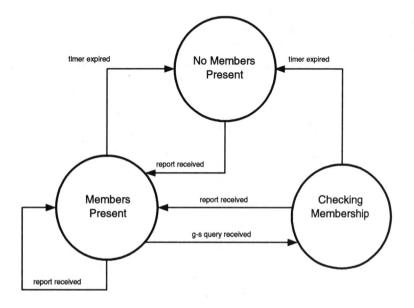

The state diagram for a router in the Non-Querier state is passive in nature because the router is only listening to Membership reports and Membership Queries and is not actively polling for group members (see Figure 3-18).

Configuring IGMP

Configuring IGMP on Cisco routers is very easy—you don't have to do anything. When a multicast routing protocol is enabled on a router interface, IGMP is automatically enabled. A number of commands exist to tailor IGMP to suit your environment. IGMP interface commands can be listed by entering interface configuration mode and typing

    router(config-if)#ip igmp ?

access-group	IGMP group-access group
helper-address	IGMP helper address
join-group	IGMP join multicast group
querier-timeout	IGMP previous querier timeout
query-interval	IGMP host query interval
query-max-response-time	IGMP max query response value
version	IGMP version

By default, all hosts on a subnet are allowed to join all multicast groups. The groups that hosts on a subnet can join are controlled using the interface command:

---

ip igmp access-group *access-list-number* [*version*].

---

access-list-number	IP standard access-list number (1–99)
version	Optional. Changes the IGMP version number. Default is 2.

EXAMPLE

Configure the ethernet 0 interface on a router such that hosts can only join multicast groups 239.0.0.0 through 239.255.255.255.

```
interface ethernet 0
ip igmp access-group 1

access-list 1 permit 239.0.0.0 0.255.255.255
```

To enable stub multicast routing, use the `ip igmp helper-address` in conjunction with the `ip pim neighbor-filter` command. This IGMP command causes the router to forward IGMP Host Reports and Leave Group messages received on the interface to the IP address specified. An example of this command and stub multicast routing is contained in Chapter 7, "Protocol Independent Multicast—Sparse Mode."

---

ip igmp helper-address *ip-address*

---

ip-address   IP address where IGMP Host Reports and Leave Group messages are forwarded

EXAMPLE

See Chapter 7.

A router interface can be configured as though there are always receivers for a multicast group present on the interface. One reason to do this is to be able to ping all multicast routers. Sending a ping to a multicast group causes all routers that have joined that group to respond. To configure a router in order to join a multicast group on an interface, use the interface configuration command:

---

ip igmp join-group *group-address*

---

group-address   Multicast group IP address

EXAMPLE ▬ ▬ ▬ ▬ ▬ ▬ ▬ ▬

Configure interface ethernet 0 to join the multicast group 225.250.250.1.

```
interface ethernet 0
ip igmp join-group 225.250.250.1
```

The default IGMP query interval on an interface is 60 seconds. Every 60 seconds the router sends IGMP host-query messages on the interface. To modify this default value, use the interface command:

> **ip igmp query-interval** *seconds*

seconds Number of seconds between host-query messages. The value can be between 0 and 65535.

EXAMPLE ▬ ▬ ▬ ▬ ▬ ▬ ▬ ▬

Change the query interface on interface serial 0 to 3 minutes.

```
interface serial 0
ip igmp query-interval 180
```

Be very careful with this command. If the query interval is longer than the query timeout value, then IGMP is effectively broken on the interface. All neighbor routers should be configured with the same value.

The default Maximum Response Time that is advertised in IGMP queries is 10 seconds. This value can be modified using the interface command:

> **ip igmp query-max-response-time** *seconds*

seconds Maximum Response Time that is advertised in IGMP queries

EXAMPLE ▬ ▬ ▬ ▬ ▬ ▬ ▬ ▬

Configure the Maximum Response Time on interface ethernet 0 to 15 seconds.

```
interface ethernet 0
ip igmp query-max-response-time 15
```

A Non-Querier router on a multi-access network becomes the Querier if the current Querier times out. The default value for the time out is twice the Query Interval. To modify the Query Timeout Value, use the interface command:

```
ip igmp query-timeout  seconds
```

seconds   Number of seconds a Non-Querier router will wait before taking over as Querier if the current Querier times out

EXAMPLE

Change the Query Timeout Value to 60 seconds on interface serial 1

```
interface serial
ip igmp query-interval 30
ip igmp query-timeout 60
```

The `ip igmp join-group` command can be used to statically configure a router to join a multicast group. When this command is used, packets for the configured group are handled at the process level. To fast-switch the packets for a static group, use the interface command:

```
ip igmp static-group  group-address
```

group-address   Group IP multicast address

EXAMPLE

Configure interface ethernet 0 to join the multicast group 225.250.250.1.

```
interface ethernet 0
ip igmp static-group 225.250.250.1
```

When PIM is enabled on an interface, IGMP version 2 is automatically enabled. To change the version, use the interface command:

```
ip igmp version {2 | 1 }
```

EXAMPLE

Configure the ethernet 0 interface to use IGMP version 1. If version 1 is configured on an interface, then the commands `ip igmp query-max-response-time` and `ip igmp query-timeout` cannot be used because they are version 2-specific.

```
interface ethernet 0
ip igmp version 1
```

Entries in the router's IGMP cache can be deleted using the Exec command:

```
clear ip igmp group [group-name | group-address [interface-type interface-number]
```

group-name   Optional. Multicast group name. Defined either in DNS or
                    by the **ip host** command
group-address   Optional. Multicast group address
interface-type   Specify the interface (ethernet 0, serial 0, and so on)

EXAMPLES

To clear a particular group, use **clear ip igmp group** 225.250.250.1.
To clear all groups on an interface, use **clear ip igmp group** ethernet 0.
To clear all groups, use **clear ip igmp group.**

IGMP Show and Debug Commands

The available show commands can be listed in Exec mode by typing

router#show ip igmp ?

groups	IGMP group membership information
interface	IGMP interface information

Additional show options can be found by entering

router#show ip igmp groups ?

Ethernet	IEEE 802.3
Hostname or A.B.C.D	IP name or group address
Loopback	Loopback interface
Null	Null interface
Serial	Serial
	Output modifiers
\<cr>	

EXAMPLE

Show all multicast groups on all interfaces

router#show ip igmp groups

IGMP-Connected Group Membership

Group Address	Interface	Uptime	Expires	Last Reporter
225.250.250.1	ethernet 0	03:05:59	Never	172.16.4.3

group-address	Multicast group address
interface	Interface where the group joined
Uptime	How long the group has been joined on the interface in hours, minutes, and seconds
Expires	The time when the group is removed from the table in hours, minutes, and seconds
Last Reported	IP address of the last host to report membership

The current state of IGMP on an interface along with IGMP timer values can be shown using the Exec command:

```
router#show ip igmp interface ?
```

Ethernet	IEEE 802.3
Loopback	Loopback interface
Null	Null interface
Serial	Serial
	Output modifiers
`<cr>`	

An individual interface can be displayed using

router#show ip igmp interface ethernet 0
ethernet 0 is up, line protocol is up
Internet address is 172.16.4.3/24
IGMP is enabled on interface
Current IGMP version is 2
CGMP is disabled on interface
IGMP query interval is 60 seconds
IGMP querier timeout is 120 seconds
IGMP max query response time is 10 seconds
Inbound IGMP access group is not set
IGMP activity: 1 joins, 0 leaves
Multicast routing is disabled on interface
Multicast TTL threshold is 0
Multicast groups joined (number of users): 225.250.250.1(1)

Finally, the operation of IGMP can be monitored using the `debug ip igmp` command:

router#debug ip igmp

05:09:55: IGMP: Received v2 Query from 172.16.4.1 (ethernet 0)
05:09:55: IGMP: Set report delay time to 7.0 seconds for 225.250.250.1 on ethernet 0
05:10:02: IGMP: Send v2 Report for 225.250.250.1 on ethernet 0
05:10:02: IGMP: Received v2 Report from 172.16.4.3 (ethernet 0) for 225.250.250.1
05:10:15: IGMP: Send Leave for 225.250.250.1 on ethernet 0

REFERENCES

RFC 1054, "Host Extensions for IP Multicasting," S. Deering, Stanford University, 1988

RFC 1112, "Host Extensions for IP Multicasting," S. Deering, Stanford University, 1989

RFC 2236, "Internet Group Management Protocol–Version 2," W. Fenner, Xerox PARC, 1997

Cisco Group Management Protocol

The *Cisco Group Management Protocol* (CGMP) is a proprietary layer 2 protocol that is used between Cisco routers and switches to limit multicast traffic on a virtual LAN (VLAN). CGMP was developed to address the problem illustrated in Figures 4-1 and 4-2.

In Figure 4-1, the network consists of a router and three ethernet network segments. Each segment contains an ethernet hub or repeater, and a packet transmitted by the router onto one of the segments is received by every host on the segment. Assume a host on network 2 wishes to receive the multicast traffic from the source on network 1. The host on network 2 sends an IGMP Join message to the router, and the router installs state for network 2, indicating that there is at least one receiver for traffic from the indicated multicast group.

Remember from Chapter 3, "Internet Group Management Protocol," that the router does not need to know how many receivers are on a network, only that there is at least one receiver. Network 3 has no receivers for the multicast group, so the router does not forward multicast traffic onto network 3. When the sender on network 1 transmits a multicast packet, the router forwards the traffic onto network 2, but not onto net-

Figure 4-1
At least one IGMP-registered receiver is required for a router to forward multicast traffic.

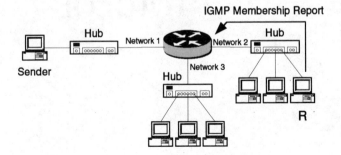

Figure 4-2
Multicast traffic is received by all hosts on a shared hub network.

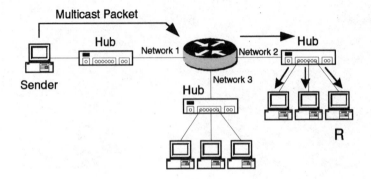

work 3. The hub on network 2 sends a copy of the packet and all subsequent packets to all hosts attached to the hub. The hosts that do not want to receive the multicast traffic must process the frame in order to determine that the frame was not intended for them.

Obviously, this is not an ideal situation. The ideal situation is to limit the multicast traffic not only to networks that have receivers, but also to limit the traffic to receivers on a network that want to receive it.

Layer-three multicast routing protocols are used to limit multicast traffic to networks that have receivers which have indicated their desire to receive the traffic. Later chapters cover layer three multicast routing protocols and their implementation.

In order to remedy the situation depicted in Figure 4-2, we will replace the hub with an ethernet switch. Assume we have an ethernet switch with 50 attached users and that virtual LANs are not being implemented. Without VLANs, every host is on the same IP subnet, and broadcast traffic from one host is flooded to all hosts on the switch (see Figure 4-3).

The situation in Figure 4-3 can be improved by reducing the size of the broadcast domain using VLANs. A VLAN is comprised of hosts in a common IP subnet. For example, if we want to reduce the size of the broadcast domains in Figure 4-3 from 50 to 25 hosts, we would need two VLANs or two logical IP subnets (LIS). Figure 4-4 contains a network where we can accomplish the same broadcast domain size reduction using two switches and no VLANs. Whenever you have more than one LIS, you need a router for intersubnet traffic.

Figure 4-3
Without VLANs,
broadcast traffic is
forwarded to all
hosts.

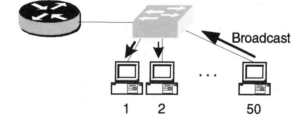

Figure 4-4
Reducing broadcast
domain size using
multiple switches

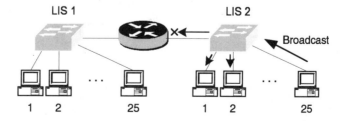

When the broadcast frame reaches the router, it will not be propagated to LIS 1 because routers do not forward broadcast traffic.

The network in Figure 4-4 can be implemented using one switch and two VLANs (see Figure 4-5). Each port on the switch is assigned to either VLAN 1 or VLAN 2 and the router has two logical interfaces configured on one physical interface.

Broadcast traffic from host 25 on VLAN 1 is only forwarded to other hosts on VLAN 1; hosts on VLAN 2 do not receive the broadcast traffic, and inter-VLAN unicast IP traffic must go to the router. In Figure 4-6, host 25 on VLAN 1 is sending unicast IP traffic to host 2 on VLAN 2. The sequence of events to accomplish this are as follows:

1. Host 25 on VLAN 1 wants to send traffic to host 2 on VLAN 2. The destination address is on a different IP subnet, so host 25 sends the packet to the default gateway, which is the router.

2. The router examines the destination address and determines the traffic is for VLAN 2, so the packet is sent back to the switch.

3. The switch examines the destination MAC address and forwards the packet to host 2 on VLAN 2.

The broadcast problem has been solved, but what about the multicast traffic? Have we improved the situation by replacing the shared hub with

Figure 4-5
Reducing broadcast
domain size using
VLANs

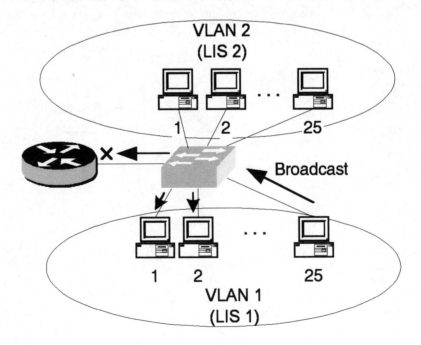

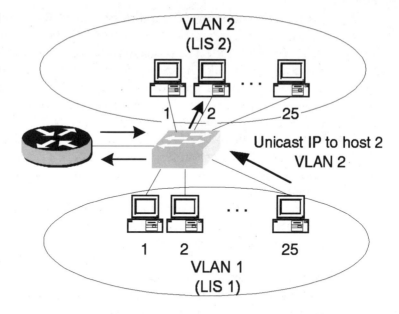

Figure 4-6
Sending inter-VLAN
traffic

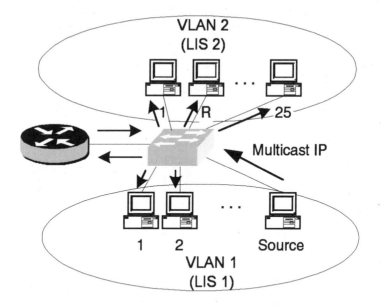

Figure 4-7
Forwarding of
multicast traffic on
VLANs

an ethernet switch? In Figure 4-7, one of the hosts on VLAN 1 is now a multicast sender and one host from VLAN 2 has joined the multicast group using IGMP. What will happen when the source sends a multicast packet?

Everyone will receive the multicast packet! Wait a minute, this is worse than the broadcast traffic. At least VLAN 2 did not receive the broadcast traffic from VLAN 1. The problem is that the switch (at least for now) treats multicast traffic like it was broadcast traffic, but the router does not. Therefore, the multicast traffic on VLAN 1 is forwarded to all hosts on VLAN 1 and the router. The router has state for the multicast group on VLAN 2 because there is a receiver on VLAN 2. The router forwards the multicast traffic to VLAN2, which treats the traffic as a broadcast and forwards it to every host on the VLAN. Looks like we need another protocol. And that protocol should cause multicast traffic to be forwarded as shown in Figure 4-8.

One method to overcome the multicast problem on switches is to manually configure the ports on the switch to receive multicast traffic. The *content addressable memory* (CAM) table on the switch contains a mapping of ethernet addresses to ports that the switch uses to forward traffic. A port can have multiple mappings because a hub can be tied to a switch port and multiple hosts with different ethernet addresses would depend on the port for traffic. Assume a host connected to switch port 1/4 wishes to receive traffic from the multicast group 224.65.10.154. The ethernet multicast address corresponding to this group is 01:00:5E:41:0A:9A (refer to Chapter 5) and we could put the mapping in the CAM table using the command

```
set cam permanent 01-00-5E-41-0A-9A 1/4
```

Figure 4-8
The ideal multicast traffic forwarding scenario

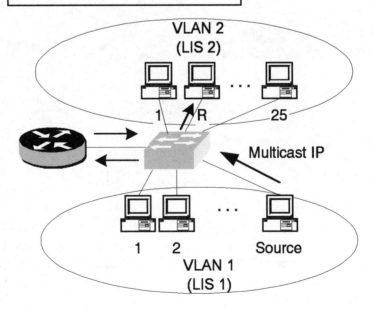

When multicast traffic arrives at the switch for group 224.65.10.154, the traffic would only be sent out through port 1/4 . What other multicast groups would have their traffic sent on only port 1/4 ? Remember that 32 different multicast groups map to the same multicast ethernet address (see Table 4-1). If traffic arrives from any one of those 32 groups, then it is sent only on port 1/4 .

Traffic for any multicast address not in the CAM table would be flooded to every port in the VLAN. This seems to be a solution to our problem. All we need to do every time a user wants to receive multicast traffic is to just add an entry to the CAM table (after we convert the IP multicast address to an ethernet multicast address). Whenever the user wants to leave the group, we just simply delete the entry from the CAM table using

```
no set cam permanent 01-00-5E-41-0A-9A 1/4
```

What could be easier? Hopefully you can see that this would be an administrative nightmare. Assuming you have hundreds or even thousands of users and only a fraction of them receive multicast traffic, this would turn into a full-time and rather boring job, but again this is not the ideal situation. Even though it achieves what we wanted, the solution is not dynamic and requires too much intervention.

To achieve the ideal multicast forwarding scenario, we need a protocol based on a layer two, or ethernet addresses, and one that is dynamic. And it should come as no surprise that this protocol is the CGMP. One of the main concerns when CGMP was designed was that no modifications should need to be made to existing multicast protocols on either hosts or

TABLE 4-1

Class D multicast IP addresses that map to the multicast ethernet address 01:00:5E:41:0A:9A

224.65.10.154	225.65.10.154	226.65.10.154	227.65.10.154
228.65.10.154	229.65.10.154	230.65.10.154	231.65.10.154
232.65.10.154	233.65.10.154	234.65.10.154	235.65.10.154
236.65.10.154	237.65.10.154	238.65.10.154	239.65.10.154
224.193.10.154	225.193.10.154	226.193.10.154	227.193.10.154
228.193.10.154	229.193.10.154	230.193.10.154	231.193.10.154
232.193.10.154	233.193.10.154	234.193.10.154	235.193.10.154
236.193.10.154	237.193.10.154	238.193.10.154	239.193.10.154

routers. Therefore, CGMP must add additional functionality without altering the operation of IGMP or any of the layer three multicast routing protocols. The relationship between IGMP, CGMP, routers, and switches is shown in Figure 4-9.

In Figure 4-9, it looks as if the host is sending the IGMP packets directly to the router and bypassing the switch. This is a logical diagram and, of course, the IGMP packet must pass through the switch. The diagram shows that IGMP is a protocol used between hosts and routers, and CGMP is the protocol used between routers and switches. The fundamental operation when using IGMP and CGMP is as follows:

1. A host sends an IGMP Join to the router for a particular IP multicast group.

2. The router, if CGMP is enabled, sends a message to the switch containing the unicast ethernet address of the host and the multicast ethernet address of the group the host is joining.

3. The switch, if CGMP is enabled, installs the entry in the CAM table.

The format of a CGMP packet is given in Figure 4–10.

Figure 4-9
Logical relationship between IGMP and CGMP

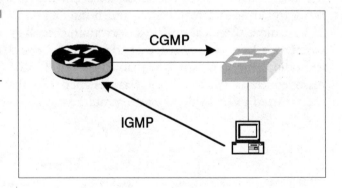

Figure 4-10
CGMP packet format

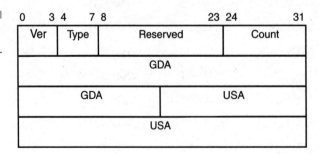

Ver— CGMP version number = 1

Type— 0 = Join, 1 = Leave

Reserved— Set to 0 and ignored

Count— Number of GDA/USA pairs in the message

GDA— Six-byte multicast group destination ethernet address

USA— Six-byte unicast source address, which is the address of the host

CGMP must be enabled on the switch and the router using the commands listed below. On the router interface connected to the switch use

```
ip cgmp
```

and on the switch use

```
set cgmp enable
```

EXAMPLE

Enable `cgmp` on router interface ethernet 0

```
interface ethernet 0
ip cgmp
```

How does the switch know to which port the router is connected? The router sends a CGMP Join message to the switch (if CGMP is enabled on the router interface) with the GDA set to zero and the USA set to the MAC address of the router port (see Figure 4-11).

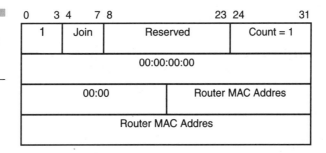

Figure 4-11
CGMP Join message from a router to a switch

When all the receivers for a particular multicast group leave the group, the router deletes state for the group on the interface and sends a CGMP leave message for the group to the switch. The Group Leave message contains the multicast MAC address for the group and the USA field is zero. An example CGMP Group Leave message is shown in Figure 4-12 for multicast group 224.65.10.154.

Upon receipt of the Group Leave message, the switch deletes all entries for the multicast group from the CAM table. What happens to multicast traffic for a group that has had all CAM entries deleted from the switch? The switch floods all packets from this group to every host in the VLAN. If all receivers for all groups no longer wish to receive multicast traffic, the router sends a CGMP Leave message with both the GDA and USA fields set to zero, as shown in Figure 4-13. All multicast groups are deleted from the CAM table and all multicast packets are flooded to all hosts in the VLAN. This may seem like a problem, but if the multicast traffic does not originate from a source connected to the switch but from a source that goes through the router, then this is not a problem.

If no receivers are on the switch, then the multicast routing protocols prevent the traffic from reaching the switch. Well, sometimes. As we shall see, some of the multicast routing protocols periodically flood traffic on all router interfaces, even if no receivers are present. When this occurs, the switch floods the multicast traffic on all ports.

Figure 4-12
Router CGMP Leave message from a router to a switch for a particular multicast group (224.65.10.154)

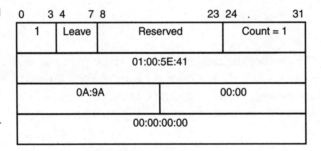

Figure 4-13
Router CGMP Leave message from a router to a switch for all multicast groups

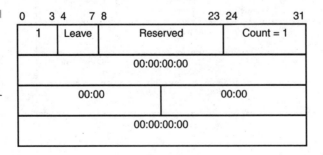

CGMP messages are layer two messages and are sent to the ethernet address 01:00:0C:DD:DD:DD.

Monitoring CGMP

The operation of CGMP is easily verified by using debug and show commands on the router and switch. The network we will use to demonstrate the operation of CGMP is shown in Figure 4-14. The router will begin the CGMP process by sending a Join to the switch.

```
router#debug ip cgmp

07:59:15: CGMP: Sending self Join on Ethernet0
07:59:15: GDA 0000.0000.0000, USA 0010.7b3a.6171
08:00:15: CGMP: Sending self Join on Ethernet0
08:00:15: GDA 0000.0000.0000, USA 0010.7b3a.6171
```

Initially, the host sends an IGMP Group Membership Report to the router. To view this, execute the command **debug ip igmp** on the router:

```
router#debug ip igmp

09:04:55: IGMP: Received v2 report from 172.16.1.1 (Ethernet0) for 224.65.10.154.
```

To verify that the router has created an entry for the group, use the show ip igmp group command.

```
router#show ip igmp group

IGMP Connected Group Membership
Group Address   Interface   Uptime     Expires    Last Reporter
224.65.10.154   Ethernet0   00:00:12   00:02:48   172.16.1.1
```

Figure 4-14
Host IGMP messages pass through the switch to the router.

Port 3/2   Port 3/1

IP Address 172.16.1.1
Multicast Group 224.65.10.154

IGMP Group Membership Report

Figure 4-15
After receiving an
IGMP Report from
the host, the router
informs the switch
with a CGMP Join
message.

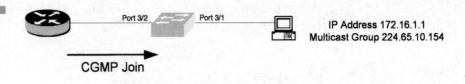

Figure 4-16
The Host IGMP Leave
message triggers
Membership Queries
from the router.

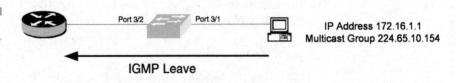

The router then sends a CGMP Join to the switch (refer to Figure 4-15), which can be monitored using both the IGMP and CGMP debug commands.

```
router#debug ip igmp
02:11:18: CGMP: Received IGMP Report on Ethernet0 from 172.16.1.1 for 224.65.10.154.
02:11:19: CGMP: Sending Join on Ethernet0
GDA 0100.5E41.0A9A, USA 0010.7b3a.6171
```

When switch B receives the CGMP Join message from the router, a static CAM entry is created for the host.

```
switch (enable) show cam dynamic
```

VLAN	Dest MAC/Route Des	Destination Ports or VCs
1	0010.7b3a.6171	3/1

B (enable) show cam static

VLAN	Dest MAC/Route Des	Destination Ports or VCs
1	01-00-5e-41-0a-9a	3/1

Once the static CAM entry is in the table, multicast traffic that is received by the switch for group 224.65.10.154 is sent only to port 3/1. When the host decides to leave the group, the host sends an IGMP Leave message to the router (see Figure 4-16). Here we are assuming that the host is using IGMP version 2.

When the router receives the Leave message from the host, the router sends multiple Membership Queries for the group to determine if there are any members remaining.

```
router#debug ip igmp
09:04:54:   IGMP: Received Leave from 172.16.1.1 (Ethernet0) for 224.65.10.154.
09:04:55:   IGMP: Send v2 Query on Ethernet0 to 224.65.10.154.
09:04:56:   IGMP: Send v2 Query on Ethernet0 to 224.65.10.154.
```

If there is no response to the query for the group, then the router deletes the state for the group on the interface and sends a CGMP Leave for the group to the switch.

```
router#debug ip igmp
02:11:18: IGMP: Deleting 224.65.10.254 on Ethernet0
02:11:19: CGMP: Sending Leave on Ethernet0
GDA 0100.5E41.0A9A, USA 0000.0000.0000
```

What happens when the router receives an IGMP v1 Leave message? Hopefully, as you remember from Chapter 3, that there are no IGMP v1 Leave messages. If the host leaves the group, the traffic for group 224.65.10.254 continues to be forwarded to the host until the state for the group expires on the router. When the state for the group does so, a CGMP Leave message is sent to the switch, deleting the entry from the CAM table.

The process of leaving a group can be made more efficient if the switch can monitor IGMP Leave messages. This option is called Fast IGMPv2 Leave processing and is enabled on the switch with the command shown below.

```
switch (enable) set cgmp leave enable
```

With CGMP Leave enabled on the switch, the switch processes the IGMPv2 Leave messages and does not send them to the router. If the switch knows that other receivers for the group are on the same port or VLAN, then no action is required. If the switch knows that this is the last

TABLE 4-2

Router CGMP
Command
Summary

Command	Description
ip cgmp	Enables CGMP on an interface or subinterface
ip cgmp proxy	Enables CGMP and DVMRP proxy on an interface or subinterface
clear ip cgmp [interface]	Clears all CGMP groups
show ip igmp interface [interface]	Shows if CGMP is enabled on an interface
debug ip cgmp	Debugs CGMP traffic

TABLE 4-3

Switch CGMP
Command
Summary

Command	Description
set cgmp enable	Enables CGMP on the switch
set cgmp disable	Disables CGMP on the switch
show multicast router	Lists the ports on the switch that are router ports
show multicast group	Displays active groups
clear cgmp statistics	Clears the CGMP statistics
debug ip cgmp	Debugs CGMP traffic

receiver to leave the group, then an IGMP Leave message is sent to the router. To disable this feature, use:

```
switch(enable) set cgmp leave disable
```

CGMP Command Summary

Tables 4-2 and 4-3 contain a summary of the router and switch commands pertaining to CGMP. The router command, ip cgmp proxy, will be covered in Chapter 5, "Distance Vector Multicast Routing Protocol."

EXAMPLE

View the switch CGMP statistics for VLAN 2

```
switch> show cgmp statistics 2
CGMP enabled
CGMP statistics for vlan 2:
valid rx pkts received            257
invalid rx pkts received          0
valid cgmp joins received         252
valid cgmp leaves received        5
valid igmp leaves received        0
valid igmp queries received       0
igmp gs queries transmitted       0
igmp leaves transmitted           0
failures to add GDA to EARL       0
topology notifications received   0
number of packets dropped         0
```

EXAMPLE

Verify the CGMP is enabled on the router

```
router#show ip igmp interface ethernet 0
Ethernet0 is up, line protocol is up
Internet address is 172.16.4.3/24
IGMP is enabled on interface
Current IGMP version is 2
CGMP is enabled on interface
IGMP Query Interval is 60 seconds
IGMP Querier Timeout is 120 seconds
IGMP Max. Query Response Time is 10 seconds
Inbound IGMP Access group is not set
IGMP activity: 4 joins, 2 leaves
Multicast routing is enabled on interface
Multicast TTL threshold is 0
Multicast Designated Router (DR) is 172.16.4.3 (this system)
IGMP Querying router is 172.16.4.1
Multicast groups joined (number of users):
 224.0.1.40(1) 225.250.250.1(1)
```

Distance Vector Multicast Routing Protocol

We have seen in the previous two chapters how hosts indicate their desire to join or leave a multicast group using the *Internet Group Management Protocol* (IGMP) and how switches and routers exchange multicast information using the *Cisco Group Management Protocol* (CGMP). In this chapter, we begin our investigation of multicast routing protocols, which are designed to efficiently (hopefully!) determine a path from multicast sources to multicast receivers. Before we jump into our first multicast routing protocol, we must first illuminate the general differences between unicast and multicast routing protocols.

Unicast Versus Multicast Routing

An IP unicast routing protocol (RIP, IGRP, EIGRP, OSPF, and BGP) is used to determine a path from a sender (source) to a *single* receiver (destination). Each router along the path from the source to the destination must contain a routing table that indicates which interface to use to forward the packet in order to reach the final destination. This route can either be learned by a dynamic IP routing protocol, a static route, or a default route. As the packet is routed through the network, routers inspect the destination IP address to determine the next hop to the final destination and the source address is not used in making the routing decision.

Of fundamental importance to this discussion is the fact that the destination IP address is a Class A, B, or C *unicast* address. In Figure 5-1, we have a simple network with a source (172.16.1.1) that is sending to a destination (172.16.5.1). It is a simple matter for each router to determine the path to the destination. Assume that only default and directly connected routes are being used in routers A, B, and C. When the packet from the source arrives at router A, the destination address in the IP packet is examined and checked against the routing table. Router A has four routes, three are directly attached, and one is a default route that says "send every packet that is not destined for one of my three directly attached networks out the serial link." Routers B and C have similar routing tables. As the packet travels through the network, each router checks the destination IP address, consults the routing table, and forwards the packet out the proper interface.

Figure 5-1

Routing of a unicast IP packet from source to destination

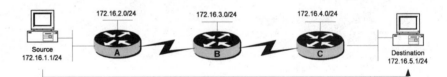

Reverse Path Forwarding

The situation becomes very interesting if the destination address is a multicast or Class D IP address. This is the first general difference between unicast and multicast—there may be multiple receivers with the same address, possibly on different networks, as shown in Figure 5-2. Each host that wants to receive multicast traffic for group 225.65.10.154 will use IGMP to inform the local router using a Join message. When the multicast packet reaches router A, the router determines that the packet is multicast because the address is Class D. The IGMP table is consulted and router A sees that at least one host on a directly attached network (172.16.2.0) has joined the group so the packet is forwarded onto that network. If downstream hosts are to receive the multicast traffic, then router A must forward the traffic on the serial interface and so must router B. If there are no downstream receivers, then it does not make sense for router A to forward the traffic to B because this is a waste of valuable bandwidth.

Therefore, a multicast router needs a mechanism to determine on which interfaces to forward multicast traffic. One method is to simply forward the multicast traffic out all interfaces except for the interface on which the traffic was received. What could possibly go wrong? The network in Figure 5-3 illustrates a problem that can occur if multicast traffic is simply forwarded out all interfaces except for the one on which the traffic was received:

1. The sender sends a multicast packet to router A.

2. Router A forwards the traffic to routers B and C.

3. Routers B and C forward the traffic to router D and to the attached receivers.

4. Router D forwards the traffic to the receiver and then back to routers B and C.

The multicast traffic then circulates in the network until the TTL field in the IP packet goes to zero. Oops! This is probably not a good idea. A

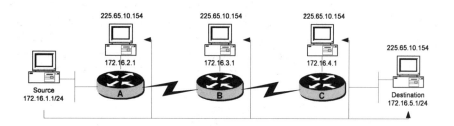

Figure 5-2
Routing of a multicast packet from source to receivers

Figure 5-3
Formation of a
multicast routing
loop

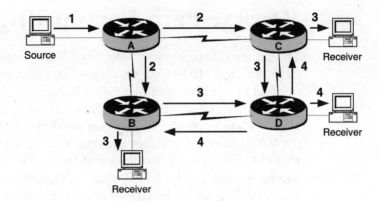

technique that is employed with multicast routing protocols to prevent
this situation from occurring is called *Reverse Path Forwarding* (RPF). RPF
requires that a unicast routing table exist in each multicast router. When
a router receives a multicast packet, the router checks to see if the packet
was received on the interface that is on the shortest path back to the
source. In other words, the interface that is on the shortest path back to
the source is the interface the router would use if forwarding a unicast
packet to the source. This is the other major general difference between
unicast and multicast routing protocols.

A multicast routing protocol examines both the source and destination
IP addresses when a forwarding decision is being made. The destination
address, along with the IGMP table, is used to determine if any hosts
require the traffic on a particular interface. The RPF technique is used to
see if the multicast packet was received on the interface that would be
used to send a unicast packet to the source. If the multicast packet was
received on the interface that would be used to forward a packet to the
source, then the multicast packet is forwarded out the appropriate interfaces. If the multicast packet was not received on the interface that would
be used to send a packet to the source, then the multicast packet is discarded. Figure 5-4 shows the flow of multicast packets when RPF is
employed.

The router interface that is the RPF back to the source is indicated for
each router. Router D has two equal paths back to the multicast source,
one through router B and one through router C. We will assume that the
interface back to router B is chosen as the RPF interface. Soon we will see
how a particular interface is chosen as the RPF interface.

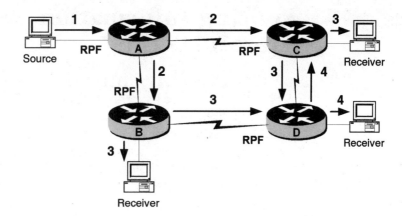

Figure 5-4
Using Reverse Path
Forwarding (RPF) to
eliminate multicast
routing loops

With RPF, the sequence of events in Figure 5-4 is as follows:

1. The multicast source sends a packet to router A.

2. Router A determines that the multicast packet was received on the RPF interface; thus, router A forwards the packet out all interfaces except for the one on which the packet was received.

3. Routers B and C receive the multicast packet on their RPF interfaces, so the packet is forwarded out all interfaces except for the one on which the packet was received.

4. Router D receives the multicast packet on two interfaces but only accepts the packet from the RPF interface. Router D then forwards the packet out the interface to router C and the interface to the attached receiver. However, router C rejects the multicast packet from router D because it did not arrive on the RPF interface.

DVMRP and RIP

The RPF technique to prevent multicast routing loops depends on the available IP routing information contained in the router. As stated earlier, the router can use static routes, default routes, or dynamic routing information to build the routing table. A dynamic routing protocol is almost always preferred and DVMRP is no exception. DVMRP utilizes its own dynamic routing protocol for route exchange and routing table construction. The routing protocol used by DVMRP is based on the *Routing Information Protocol* (RIP), so we will review RIP to gain an understanding of the mechanisms involved and the problems that can occur with a distance vector routing protocol.

Routing Information Protocol (RIP)

RIP Version 1 is specified in RFC 1058 and belongs to the class of routing protocols called *Interior Gateway Protocols* (IGP). An IGP is used for routing within a single autonomous system. An *autonomous system* (AS) is one in which the routing policies are under a common authority and utilize a common routing scheme. An *Exterior Gateway Protocol* (EGP) is used to route between autonomous systems (see Figure 5-5).

RIP is a distance-vector routing protocol, which only uses a hop count when making a routing decision. A hop count is the number of routers that a packet has to traverse in order to reach its destination. If two unequal speed or bandwidth routes to the same destination exist but with the same hop count, then RIP considers both routes to be the same distance (see Figure 5-6), which is an obvious limitation of the protocol.

RIP follows a simple algorithm for constructing a routing table. When a router is initially booted, the only networks it is aware of are those that are directly connected. A RIP routing table contains the destination network, the hop count or metric to the destination network, and the interface a packet should be sent through to reach the destination network. Routers A and B in Figure 5-7 would have initial routing tables as shown in Tables 5-1 and 5-2.

Routers C through F would have similar routing tables. Every 30 seconds RIP broadcasts the entire routing table on every RIP-configured

Figure 5-5
Interior and Exterior Gateway Routing Protocols

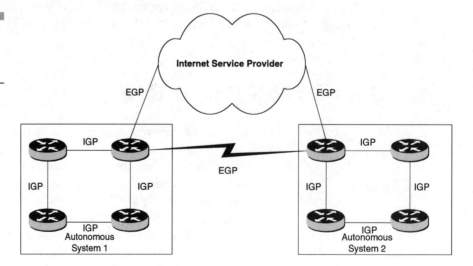

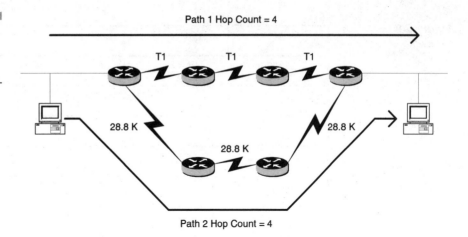

Figure 5-6
All equal-hop paths are considered equal by RIP.

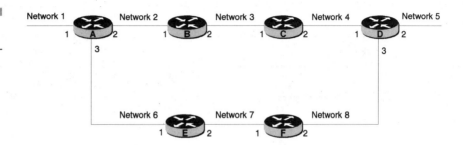

Figure 5-7
Sample RIP network

TABLE 5-1

Initial Routing Table for Router A

Destination Network	Hop Count	Interface
1	1	1
2	1	2
6	1	3

TABLE 5-2

Initial Routing Table for Router B

Destination Network	Hop Count	Interface
2	1	1
3	1	2

interface using the format in Figure 5-8. One RIP message can contain up to 25 networks. If a routing table contains more than 25 entries, multiple RIP messages will have to be transmitted.

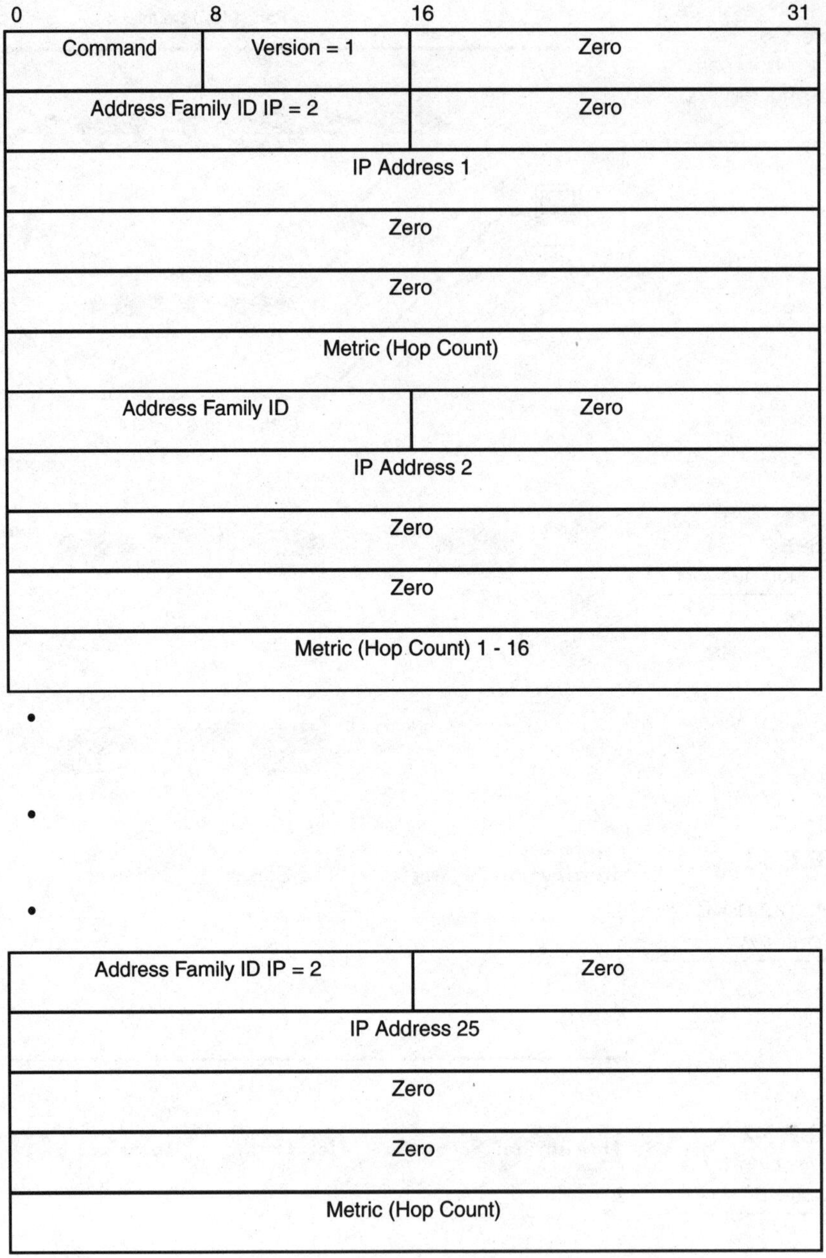

Figure 5-8
RIP Message format

0	8	16	31
Command	Version = 1	Zero	
Address Family ID IP = 2		Zero	
IP Address 1			
Zero			
Zero			
Metric (Hop Count)			
Address Family ID		Zero	
IP Address 2			
Zero			
Zero			
Metric (Hop Count) 1 - 16			

•

•

•

Address Family ID IP = 2	Zero
IP Address 25	
Zero	
Zero	
Metric (Hop Count)	

The command field in the RIP message can be used to request all or part of a routing table (command = 1), or signify a response to a request (command =2). Other values are specified in RFC 1058, but they are now considered obsolete. Usually a router sets the command field to one and then broadcasts the entire routing table.

When a router receives a RIP message, a simple algorithm is used to determine if the route(s) should be added to the routing table:

1. If a route in the update is not in the routing table, then add the route to the table and increase the metric by one.

2. If the route in the update is in the routing table, add it to the local table only if the metric is less than the metric for the current route and the update was received on a different interface. If the update was received on the same interface as the one in the routing table, then accept the route and the metric.

When router B transmits the first RIP message, router A only installs the route to network 3 with a hop count of 2, but does not install the route to network 2 because the route already exists with a metric equal to router B's metric. The routing table for router A contains four routes, as shown in Table 5-3.

Router A now knows that if it has a packet destined for network 3 it can send it to router B through interface 2. After a period of time, all the routers in the network of Table 5-3 will contain entries in their routing tables for every network. The complete routing table for router A is contained in Table 5-4.

Notice in Figure 5-7 that router A can reach network 5 through interface 3 with a hop count of four or through interface 2 with a hop count of four. Which route will router A place in the routing table? The answer depends on whether it receives the RIP message from router E first or from router B. Both routers B and E will advertise a route to network 5 with a hop count of three. According to the RIP algorithm, router A will install the route from the first RIP message received and ignore the route from the second.

In Figure 5-8, the metric is shown to have a range of values between one and 16. A hop count of 16 signifies that the corresponding network

TABLE 5-3	**Destination Network**	**Hop Count**	**Interface**
Initial Routing Table for Router A	1	1	1
	2	1	2
	6	1	3
	3	2	2

TABLE 5-4

Final Routing
Table for Router A

Destination Network	Hop Count	Interface
1	1	1
2	1	2
3	2	2
4	3	2
5	4	2
6	1	3
7	2	3
8	3	3

is unreachable. Such a value is considered to be infinity by RIP, which is another limitation of the protocol. Networks that are more than 15 hops away cannot be reached. Many corporate networks have hundreds of routers and their size makes RIP unusable as a routing protocol.

RIP is also a slowly converging protocol. Convergence is a measure of how long it takes to propagate a route through the network when there is a change. Assuming we boot all the routers in Figure 5-7 simultaneously, it will take 60 seconds (if all routers immediately send their initial RIP message) for the route to network 5 to reach router A. If router D loses the connection to network 5, it will advertise a hop count of 16 (infinity) to network 5. Router A will not know that the network is unreachable for 60 seconds (a very long time) and will continue to send packets to network 5 until it learns the network is unreachable. Actually, all the routers do not send their initial routing tables at the same time. The 30-second timer for RIP updates is offset by a random amount to prevent the routers from transmitting simultaneously.

Two additional timers are also associated with RIP updates, the timeout timer and the garbage-collection timer. When a new route is installed in the routing table, the timeout timer is initialized to zero and begins to count. Every time a RIP message containing the route is received, the timeout timer is reset to zero. If a RIP message containing the route is not received for 180 seconds, the metric for the route is set to 16 and a garbage-collection timer for the route is started. If 120 seconds pass without receiving the route in a RIP message, the route is removed from the routing table. If a message is received containing the route before the garbage-collection timer reaches 120, the timer is cleared and the route is installed in the routing table.

Count to Infinity Problem

In Figure 5-9, router A has lost connectivity to network 1. Router A adjusts the metric in the routing table for network 1 to 16. Assume router B transmits its routing table before router A.

The message from router B contains a route to network 1 with a hop count of two. This is better than the route currently in router A's routing table, so the route is installed. Router A now advertises that it can reach network 1 with a hop count of three. Because router B receives this information on the same interface as the route currently in the table, it installs the route with a hop count of four. Router B now advertises to router A a hop count of four for network 1 and router A installs it with a hop count of five and so on ad infinitum (or at least to 16).

While the routers are counting to 16, we have a routing loop. Packets that A has to send to network 1 are sent to router B and router B sends them to router A and so on. The routing loop will be broken when the routers finally count to 16, but with 30-second updates this could take some time. Meanwhile, the network is being flooded with packets essentially making the network unusable.

SPLIT HORIZON   Split horizon is a technique used to solve the counting to infinity problem. With split horizon, a router does not advertise a route over the interface from which it learned the route. This prevents router B from advertising the route to network 1 back to router A. Within 30 seconds, router A would advertise a hop count of 16 to network 1, alerting the network that the network is unreachable.

SPLIT HORIZON WITH POISON-REVERSE   This technique allows a router to send updates about routes over the interface that they were learned from, but the hop count is set to 16. For our example, router B

Figure 5-9
Rip Count to
Infinity Problem.

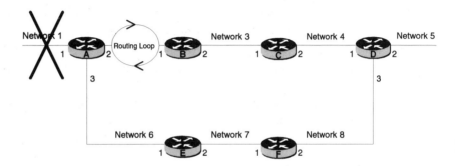

would advertise a route to network 1 with a hop count of 16, preventing routing A from placing it in the routing table. DVMRP uses a modified version of poison-reverse for determining downstream dependencies.

HOLD DOWN   Hold down causes a router to ignore routing updates about a route for a period of time after the route has been declared unreachable. For our example, router A determines that network 1 is unreachable. With hold down, router A will ignore advertisements about network 1 from routers B and E during the hold down period, which will allow router A to transmit its routing table, informing the network that network 1 is unreachable.

TRIGGERED UPDATES   Although split horizon solves the routing loop problem between two routers, a situation could occur when three or more routers form a routing loop. Split horizon cannot prevent this from happening. Triggered updates require a router to immediately transmit the routing table when a change occurs, which speeds up the convergence of the network but has the potential for creating broadcast storms. Another situation could arise where a router receives a triggered update and then a regular update from another router reinstalling the route. In short, this is not a technique that solves all the convergence problems of RIP, although the ones mentioned do add a measure of stability to a RIP network.

RIP and VLSM

Simply stated, don't use VLSM with RIP. You can do it, but it won't work and it can cause a lot of head scratching if you don't realize what is happening.

If you look back at the RIP message format in Figure 5-8, you will notice that a very important piece of information is missing, the subnet mask! When RIP is constructing the routing message for an interface, RIP only includes those networks that have the same subnet mask as the interface on which the message is to be transmitted. In Figure 5-10, we have a router with four interfaces. Two of the interfaces use a /20 subnet mask and two of the interfaces use a /24 subnet mask.

Downstream routers on interfaces 1 and 2 would never learn about networks 1.0 and 2.0, and routers downstream of interfaces 3 and 4 would never learn about networks 16 and 32. If all the subnet masks are equal, then there is not a problem. Without transmitting the subnet mask, RIP cannot take advantage of the properties of VLSM, yet another limitation.

Figure 5-10
RIP and VLSM

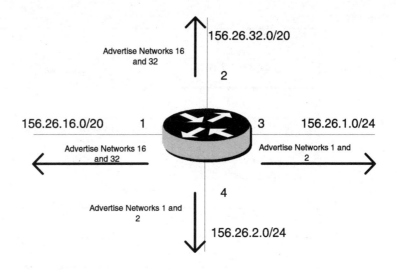

RIP Version 2

RFC 1723, 1994, contains extensions to RIP version 1. Most notable is the RIP message format (see Figure 5-11). The shaded entries are the additions that have been made in version 2. The route tag can be used to indicate routes that have been learned from other RIP routers or from another IGP, such as OSPF, or from an EGP, such as BGP. The subnet mask is probably the most important addition allowing designers to use VLSM with RIP V2.

Unfortunately, RIP V2 still suffers from the other limitations of RIP V1 as summarized in Table 5-5.

DVMRP Operation

The basic operation of DVMRP consists of four processes. The first process is neighbor discovery, which is used to find other DVMRP-capable and enabled routers attached to a common network. The second process is that of route exchange. Although the DVMRP route exchange process is similar to RIP, there are important differences that will be demonstrated. The purpose of a multicast routing protocol is the efficient delivery of multicast datagrams to destinations that want to receive them. Therefore, DVMRP must interoperate with IGMP to determine if multicast packets need to be forwarded onto a network (receivers are present) or if the packets need to be

Figure 5-11
RIP Version 2
Message format

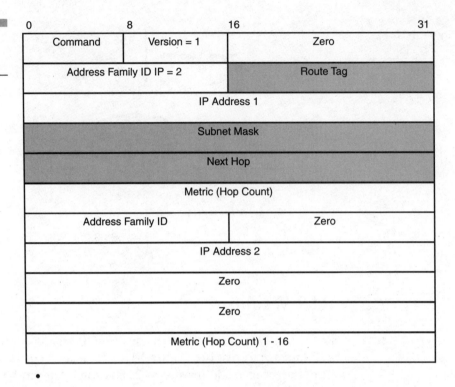

prevented from reaching a network (no receivers present). DVMRP can dynamically add or delete networks from the list of networks that desire to receive multicast traffic from a particular group. The final two basic

TABLE 5-5

RIP Limitations

Slow Convergence

Routing to Infinity

Can't handle VLSM (V1)

Unable to detect routing loops

Only metric is hop count

Small network diameter (15 hops)

If multiple routes to a destination exist, will only use one (no load balancing)

DVRMP processes are used to achieve this dynamic nature. Networks are added to the forwarding list using Graft messages, while networks are removed from the forwarding list using Prune messages.

DVMRP messages are sent using the IP packet format (see Figure 5-12) with no options and with the protocol field set to 2, identifying the packet type as an IGMP message. The type field is set to 19 (0×13) to identify the IGMP packet as a DVMRP message and the code field is used to differentiate between the various DVMRP packets, as shown in Table 5-6.

DVMRP Neighbor Discovery

When DVMRP is initially enabled on a router, the DVMRP process determines if the router has any DVMRP neighboring routers. The purpose of neighbor discovery is to locate other DVMRP routers that are directly connected in order to determine the capabilities of neighbor routers and to enable a keep-alive function.

Neighbor probes are sent on all DVMRP-enabled interfaces every 10 seconds. If a previously discovered neighbor does not respond with its own keep-alive (neighbor probe) message within 35 seconds, then the neighbor is declared down. Routers that have tagged a neighbor as down are required to follow the actions listed in the following steps.

1. Any routes that have been learned from the dead neighbor are placed in the hold-down state.

2. If traffic was being forwarded to this router (it was a downstream router), then this dependency should be removed.

Figure 5-12
Encapsulation of a
DVMRP packet in an
IP datagram

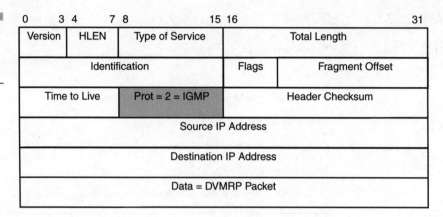

0	3 4	7 8	15 16	31
Version	HLEN	Type of Service	Total Length	
Identification			Flags	Fragment Offset
Time to Live		Prot = 2 = IGMP	Header Checksum	
Source IP Address				
Destination IP Address				
Data = DVMRP Packet				

•

•

•

Data

TABLE 5-6

DVMRP Packet
Type Identifiers

Packet Type	Code
Probe	1
Route Report	2
Ask-Neighbors2	5
Neighbors2	6
Prune	7
Graft	8
Graft Ack	9

3. If the dead neighbor was the designated forwarder on a multi-access network, then a new designated forwarder needs to be elected.

4. If the dead neighbor was an upstream router, then forwarding entries must be flushed.

5. If Grafts from this neighbor need to be acknowledged, then they can be canceled.

6. If the neighbor is the last downstream router on the interface and no other receivers are on the network, then the interface should be pruned.

Neighbors are discovered using IGMP packets with the format shown in Figure 5-13. The type code of 0×13 indicates that this a DVMRP message. Neighbor discovery packets are identified by setting the code field to 1. The checksum field in all DVMRP packets is the standard 16-bit ones compliment of the ones compliment sum of the packet.

The Generation ID field is used to determine if a neighbor router has been rebooted. When a router discovers that the generation ID field has changed, the router can assume that the neighbor has been restarted. When this occurs, the router that detected the change in neighbor generation ID flushes any prune information that it has from the neighbor and then sends a unicast copy of the routing table to the neighbor. The network in Figure 5-14 illustrates the neighbor discovery process.

When DVMRP is enabled on the ethernet interface on router A, a DVMRP probe packet is sent out from that interface. Router A has not discovered any DVMRP neighbors at this point, so the neighbor list in the probe packet is empty (see Figure 5-15).

The neighbor probe interval is 10 seconds. Router A will continue to send neighbor probe packets with an empty neighbor list until DVMRP is enabled on the ethernet interface of router B. Assume DVMRP is

Figure 5-13

DVMRP neighbor discovery packet format

Type = 0x13	Code = 1	Checksum	
Reserved	Capabilities	Minor Ver	Major Ver
Generation ID			
Neighbor IP Address 1			
Neighbor IP Address 2			
. . .			
Neighbor IP Address N			

Figure 5-14
Network used to
illustrate the DVMRP
neighbor discovery
process

Type = 0x13	Code = 1	Checksum	
Reserved	Capabilities	Minor Ver	Major Ver
Generation ID			

Figure 5-15
DVMRP neighbor
discovery packet
format, initial
contents

Type = 0x13	Code = 1	Checksum	
Reserved	Capabilities	Minor Ver	Major Ver
Generation ID			
Neighbor IP Address 1 = 172.16.1.1 = Router A			

Figure 5-16
Neighbor probe
packet sent by
router B.

enabled on router B, which receives a neighbor probe from router A before
it sends its initial probe. Router B will place the IP address of router A
into the neighbor list of the probe packet and then transmit the probe
having the format of Figure 5-16.

When router A receives the probe from router B and detects its IP
address, then router A has established a two-way adjacency with router B.
When router A sends the next probe, the packet will now contain the IP
address of router B, which will form a two-way adjacency with router A.
Once the two-way adjacency has been formed, the routers can exchange
their routing information.

The neighbor discovery process also determines if any DVMRP enabled
routers are directly attached to any of the router's interfaces. If no neighbors are discovered, then the network is a leaf network, meaning that no
other DVMRP routers are on the network that will forward the multicast
traffic. On leaf networks, the router only needs to consult the IGMP tables
to determine if any receivers for a particular multicast group are on the network. For non-leaf networks, networks on which there is a DVMRP neighbor, other techniques are required to determine if multicast traffic needs
to be forwarded (see Figure 5-17).

DVMRP Route Exchange

DVMRP initially advertises directly connected networks. As other networks are learned through the route advertisement process and routes are added to the local DVMRP routing table, more routes may be advertised.

Unlike RIP route advertisements, DVMRP routes are sent in an abbreviated format, as shown in Figure 5-18. Route advertisements consist of three components: the netmask, the network, and the metric. The netmask is assumed to be of the form 255.x.x.x because the standard subnet masks for class A, B, and C addresses begins with 255. Because the first octet of every subnet mask is assumed to be 255, then the first octet does not need to be included in the route report. This is why the length of the netmask fields in Figure 5-18 is shown as only three bytes. For example, if the netmask in the route report has a value of 255.255.128, then the full netmask has the value 255.255.255.128.

Another method used to reduce the size of the route report is to list one netmask for all networks having the same netmask, instead of listing a netmask for every network. If we are advertising networks 172.16.1.0/24 and 172.16.2.0/24, for example, then we could list the two networks, 172.16.1.0 and 172.16.2.0, and one netmask, 255.255.0 (remember the assumed 255 at the beginning of the netmask). For routing, we only need to know the network address that corresponds to the non-zero values of the netmask. To reduce the packet size further, only the portion of the network that corresponds to a non-zero value of the netmask needs to be reported. With a netmask of 255.255.255.0, we only need to report 172.16.1 and 172.16.2 for the networks mentioned previously. The metric parameter must be listed for each advertised network and the metric values will be explained shortly.

Looking back at Figure 5-18, it is not clear how to differentiate when one set of netmask-network-metric groups ends and another group begins. The delineation between groups is accomplished by setting the most significant

Figure 5-17
DVMRP leaf and non-leaf networks

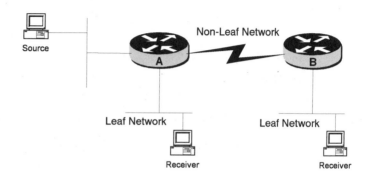

Figure 5-18
DVMRP Route Report
packet format

Type = 0x13	Code = 2	Checksum	
Reserved		Minor Ver	Major Ver
Mask 1 (3 bytes)			SrcNet11
SrcNet11		Metric 11	SrcNet11
SrcNet12		Metric 12	Mask 2
Mask 2		SrcNet21	
SrcNet21		Metric 21	Mask 3

bit of the last metric value for the last network in the group, which is equivalent to adding 128 to the metric.

Let's look at an example. Assume a DVMRP router has the following routes in the local routing table.

Network	Netmask	Metric
156.26.1.0	255.255.255.0	1
144.223.0.0	255.255.0.0	2
12.0.0.0	255.0.0.0	3
191.56.3.0	255.255.255.0	4
130.10.10.0	255.255.0.0	5
188.44.0.0	255.255.0.0	6

The first step in determining the DVMRP route report format is to group the networks to be advertised according to their netmask.

Network	Netmask	Metric	Network Reported
12.0.0.0	255.0.0.0	3 + 128 = 131	12
144.223.0.0	255.255.0.0	2	144.223
130.10.10.0	255.255.0.0	5	130.10
188.44.0.0	255.255.0.0	6 + 128 = 134	188.44
156.26.1.0	255.255.255.0	1	156.26.1
191.56.3.0	255.255.255.0	4 + 128 = 132	191.56.3

Notice that 128 (the most significant bit set) has been added to the last metric of the last network in each group. With the route information listed above, the route report packet can be built and is shown in Figure 5-19.

Figure 5-19
Example DVMRP
Route Report packet

Type = 0x13	Code = 2	Checksum	
Reserved		Minor Ver	Major Ver
0.0.0			12
131	255.0.0		
144.223		2	130.
10	5	188	44
134	255.255.0		
156.26.1			1
191.56.3			132

One special case is that of the default route. The default route is represented by the mask-network pair 00 00 00/00 . The mask indicates a standard Class C address and normal processing indicates that the mask is 255.0.0.0. This case needs to be interpreted correctly, so the mask for the default route is 0.0.0.0 and not 255.0.0.0.

The processing of DVMRP route reports is much more complex than RIP route processing. The rules that follow dictate how a DVMRP router will treat the routes received in a route report:

1. If the route is received from a neighbor, then accept it. If the route report is received from a router for which a two-way adjacency was not established (not a neighbor), then reject the route report.

2. If the metric of a route in the report plus the metric of the receiving router is greater than or equal to infinity (32), then set the metric to infinity (32).

3. If the metric of a route in the report is greater than or equal to infinity, then no change to the metric will be made (we will see why).

4. If a route is not in the routing table (a new route) and the metric plus the metric of the receiving router is less than infinity (32), then the route is added to the routing table.

5. If a route is in the routing table, then another set of rules comes into effect.

a. If the metric is between but not equal to 32 (infinity) and 64
(2 × 32), then the sending router is informing the receiving
router that it is dependent on the receiving router for multicast
traffic from any source on that network. Another way of stating
this is that the receiving router is on the shortest path back to
any source on that network. Figure 5-20 illustrates this situation.

In Figure 5-20, we assume that routers A and B have completed
the neighbor discovery process and that they have formed a
two-way adjacency. As part of its route report, router B says
that it can reach network 172.16.2.0/24 with a metric of one
(directly attached). In some cases, metrics can be assigned to an
interface, but typically the metric is set to one, indicating that
the network is one hop away. Router A installs this route in its
routing table because this is a new route.

Router A also determines that traffic from any multicast source
on network 172.16.2.0/24 has to pass through router B to get to
router A. In this situation, router A will poison-reverse the
route by adding infinity (32) to the metric and reporting the
route back to router B. Router A has a metric of 2 for network
172.16.2.0/24 and the poison-reverse value is 34 (2 + 32). When
router B receives this metric (34), then it knows that router A
depends on it for multicast traffic from network 172.16.2.0/24.
This information is important when pruning occurs.

Figure 5-20
DVMRP poison-
reverse used to
indicate route
dependency

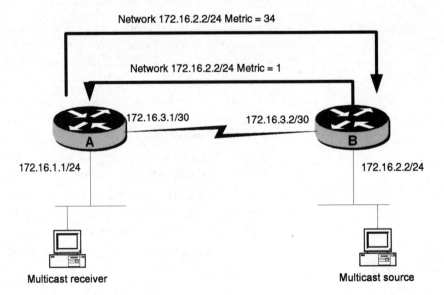

Network 172.16.2.2/24 Metric = 34

Network 172.16.2.2/24 Metric = 1

172.16.3.1/30   172.16.3.2/30

A   **B**

172.16.1.1/24   172.16.2.2/24

Multicast receiver   Multicast source

The function of poison-reverse can easily be seen in the network of Figure 5-21. Router A advertises to routers B and C that it can reach the source in one hop. Routers B and C add one to the metric and advertise the metric as two. Router D then adds one to the metric and advertises the distance as three. Router E receives two advertisements for the source with metrics of two and three, chooses the smallest metric as the RPF interface, and poison-reverses the route. So when router E transmits its routing table to C, the metric is 35, indicating that router E is dependent on router C for traffic from the source.

b. If the metric plus the metric of the receiving router is greater than the metric of the route already in the routing table, then check the address of the sending router. If the address of the sending router is different than the address of the sending router for the route in the table, ignore the route. If the address of the sending router is the same as the address of the sending router for the route in the table, then replace the metric in the table for that route.

c. If the metric plus the metric of the receiving router is less than the metric of the route in the table, then replace the route in the table. If the address of the sending router is different than the address of the sending router in the table, then poison-reverse the route.

d. If the metric plus the metric of the receiving router is equal to the metric in the routing table and the address of the sender matches the address of the sender in the routing table, then refresh the route. If the address of the sender is not the same as the address of the sender in the routing table and the

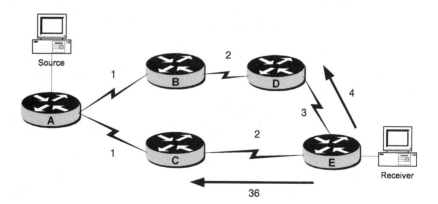

Figure 5-21
DVMRP poison-
reverse example

new sender's IP address is lower, use this neighbor as the upstream router.

e. If the metric of the received route is greater than or equal to 2×32 (64), then ignore the route.

Figure 5-22 illustrates rule 5b:

1. Router B sends a route report to router C advertising network 172.16.1.0/24.

2. This is a new route for router C, so the route is installed in the routing table and the poison-reverse route is sent back to router B.

3. Router A sends a route report containing the network 172.16.1.0/24 with the same metric being advertised by router B.

4. Router C now selects router A as the upstream router for multicast traffic from network 172.16.1.0/24 because router A has a lower IP address than router B and sends a poison-reverse to router A for this network. An updated poison-reverse is also sent to router B (without the addition of infinity) to inform router B that router C is no longer dependent on router B for multicast traffic from network 172.16.1.0/24.

In the case of a multi-access network such as ethernet, only one router needs to forward multicast traffic onto the network. For the network in Figure 5-23, each router is a designated forwarder for a particular multicast source. The designated forwarder for each multicast source is the router that has the smallest metric back to the source. If two or more routers attached

Figure 5-22
Illustration of rule 5b

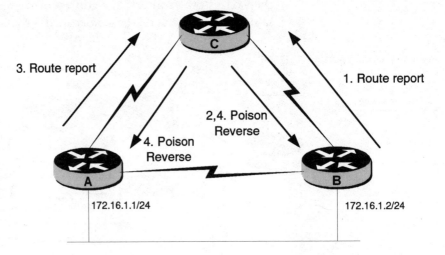

3. Route report

1. Route report

2,4. Poison Reverse

4. Poison Reverse

172.16.1.1/24

172.16.1.2/24

to a multi-access network have the same metric back to the source, then the router with the lowest IP address is elected designated forwarder.

For network 172.16.1.0 in Figure 5-23, there are three multicast sources for which a designated forwarder needs to be elected. For source 1, the choices are router A or router B. Both have an identical metric back to source 1, so the IP address of the routers is used to break the tie. In this case, router A becomes the designated forwarder because it has a lower IP address. For source 2, router B is the designated forwarder because it is the only router attached to network 172.16.1.0/24 that has a path back to source 2. The same argument applies for router C and source 3. In this scenario, we have three designated forwarders on the multi-access network, one for each source.

Source-Based Multicast Trees

The routing table that is constructed using DVMRP route exchange produces multicast delivery trees that are source-based. The term "source-based" simply means that forwarding paths are based on the shortest path back to the source (remember RPF?). Therefore, for every multicast source, there is a corresponding multicast tree that connects the sender to all receivers through the RPF interface. For example, the network in Figures 5-24a and 5-24b contains two multicast sources. It is not important which multicast address the sources are sending packets to, only the location of the sources when constructing the delivery tree.

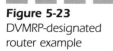

Figure 5-23
DVMRP-designated router example

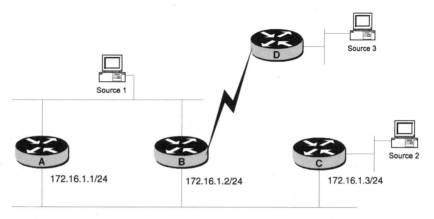

Network 172.16.1.0/24

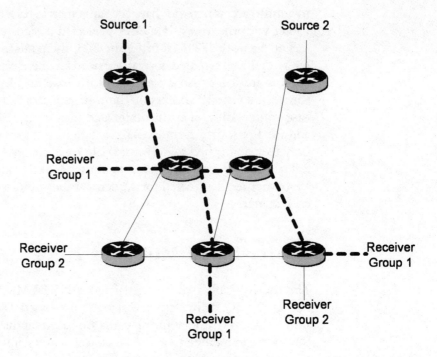

Figure 5-24a
Source-based
multicast delivery tree
for source 1

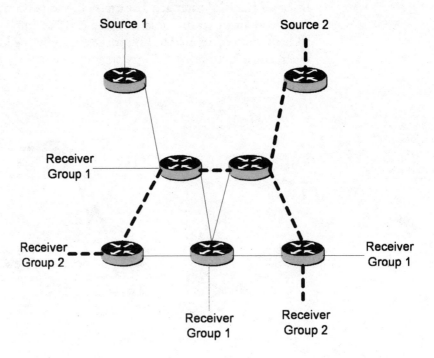

Figure 5-24b
Source-based
multicast delivery tree
for source 2

DVMRP Pruning and Grafting

Membership in a multicast group is dynamic and receivers can join or leave a multicast group using IGMP. Forwarding multicast traffic onto networks that have no receivers or downstream routers is an inefficient use of network resources, so DVMRP uses prunes and grafts to dynamically alter the structure of the source-based trees. To illustrate the situations when pruning and grafting comes into effect, we will examine some simple network scenarios where these mechanisms come into play. In Figure 5-25, we have a network with one multicast source and one multicast receiver.

Router A and B have no leaf networks, a network with only multicast receivers and no forwarding routers. The receiver on router C has signaled, using IGMP, that it desires to receive traffic from the multicast group (which has as its source the host attached to router A).

How do routers A and B know to forward traffic to router C so the host may receive it? Initially, DVMRP assumes that all networks have receivers and so it floods the multicast traffic received on the RPF interface on all networks. Routers A and B know that they are upstream routers in relation to router C due to the fact that router C has used poison-reverse for the network containing the source.

Assume now that the receiver no longer wishes to receive multicast traffic from the source. The host then sends an IGMP Leave message for the group, and router C queries the network and discovers that no hosts want to receive multicast traffic. At this point, there is no reason for any of the routers to forward multicast traffic from the source because there are no longer any receivers. Router C sends a Prune message to router B, and because no other networks require the forwarding of multicast traffic by router B, router B sends a Prune message to router A. Router A now has no downstream routers requiring multicast traffic, so router A prunes its serial interface.

Prunes are also necessary when hosts need to receive multicast traffic on an attached network. The network of Figure 5-26 contains a multi-access

Figure 5-25
DVMRP network
used to illustrate
pruning and grafting

Source

A   B   C

Receiver

Figure 5-26
Pruning interfaces on
a multi-access
network

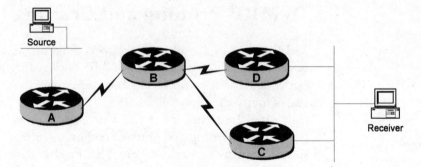

ethernet segment. From our earlier discussion, we know that either router C or D will become the designated forwarded for the ethernet network, based on the metric back to the source, or in the case of a tie, the IP address. Whichever router is not elected as designated forwarder must prune its serial interface from the source tree, so only one router will forward the multicast traffic to the receiver.

The actions that a router must take when a Prune message is received are as follows:

1. If the Prune is received from a router that the receiving router has not formed a two-way adjacency with, then discard the message.

2. Examine the Prune message and determine if the message is the proper format.

3. If the Prune message does not apply to source information active on the router, then discard the message.

4. If the neighbor that sent the prune is not a dependent neighbor for the network to be pruned, then discard the message.

5. If there is an active Prune from this neighbor for the indicated source network and group, then reset the timer to the value received in the Prune message.

6. If there is not an active Prune from this neighbor for the indicated source network and group, then set a time-out using the value in the Prune message.

7. If all dependent downstream routers on this network have been sent Prunes, then determine if any group members are on the network. If there are no group members, then send a Prune message to the upstream router.

The actions a router must take when sending a prune are as follows:

1. If the upstream router cannot receive Prunes, then do not send a Prune. This can be determined from the neighbor's DVMRP version and capabilities.

2. If any Graft messages need to be acknowledged, cancel them.

The Prune packet format is shown in Figure 5-27.

The Prune lifetime is the amount of time the Prune is in effect. DVMRP is a broadcast and Prune protocol, so when the Prune expires, the multicast traffic will again be forwarded until another Prune is received.

Grafting is the opposite of pruning. When a pruned network needs to again receive multicast traffic from a particular source for a multicast group, then the network needs to be added, or grafted, back onto the multicast source based tree. Graft messages are sent upstream until they reach the source tree for the particular multicast source and are acknowledged at each hop. Graft messages are sent under the following conditions:

1. If a host joins a multicast group (using IGMP) on a network that has been pruned for that group.

2. A DVMRP router is enabled on a pruned network and is dependent on the upstream router.

3. A router on a pruned network restarts (signaled by the generation ID).

4. If a Graft acknowledgment is not received for a previous Graft message.

The format of the Graft and Graft acknowledgment packets are shown in Figures 5-28 and 5-29. The values of the various DVMRP timers are listed in Table 5-7.

Figure 5-27
DVMRP Prune
packet format

Type = 0x13	Code = 7	Checksum	
Reserved		Minor Ver	Major Ver
Source Address			
Group Address			
Prune Lifetime			

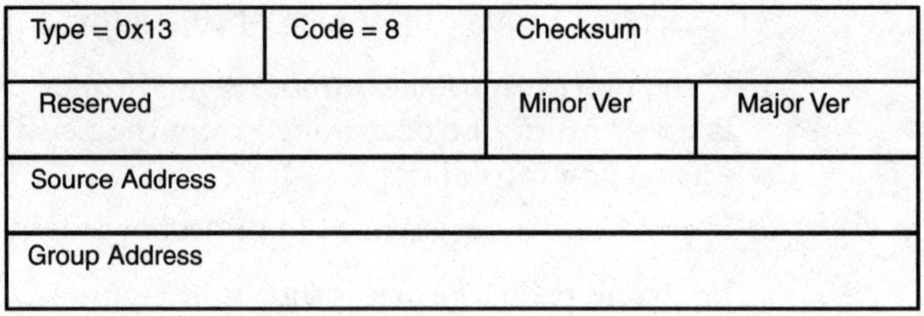

Figure 5-28
DVMRP Graft
packet format

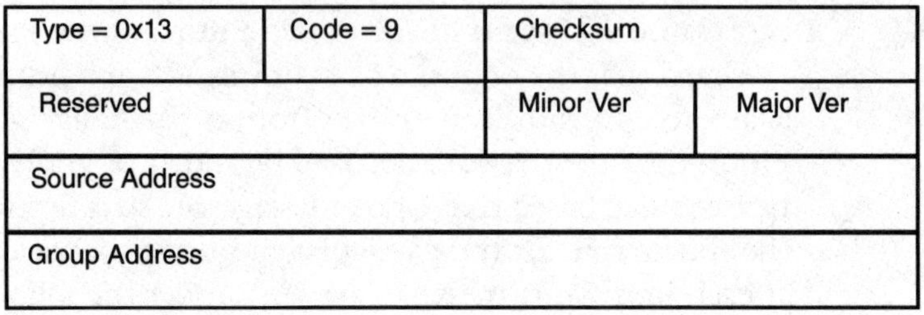

Type = 0x13	Code = 8	Checksum	
Reserved		Minor Ver	Major Ver
Source Address			
Group Address			

Figure 5-29
DVMRP Graft
acknowledgment
packet format

Type = 0x13	Code = 9	Checksum	
Reserved		Minor Ver	Major Ver
Source Address			
Group Address			

TABLE 5-7

DVMRP Timers
and Values

Timer	Value in Seconds
Probe Interval	10
Neighbor Timeout Interval	35
Minimum Flash Update Interval	5
Router Report Interval	60
Route Expiration Time	140
Route Hold-Down	120
Prune Lifetime	Variable (less than two hours)
Prune Retransmission Time	3 with exponential back-off
Graft Retransmission Time	5 with exponential back-off

Tracing and Troubleshooting

DVMRP contains a mechanism for determining the characteristics of a
particular router. The first part of this mechanism is to send a unicast
request to a DVMRP router requesting this information. The packet is
called an Ask-Neighbors2 and it has the format shown in Figure 5-30. The
response to an Ask-Neighbors2 packet is the Neighbors2 response packet,
whose format is shown in Figure 5-31.

Figure 5-30
DVMRP Ask-
Neighbors2 packet

Type = 0x13	Code = 5	Checksum	
Reserved		Minor Ver	Major Ver

Figure 5-31
DVMRP Neighbors2
packet format

Type = 0x13	Code = 6	Checksum	
Reserved	Capabilities	Minor Ver	Major Ver
Local Address 1			
Metric 1	Threshold 1	Flags 1	Nbr Count 1
Neighbor 1			
Neighbor 2			
. . .			
Neighbor n			
Local Address k			
Metric k	Threshold k	Flags k	Nbr Count k
Neighbor 1			
Neighbor 2			
. . .			
Neighbor m			

The capabilities field lists the characteristics of the router, and the possible values are listed in Table 5-8 and the flags values in Table 5-9. The Neighbors2 packet contains a section for each interface on the router from which the information was requested. For each router interface, the Neighbors2 packet contains the metric of the interface, the interface flags, the number of neighbors on the network connected to the interface, and the neighbors' addresses.

TABLE 5-8

DVMRP Router
Capabilities

Bit	Flag	Description
0	Leaf	This is a leaf router
1	Prune	Router understands pruning
2	GenID	Router sends generation IDs
3	Mtrace	Router handles Mtrace requests
4	SNMP	Router supports the DVMRP MIB

TABLE 5-9

DVMRP Interface
Flags

Bit	Flag	Description
0	Tunnel	Neighbor reached via a tunnel
1	Source Route	Tunnel uses IP source routing
2	Reserved	No longer used
3	Reserved	No longer used
4	Down	Operational status down
5	Disabled	Administrative status down
6	Querier	Querier for the interface
7	Leaf	No downstream neighbors on this interface

DVMRP Tunnels and the Internet Multicast Backbone

Tunnels are used to transport one protocol within another. For example, in Figure 5-32, we have a network that is running IP and IPX applications, but only IP is enabled between routers A and B. For the IPX traffic from router A to get to the client attached to router B, the IPX datagram is sent through an IP tunnel connecting the two routers.

Assume that the Netware server in Figure 5-32 is sending an IPX packet to the Netware client. The data from the server is encapsulated in an IPX packet at layer 3 and sent to the ethernet module at layer 2. The ethernet module then encapsulates the IPX packet in an ethernet frame with destination and source ethernet addresses. The IPX packet is treated as data inside the ethernet frame. When router A receives the frame, the data is removed and router A determines that this is an IPX packet destined for

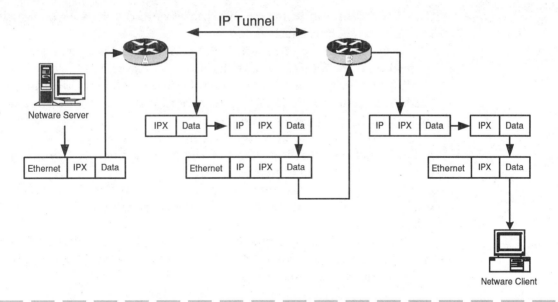

Figure 5-32   Tunneling IPX in IP

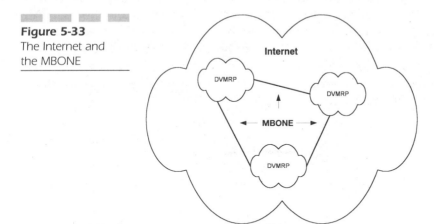

Figure 5-33
The Internet and
the MBONE

the IPX network attached to router B. Because IP is the only protocol enabled between the routers, a tunnel needs to be configured to carry the IPX packet in an IP packet. Assuming the tunnel has been configured, router A encapsulates the IPX packet in an IP packet. Notice that we are encapsulating one layer 3 protocol, IPX, in another layer 3 protocol, IP. This is typically the characteristic of tunneling. When the IP packet reaches the other end of the tunnel, router B removes the IPX packet from the IP packet and forwards the IPX packet onto the network on which the Netware client is attached.

The *Internet Multicast Backbone* (MBONE) is a logical multicast network overlaid onto the physical unicast Internet (see Figure 5-33).

Multicast traffic that travels between DVMRP sections of the Internet needs to be sent over an IP tunnel that encapsulates the multicast packet into a unicast packet (see Figure 5-34).

The two DVMRP routers and the tunnel form the logical or virtual multicast network that is a subset of the physical Internet. Tunnels are needed because not all routers on the Internet support multicast routing. Even if they did, the maximum hop count for DVMRP is 32, which is not sufficient to span the entire Internet. DVMRP tunnels are IP in IP tunnels, as shown in Figure 5-35.

Cisco routers do not implement DVMRP but can interact with DVMRP, as we shall see in later chapters. CGMP can act as a proxy for a non-Cisco DVMRP router using the interface command

```
ip cgmp proxy
```

Consider the network in Figure 5-36. Here we have a non-Cisco DVMRP router connected to a Cisco switch that has CGMP enabled, and with CGMP enabled on the interface connected to the switch. With CGMP proxy enabled on the router, the router listens to the DVMRP messages and determines the groups for which DVMRP will be forwarding traffic. The proxy router then informs the switch using CGMP about any DVMRP hosts attached to the switch that wish to receive the traffic.

Figure 5-34
A DVMRP tunnel

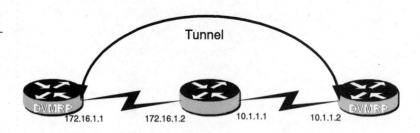

Destination 10.1.1.2	Source 172.16.1.1	Protocol 4	Data

Figure 5-35
Multicast traffic encapsulated in an IP in IP tunnel

Destination 224.0.0.4	Source 156.26.32.1	Protocol	Multicast Data

Figure 5-36
Cisco router acting as
a proxy for the
DVMRP router and
host.

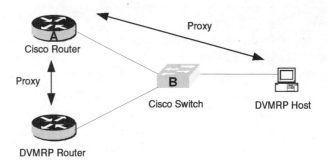

DVMRP Router Commands

Cisco does not support a full DVMRP implementation but does support a number of commands that affect DVRMP information that is being injected into the network. The DVMRP commands available are listed below with an explanation of their use. These commands are used when integrating PIM and DVMRP networks and are covered in more detail in Chapter 8, "PIM-DVMRP Networks."

```
ip dvmrp unicast routing
Type: interface
```

This command allows Cisco routers to exchange DVMRP routing information. Routes received in a DVMRP report message are cached by the router in a DVMRP routing table. If PIM is running, then these routes will be preferred over routes in the unicast table.

```
ip dvmrp route-hog notification <route-count>
default--route-count = 10,000
Type: global
```

The `route-hog notification` command is used to send notification by way of a syslog message when the number of DVMRP routes has exceeded the `route-count` limit. There may be a misconfigured router on the MBONE, which is advertising a large number of routes.

```
ip dvmrp route-limit <route-count>
default--route-count = 7000
Type: global
```

The `route-limit` command limits the number of DVMRP routes advertised on a DVMRP-enabled interface. The interface could be a DVMRP tunnel, an interface with a DVMRP neighbor, or an interface configured with `ip dvmrp unicast-routing`. This command prevents injecting more routes than the `route-count` parameter into the MBONE.

```
ip dvmrp distance <administrative-distance>
Type: interface
```

This command sets the administrative distance for DVMRP routes to the value specified.

```
ip dvmrp metric <metric> [list <access-list>]
{[<protocol> <process-id>] | dvmrp]}
Type: interface
```

If PIM is configured on an interface and there are DVMRP neighbors, the router send DVMRP report messages. This command is used to set the metrics for unicast routes that are reported to the DVMRP neighbor. If an `access-list` is used, either standard or extended, then only those destinations permitted by the access-list will have the specified metric applied to the routes. The `<protocol>` `<process-id>` pair is used to limit the application of the metric to routes learned by the specified protocol. The DVMRP parameter is used to apply the metric only to routes from the DVMRP routing table. The command can be used multiple times on an interface.

```
ip dvmrp accept-filter <access-list> [neighbor-list <nbr-acl>] [<distance>]
Type: interface
```

This is used to filter incoming DVMRP reports. If the destination matches the `<access-list>` from neighbors in the `<nbr-acl>`, then the routes are stored in the DVMRP routing table with `<distance>`.

```
ip dvmrp default-information originate | only
Type: interface
```

The default network 0.0.0.0 will be advertised to DVMRP neighbors on the interface with a default metric of 1. It only has effect if the neighbor is an mrouted 3.4 system. If the keyword only is used, then no other DVMRP routes will be reported. The keyword originate allows more specific routes to be advertised.

```
ip dvmrp metric-offset [in | out] <increment>
default: in
increment default: in 1 out 0
Type: interface
```

The value of increment is added to either incoming or outgoing DVMRP route reports.

```
ip dvmrp reject-non-pruners
Type: interface
```

If a DVMRP neighbor does not support pruning and grafting, then a neighbor relationship will not be established.

```
ip dvmrp summary-address <address> <mask> metric <value>
Type: interface
```

This configures a summary address to be advertised out of the interface.

```
ip dvmrp auto-summary
Type: interface
```

This enables DVMRP auto-summarization.

```
ip dvmrp output-report-delay <delay-time> [<burst>]
default: delay = 100 milliseconds burst = 2
Type: interface
```

This configures the interpacket delay between DVMRP reports in milliseconds. A set number of packets given by the burst parameter will be transmitted with a delay given by the delay-time parameter.

```
tunnel mode dvmrp
Type: interface (tunnel)
```

This is used on a tunnel interface connecting a Cisco router to an mrouted machine. Usually it is used to connect to the MBONE.

REFERENCES ▬ ▬ ▬ ▬ ▬ ▬ ▬ ▬

RFC 1058, "Routing Information Protocol," C. Hedrick, Rutgers University, 1988

RFC 2453, "RIP Version 2," G. Malkin, Bay Networks, 1998

RFC 1075, "Distance Vector Multicast Routing Protocol," D. Waitzman, C. Partridge, S. Deering, 1988

IETF Internet Draft, "Distance Vector Multicast Routing Protocol," T. Pusateri, 1998, draft-ietf-idmr-dvmrp-v3-07.txt

Protocol Independent Multicast— Dense Mode

Protocol Independent Multicast-Dense Mode (PIM-DM) is similar to *Distance Vector Multicast Routing Protocol* (DVMRP) in a number of ways. Both are referred to as dense mode protocols. A dense mode protocol operates in an environment where the multicast sources and multicast receivers are located in the same area, such as a *local area network* (LAN). Dense mode protocols also assume that bandwidth is not a limiting factor. Both protocols operate using a broadcast and prune methodology where multicast routers assume everyone wants to receive multicast traffic. Under this model, traffic from a multicast source is sent on all downstream interfaces until an interface is pruned from the multicast tree. An interface has a limited prune time after which the interface is grafted back onto the multicast delivery tree and multicast traffic is again flooded onto the network. Both protocols create source-based delivery trees that connect each specific multicast source with each downstream receiver. Source trees are dynamically created for each source using the *Reverse Path Forwarding* (RPF) technique. The major difference between DVMRP and PIM-DM is that DVMRP uses a built-in multicast routing protocol while PIM-DM relies on the configured unicast routing protocol. This means that you can use any of the IP routing protocols (RIP, IGRP, EIGRP, or OSPF) with PIM-DM.

PIM-DM is independent of the IP routing protocol chosen to run on your network, hence the name, Protocol Independent Multicast. This also means that in the same network DVMRP and PIM could possibly construct divergent source based delivery trees as shown in Figures 6-1, 6-2, and 6-3. In Figure 6-1, DVMRP is being used as the multicast routing protocol. Since DVMRP builds routing tables based on RIP, the source based tree for the network in Figure 6-1 would be through the 28.8K connections since this path offers a lower hop count than the path through the T1 connections.

In Figure 6-2, OSPF is the unicast routing protocol which has a metric based on the link speed and not the hop count. In this case, the shortest path from the receiver to the source is through the T1 connections instead

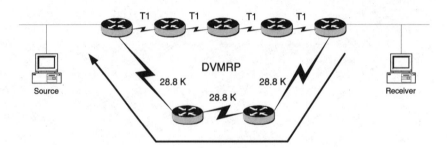

Figure 6-1
DVMRP source-based tree

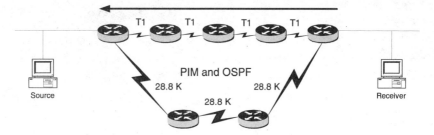

Figure 6-2
PIM-DM source-based
tree in an OSPF
environment

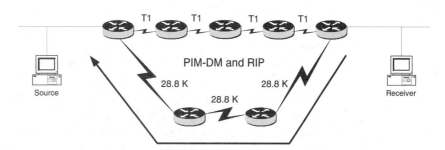

Figure 6-3
PIM-DM source-based
tree in an RIP
environment

of the 28.8K connections. Figure 6-3 shows that PIM-DM is independent of the unicast routing protocol in the sense that it doesn't matter which unicast routing protocol is used since PIM-DM will still operate. Figure 6-3 does show that PIM-DM is, in some ways actually, dependent on the selected unicast routing protocol since the source based delivery tree can be different depending on the protocol used.

PIM-DM Version 1, Protocol Operation

The source based trees that are constructed in a PIM-DM environment are created in the same manner as DVMRP as shown in Figure 6-4.

In Figure 6-4, router A receives a multicast packet from the source and examines the source IP address of the packet to see if the packet was received on the *Reverse Path Forwarding* (RPF) interface. The RPF interface is used to send a unicast packet back to the source. Becasuse the source is directly attached to router A, the interface is the RPF. Router A then floods the packet on all interfaces except for the interface on which the packet was received. When router B receives the packet from router A, router B will

Figure 6-4
Dynamically created
source-based trees

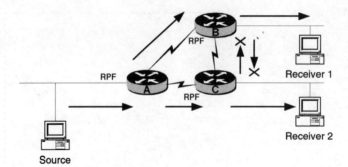

determine if the packet was received on the RPF interface for the particular source. The packet passes the RPF test and so the packet is forwarded to router C and receiver 1. Router C performs the same RPF on the packet and forwards the packet to router B and receiver 2. When B receives the packet from C and C receives the packet from B, the RPF test fails since the packet was not received on the interface that is on the shortest path back to the source. The packet is then discarded. If we take a close look at Figure 6-4, we can see that we have a source tree for each receiver that connects each receiver to the source.

The RPF interface is selected by examining the IP routing table, an example of which is given in Listing 6-1. From the sample routing table, we can determine the RPF interface for any multicast source. Remember that the multicast source is a unicast class A, B, or C address and not a multicast class D address. For example, if the router receives a multicast packet on the serial 1 interface from the source 130.10.9.1, should the packet be forwarded? By examining the routing table in Listing 6-1 we find that the unicast route back to 130.10.9.1 is through interface serial 0 so the packet did not arrive on the RPF interface. For this case, the multicast packet would be dropped and no further processing would occur. We can determine the RPF interface for each known source network by examining the routing table. Each route listed contains a forwarding interface, which is also the RPF interface. How would the router handle multicast traffic from sources not in the routing table? For this situation the default route would be used.

LISTING 6-1

Example Cisco
router IP routing
table

Codes: C—connected, S—static, I—IGRP, R—RIP, M—mobile, B—BGP
   D—EIGRP, EX—EIGRP external, O—OSPF, IA—OSPF inter area
   E1—OSPF external type 1, E2—OSPF external type 2, E—EGP
   i—IS-IS, L1—IS-IS level−1, L2—IS-IS level−2, `*`—candidate default

Gateway of last resort is not set

```
I       130.10.128.0 255.255.255.0 [100/1115174 ] via 130.10.11.3, 00:00:40, Serial1
C       130.10.252.0 255.255.255.0 is directly connected, Loopback0
I       130.10.253.0 255.255.255.0 [100/265657 ] via 130.10.11.3, 00:00:40, Serial1
I       130.10.246.0 255.255.255.0 [100/1115611 ] via 130.10.11.3, 00:00:40, Serial1
O       130.10.8.0 255.255.255.0 [110/2641 ] via 130.10.5.5, 00:12:29, Serial0
O IA 130.10.9.0 255.255.255.0 [110/5268 ] via 130.10.5.5, 00:12:29, Serial0
C       130.10.10.0 255.255.255.0 is directly connected, Ethernet0
C       130.10.11.0 255.255.255.0 is directly connected, Serial1
I       130.10.12.0 255.255.255.0 [100/1115111 ] via 130.10.11.3, 00:00:41, Serial1
I       130.10.13.0 255.255.255.0 [100/265257 ] via 130.10.11.3, 00:00:41, Serial1
O IA 130.10.251.251 255.255.255.255 [110/5263 ] via 130.10.5.5, 00:12:33, Serial0
O IA 130.10.250.250 255.255.255.255 [110/2632 ] via 130.10.5.5, 00:12:33, Serial0
O       130.10.5.5 255.255.255.255 [110/2631 ] via 130.10.5.5, 00:12:33, Serial0
O       130.10.5.1 255.255.255.255 [110/5262 ] via 130.10.5.5, 00:12:33, Serial0
C       130.10.5.0 255.255.255.0 is directly connected, Serial0
O IA 130.10.100.0 255.255.255.192 [110/2632 ] via 130.10.5.5, 00:00:13, Serial0
I       193.10.10.0 [100/1115174 ] via 130.10.11.3, 00:00:45, Serial1
```

Neighbor Discovery

PIM-DM version 1 packets are encapsulated in Internet Group IGMP packets as shown in Figure 6-5. PIM-DM packets have a common header (see Figure 6-6) which contains a code identifying the PIM-DM message type and the PIM mode, dense, sparse or sparse-dense. The message types are listed in Table 6-1 and neighbor discovery or router query messages (see Figure 6-7) are identified as type 0 (see Table 6-2). Router query messages are used to discover neighbors that are attached to a common network. Discovery may be a misleading term since there is not an explicit neighbor list section comparable to a DVMRP neighbor discovery message.

A better name for a router query message could be a neighbor inform message. When a neighbor receives a query message, the IP address of the neighbor is recorded. No explicit mechanism acknowledges that the query was received. Instead, the receiving router will simply transmit its own query message that has the effect of informing other PIM-DM routers on the network of its existence. When a query message is received from a neighbor, the interface is added to the outgoing interface list. The outgoing interface list is

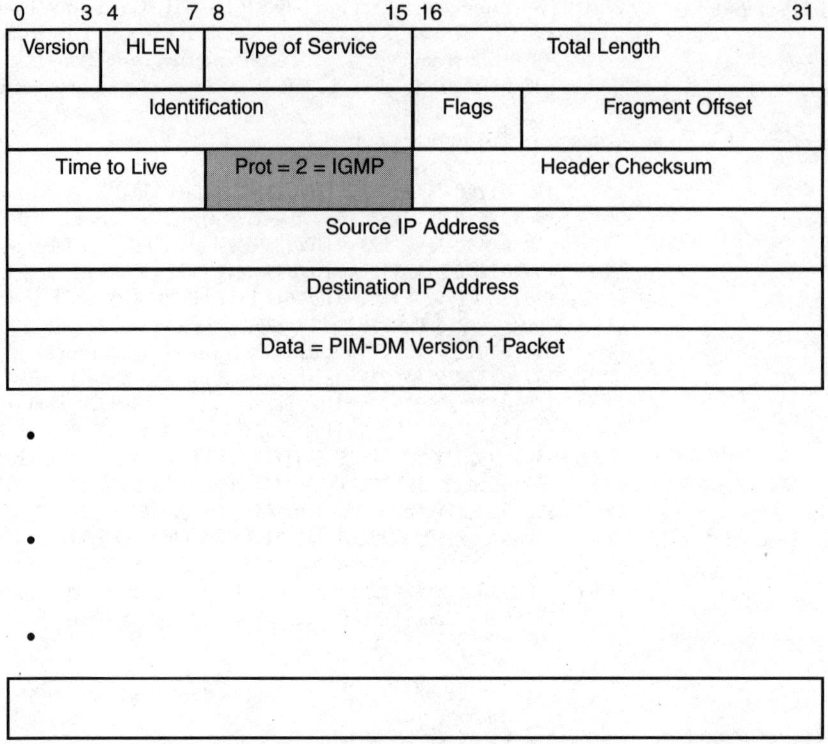

Figure 6-5
Encapsulation of a
PIM-DM version 1
packet in an IGMP
datagram

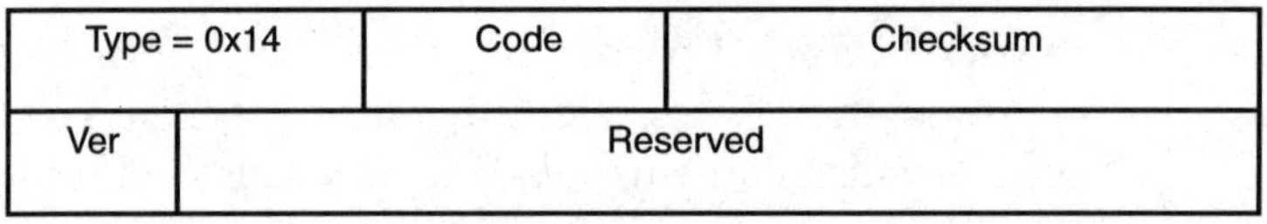

0   3 4   7 8   15 16   31

Version	HLEN	Type of Service	Total Length
Identification		Flags	Fragment Offset
Time to Live		Prot = 2 = IGMP	Header Checksum
Source IP Address			
Destination IP Address			
Data = PIM-DM Version 1 Packet			

-
-
-

Figure 6-6
PIM-DM version 1
packet header

| Type = 0x14 | Code | Checksum |
| Ver | Reserved ||

TABLE 6-1

PIM-DM version 1
Message Codes

Code	Message Type
0	Router Query
1	Register (Sparse Mode)
2	Register-Stop (Sparse Mode)
3	Join/Prune
4	RP Reachability (Sparse Mode)
5	Assert
6	Graft
7	Graft-ACK

TABLE 6-2

PIM-DM version 1
Query Message
Modes

Code	Mode
0	Dense Mode
1	Sparse
2	Sparse-Dense

Figure 6-7
PIM-DM version 1
Query Message
packet format

Type = 0x14		Code = 0	Checksum	
Ver		Reserved		
Mode	Reserved		Holdtime	

Figure 6-8
PIM-DM router query
and DR election

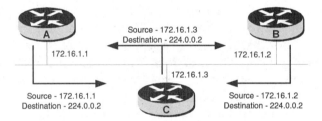

used to determine which interfaces the PIM-DM router should forward multicast traffic. Of course, if there are no other PIM-DM routers on the network, the interface would be added to the outgoing list if there are receivers requesting traffic for a particular multicast group. For a multi-access network, such as an ethernet, the query message is sent to the All-Routers multicast address, 224.0.0.2, and serves as the *Designated Router* (DR) election mechanism. For dense mode PIM, the designated router only has a function if IGMP version 1 is being used. In this case, the DR becomes the IGMP querier for the network (see Chapter 3). The elected DR is the PIM-DM enabled router with the highest IP address. The query process and DR election is shown in Figure 6-8. For this scenario, router C is elected DR since it has the highest IP address on the multi-access network.

The holdtime parameter in the router query message indicates how much time will elapse before this neighbor is declared dead. Subsequent router queries from a neighbor will reset this time so the query interval must be less than the holdtime interval. The router queries act as a keep-alive mechanism to inform neighboring routers that this router is still alive and well. If PIM-DM is disabled on the interface or the router actually crashes and burns, the holdtime for this router will expire on the neighboring routers. If the holdtime expires for a neighbor that was elected DR for the multi-access network, then a new DR will need to be elected.

PIM-DM Packet Forwarding

When a PIM-DM router receives the initial multicast packet from a source, the packet is flooded onto all interfaces in the *output interface list* (oilist). Recall that the oilist is populated with those interfaces on which neighbors were discovered or on interfaces that have multicast receivers that have indicated their desire to receive the traffic using IGMP. Figure 6-9 shows the various possibilities for forwarding of multicast traffic. Router A has discovered a PIM-DM neighbor on interface S0.

A host has signaled that it wishes to receive multicast traffic for a particular group. The host doesn't care where the multicast traffic originates, so any packets for this group from any source reaching router A will be forwarded to the host on E0.

No PIM-DM neighbors or multicast receivers have been found on interface S1 so the oilist for this interface will be null. The oilist for the ethernet interface will contain the state (*,G) indicating that router A should forward traffic for group G from any source onto the ethernet interface. The oilist for the S0 interface will contain the state (S,G) indicating that

Figure 6-9
PIM-DM packet forwarding

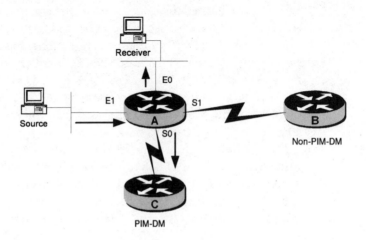

router A should forward multicast traffic for group G from source S to router C. Traffic will also be forwarded if the interface has been manually configured to receive traffic. Traffic is forwarded using the RPF technique, which you will recall, only accepts packets on the interface on the shortest path back to the source. For DVMRP this is generally unambiguous since each DVMRP router runs the same routing protocol. PIM-DM uses whatever IP routing protocol has been configured on the router to determine the RPF technique. We will see how to deal with situations involving a network running more than one IP routing protocol.

Interface States

The oilist for a router interface can be null or in the (*,G) or (S,G) state. An interface can also be in both the (S,G) and (*,G) states. In Figure 6-10, router A has PIM-DM enabled on all interfaces. When the host attaches to the E1 interface of router A, it will join the multicast group 224.0.18.10 by sending an IGMP join message to router A. Router A will add the entry (*,224.0.18.10) to the E1 interface, indicating that multicast traffic for group 224.0.18.10 from any source should be sent onto the ethernet interface. The same (*,G) state can exist in more than one oilist. Input interfaces for a multicast group will have (S,G) state and the same (S,G) state will not exist on more than one interface since a router can only have one best path back to a multicast source. The input interface is the interface over which a router expects to receive multicast traffic from a specific source. This interface is simply the RPF interface.

In Figure 6-11, router A receives a multicast packet from the source 172.16.1.2 for group 224.0.18.10. Router A creates the (S,G) state for the serial interface since a PIM-DM neighbor has been discovered on this interface. If the serial interface on router A is not on the shortest path back to the source for the downstream router, the interface will be pruned.

In Figure 6-12, we have two sources for the multicast group 224.0.18.10. Router A has a host which has joined this group using IGMP. Router A will

Figure 6-10

Router state is (*,G) when a receiver joins a multicast group.

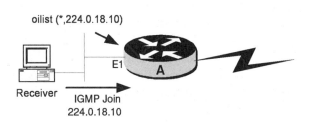

Figure 6-11
Routers maintain
(S,G) state for
multicast sources

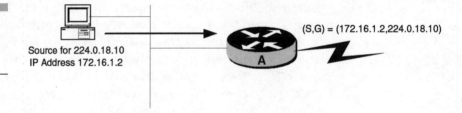

Figure 6-12
Each multicast source
will have (S,G) state
on the directly
attached router.

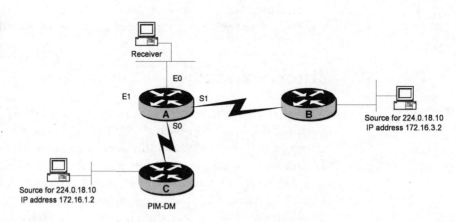

accept traffic on interface S1 from the source 172.16.3.2, from router B and
on interface S0 from the source 172.16.1.2, and from router C because these
are the RPF interfaces for the respective sources. The oilist for the serial
interface on router B will contain the (S,G) state (172.16.3.2,224.0.18.10). The serial interface on router C will contain the (S,G) state (172.16.1.2,224.0.18.10).

PIM-DM Interface Pruning

When the oilist for a particular interface becomes null, there are no
downstream PIM-DM routers or multicast receivers attached to the network. The interface does not need to transmit multicast traffic and can,
therefore, be pruned from the source-based delivery tree. In Figure 6-13,
router A initially receives multicast traffic from the source and floods the
traffic onto all interfaces in the oilist. Router B is a PIM-DM-enabled
router, but has no attached downstream PIM-DM routers or mulitcast
receivers. Router B will send a prune message to its upstream router for
this particular multicast source. When router A receives the prune from

Figure 6-13
The pruning of a
PIM-DM interface

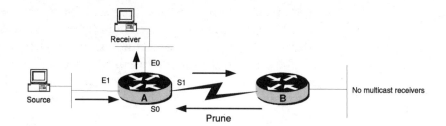

Type = 0x14	Code = 3	Checksum		
Ver	Reserved			
Upstream Neighbor Address				
Reserved		Holdtime		
Reserved	Mask Len.	Adr. Len.		Num. Grps
Group List				

Figure 6-14
PIM Join/Prune
Packet Format

router B, router A's oilist for the serial link will become null, halting the forwarding of multicast traffic to router B.

The packet format used for Prune, Join, or Graft messages is illustrated in Figure 6-14.

The Upstream Neighbor Address is where the Join/Prune packet is sent. For the network in Figure 6-13, router B sends the message to router A so the upstream neighbor address equals the IP address of router A's serial interface. The holdtime indicates the lifetime of the prune. PIM-DM is a cyclic protocol. Initially all packets are forwarded onto interfaces in the oilist. When a prune is received, traffic from the source/group indicated in the prune message no longer forwards onto the interface. The prune remains in effect until the holdtime for the prune expires. When the prune timer expires, the interface is added back to the oilist for the source group. Multicast traffic is again forwarded onto the interface. Join or graft messages can be used to add a pruned interface to the oilist before the prune holdtime expires. The *mask length* (mask len) and *address length* (adr len) fields indicate the length in bytes of the mask and the address for the group or groups to be pruned from or grafted onto the source-based delivery tree. Either the prune list or the join list may be empty, but a join/prune packet should never be sent when both the join and prune lists are empty. The format for the group list is shown in Figure 6-15. The number of groups in the group list is given by the `Num. of Groups` parameter in Figure 6-14. Each group is identified by the address and mask of the group to be pruned or joined. Following the address and mask pair is the number of join and prune sources for the group. Join sources are all listed first, followed by the prune sources represented by the encoded format of Figure 6-16.

The S bit in the encoded source address format indicates whether or not this is a sparse mode group and should be set to 0 for dense mode groups. The W bit is the wildcard bit and indicates whether the entry applies to a specific source/group (S,G), W = 0 or if the entry applies to all sources of the group (*,G), W = 1. The R bit applies to *PIM Sparse Mode* (PIM-SM). The Len field is the length of the source mask in bits and the source address is the IP address of the source to be joined or pruned.

PIM-DM Interface Grafting

Interfaces that have been pruned from the oilist for a router interface can be added back into the source-based tree for a multicast source using PIM-DM graft messages (see Figure 6-17). PIM-DM graft messages are the only messages that are acknowledged. The graft messages are acknowledged using the packet format shown in Figure 6-18.

The network in Figure 6-19 will be used as an example of PIM-DM grafting. Router A is forwarding multicast traffic to router B (step 1). Since router B has no downstream PIM-DM neighbors or multicast receivers, router B sends a prune message to router A (step 2). The oilist for the S1 interface on router A is now null and a prune timer has been set using the timer value in the prune message. If a multicast receiver attached to the ethernet on router B wishes to receive traffic, an IGMP join message is sent to router B (step 3). Router B can either wait for the prune timer on router A to expire, which will cause router A to add interface S1 to the oilist for the source, or router B can send a graft message to router A (step 4). The serial interface on router A is in the prune state for the source and has a prune lifetime timer running. Router B has (S,G) and (*,G) entries for

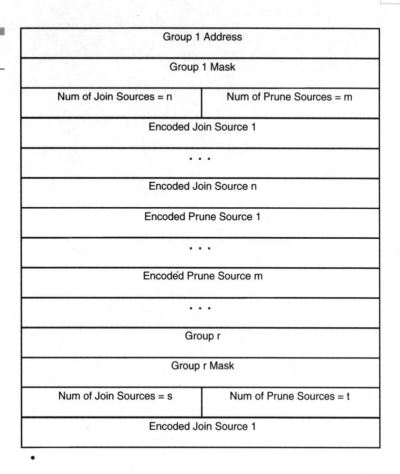

Figure 6-15
Group List format

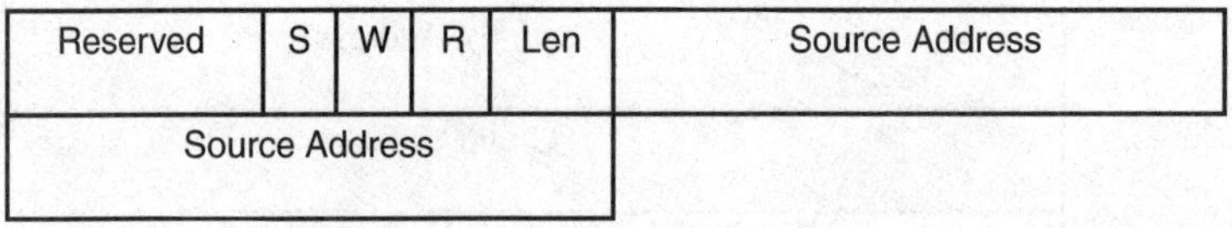

Figure 6-16
Encoded Source
Address format

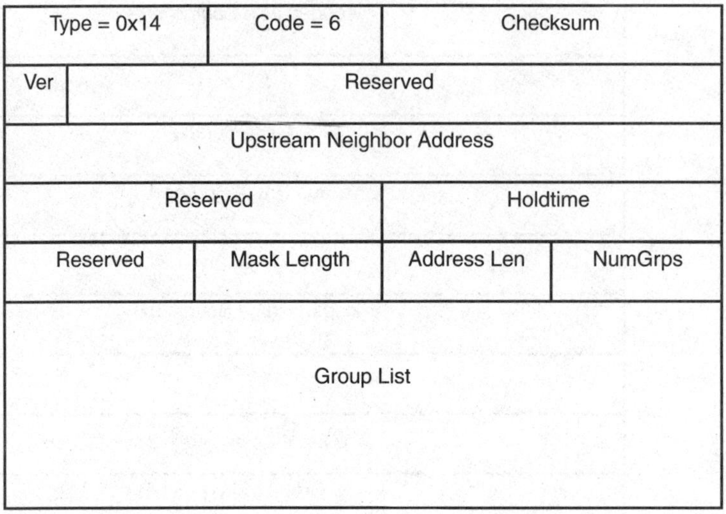

Reserved	S	W	R	Len	Source Address
Source Address					

Figure 6-17
PIM Graft Packet
format

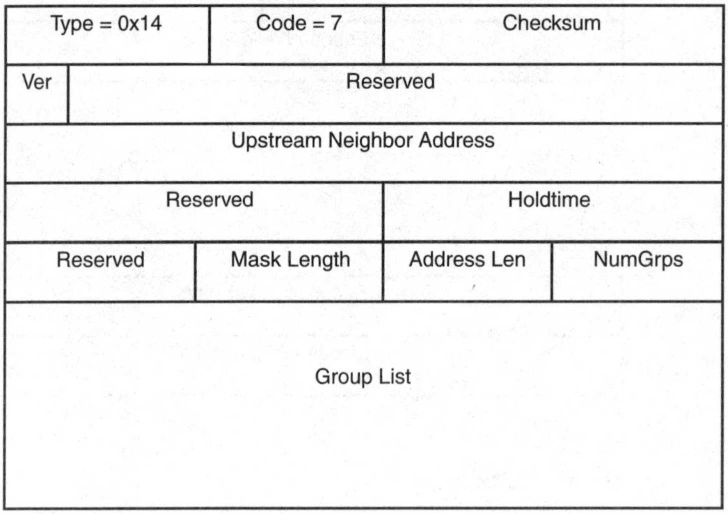

Type = 0x14	Code = 6	Checksum	
Ver	Reserved		
Upstream Neighbor Address			
Reserved		Holdtime	
Reserved	Mask Length	Address Len	NumGrps
Group List			

Figure 6-18
PIM Graft-Ack Packet
format

Type = 0x14	Code = 7	Checksum	
Ver	Reserved		
Upstream Neighbor Address			
Reserved		Holdtime	
Reserved	Mask Length	Address Len	NumGrps
Group List			

Figure 6-19
PIM-DM interface
pruning and grafting
message flow.

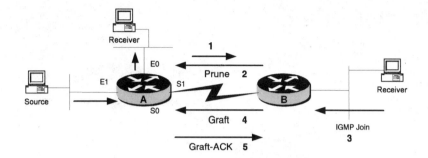

the source but these entries are in the prune state. So router B will send
a graft message to router A and A will acknowledge will graft acknowledgment message (step 5).

One very important characteristic of dense mode protocols is the
prune/broadcast cycle. In Figure 6-19, if router B never had any attached
receivers or downstream PIM-DM neighbors, then multicast traffic would
never need to be forwarded to router B. Initially, router B will prune itself
from any source-based delivery trees. Since prunes have a limited lifetime,
router B would again be sent multicast traffic from router A. Router B
would again send a prune to A, which would timeout, and cause A to forward to B. This triggers a prune, and so it goes. If you are certain that multicast traffic does not need to go to a particular router, then don't enable
PIM-DM on the interfaces.

PIM-DM Assert Message

To avoid duplicate multicast packets from traversing multi-access networks, PIM-DM uses assert messages to determine a designated forward
for a multi-access network. Figure 6-20 demonstrates the situation that
would warrant the assert mechanism. The steps of this are as follows:

1. Router A receives multicast traffic.

2. Routers B and C are PIM-DM neighbors so the multicast traffic
   is forwarded to routers B and C.

3. Router D is a PIM-DM neighbor so routers B and C will forward
   the traffic onto the ethernet LAN. Assume router B transmits
   first. Router C receives the multicast packet on an interface that
   has this group in the output interface list. This alerts router C to

Figure 6-20

Assert messages are used to prevent multiple copies of multicast traffic on a multi-access network.

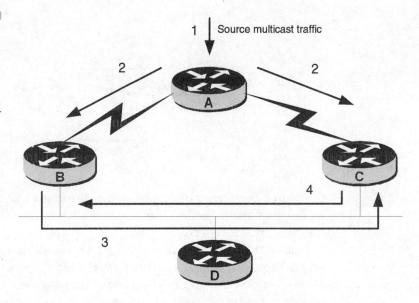

the fact that a PIM-DM neighbor on the ethernet LAN has forwarded traffic for the group.

4. Router C forwards the multicast packet to routers B and D. B notices that the packet has arrived on an output interface for the group. Router D really doesn't care since this router is not forwarding traffic for the group onto the ethernet LAN. Router D has received the same multicast packet twice, a situation that needs to be eliminated.

If a router receives a multicast packet for which it has state, either (S,G) or (*,G), on an outgoing interface, the router knows another router is forwarding packets onto the network. For example, the serial interfaces for both routers B and C are the RPF interfaces back to the multicast source. When router A receives a packet from the source, the packet is forwarded to both routers B and C. With no other mechanism in place, both routers B and C will forward the traffic to router D, creating duplicate packets on the network. Assert messages are used to avoid this situation.

An assert message contains the group address and mask for the multicast source and the router's metric back to the source (see Figure 6-21). If both routers have an equal metric back to the source, the router with the highest IP address becomes the forwarder for the network. The router that is not the forwarder will prune the interface. In Figure 6-20, router D does not send Assert messages but must listen to the Assert messages and deter-

Figure 6-21
PIM Assert
Packet format

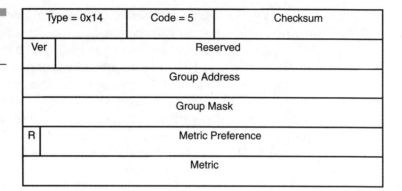

Type = 0x14		Code = 5	Checksum	
Ver		Reserved		
Group Address				
Group Mask				
R	Metric Preference			
Metric				

Figure 6-22
Routers B and C
have comparable
metrics to the
source so they
can be used in an
assert message to
elect the designated
forwarder.

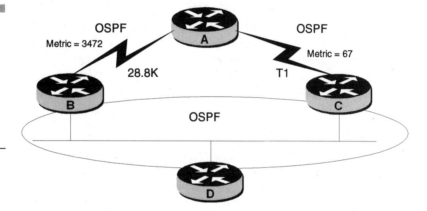

mine which router is the designated router for the LAN. This information is necessary so router D knows where to send Prune and Graft messages for the group. The assert process is straightforward if both routers are running the same IP routing protocol. Recall that PIM-DM uses whatever protocol has been configured on the router to determine the RPF interface and the metric for the RPF interface.

For the configuration in Figure 6-22, both routers on the multi-access network are running OSPF and the metrics back to the source are comparable. The OSPF metric is calculated by dividing 100,000,000 by the bandwidth of the link. The metric is the T1 link, which is approximately 67, and for the 28.8K link the metric is 3,472. By comparing the metrics of the two links back to the source, we can easily choose the T1 link because it has a smaller metric than the 28.8K link. If different routing protocols are being utilized, the metrics cannot be compared.

In Figure 6-23, router B is running OSPF and router C is running RIP. Comparing the metric back to the source for the two routers is like comparing apples and oranges. OSPF uses the speed of the interface to determine the metric and RIP uses a simple hop count. For this case, the metric preference value in the assert packet is used to determine which router will forward traffic and which router will prune the interface. Metric preference is analogous to an administrative distance for a unicast routing protocol. For example, the default administrative distance for RIP is 120 and for OSPF it is 110. Using the defaults will always cause an OSPF route to be preferred to a RIP route.

Metric preferences can be configured for each unicast routing protocol. When PIM-DM receives an assert message for a group, the metric preference is compared to its own metric preference. If they are equal, metrics can be compared to determine which router will forward traffic. If the metric preference values are different, the router with the lowest metric preference will be selected as the forwarder on the network. If we assign a lower metric value for OSPF than for RIP, the routers on the multi-access network in Figure 6-23 will select the OSPF router to forward traffic and the RIP router will prune its interface for the group.

PIM-DM Version 2

PIM-DM version 2 is specified in the IETF document draft-ietf-im-v2-dm-01.txt dated November 3, 1998. In this section we will examine the differences between PIM-DM versions 1 and 2. The first major change is that

Figure 6-23
Routers B and C have metrics that cannot be compared. The assert mechanism would use the metric preference to determine the designated forwarder.

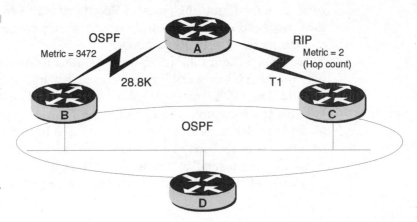

version 2 messages are no longer encapsulated in IGMP messages but are encapsulated in IP packets with protocol number 103 (Figure 6-24). PIM-DM version 2 messages are sent to the multicast group 224.0.0.13, ALL-PIM-ROUTERS.

The PIM-DM version 2 packet header, shown in Figure 6-25, has been modified from the version 1 packet header (see Figure 6-6). The types of messages identified in the packet header along with the version 1 types are listed in Table 6-3. As you can see, there have been a few modifications from Table 6-1.

The router query message that was used as the neighbor discovery mechanism in version 1 has been replaced by the Hello message (see Figure 6-26).

Figure 6-24
Encapsulation of a PIM-DM version 2 packet in an IP datagram

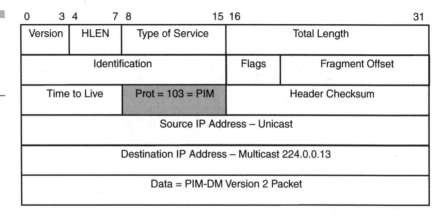

Version	HLEN	Type of Service	Total Length		
Identification			Flags	Fragment Offset	
Time to Live		Prot = 103 = PIM	Header Checksum		
Source IP Address – Unicast					
Destination IP Address – Multicast 224.0.0.13					
Data = PIM-DM Version 2 Packet					

•

•

•

Figure 6–25
PIM-DM version 2 packet header format

Ver	Type	Reserved	Checksum

TABLE 6-3 PIM Versions 1 and 2 Message Types

Type	Description Version 2	Description Version 1
0	Hello	Router Query
1	Register (Sparse Mode)	Same
2	Register-Stop (Sparse Mode)	Same
3	Join/Prune	Same
4	Bootstrap (Sparse Mode)	RP Reachability (Sparse Mode)
5	Assert	Same
6	Graft (Dense-Mode)	Same
7	Graft-Ack (Dense Mode)	Same

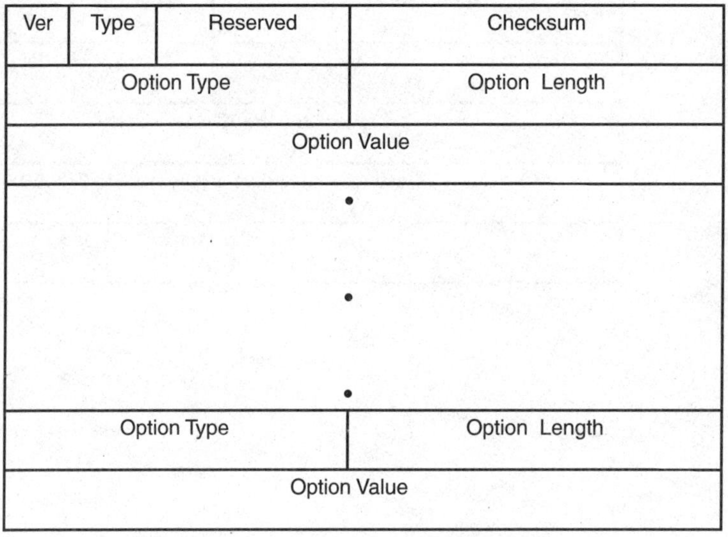

Figure 6-26 PIM-DM Version 2 Hello message format

The option fields for the Hello message are listed in Table 6-4 and the values of the hold time in Table 6-5.

A timeout value of 0xFFFF means that the neighbor never times out. This value has the affect of preventing periodic hello messages from being sent. This is especially useful on a tariff connection such as an ISDN. Periodic hellos keep the link active even in the absence of user data traffic. You may not be happy receiving an ISDN bill for nothing more than periodic hello traffic. A holdtime of zero signifies that the neighbor should immediately time out.

TABLE 6-4

Hello Message
Option Fields

Option Type	Option Length	Option Value
1	2	Hold time
2–16	Reserved	Reserved

TABLE 6-5

Hello Message
Hold Time Values

Value	Description
0xFFFF	No time out
0	Immediate time out
Any other value	Neighbor time out value

The prune/join message format has been modified as shown in Figure 6-27 (compare to the version 1 format in Figure 6-14). The encoded unicast and multicast address formats are shown in Figures 6-28 through 6-31.

Encoding value is 0 and represents the native encoding for the address family (see Table 6-6).

The Graft and Graft Acknowledgment message formats have not changed from version 1.

PIM-DM Router Configuration

Configuring PIM-DM on Cisco routers is a relatively simple exercise. The first step is to enable multicast routing in global configuration mode using the command:

```
ip multicast-routing
```

Next, enable PIM-DM on the router interfaces using the interface command:

```
ip pim dense-mode
```

The router in Figure 6-32 has a basic configuration shown in the diagram. Although the configuration has EIGRP as the routing protocol, any of the IP routing protocols could have been used.

Figure 6-27
PIM version 2
Join/Prune Packet
format

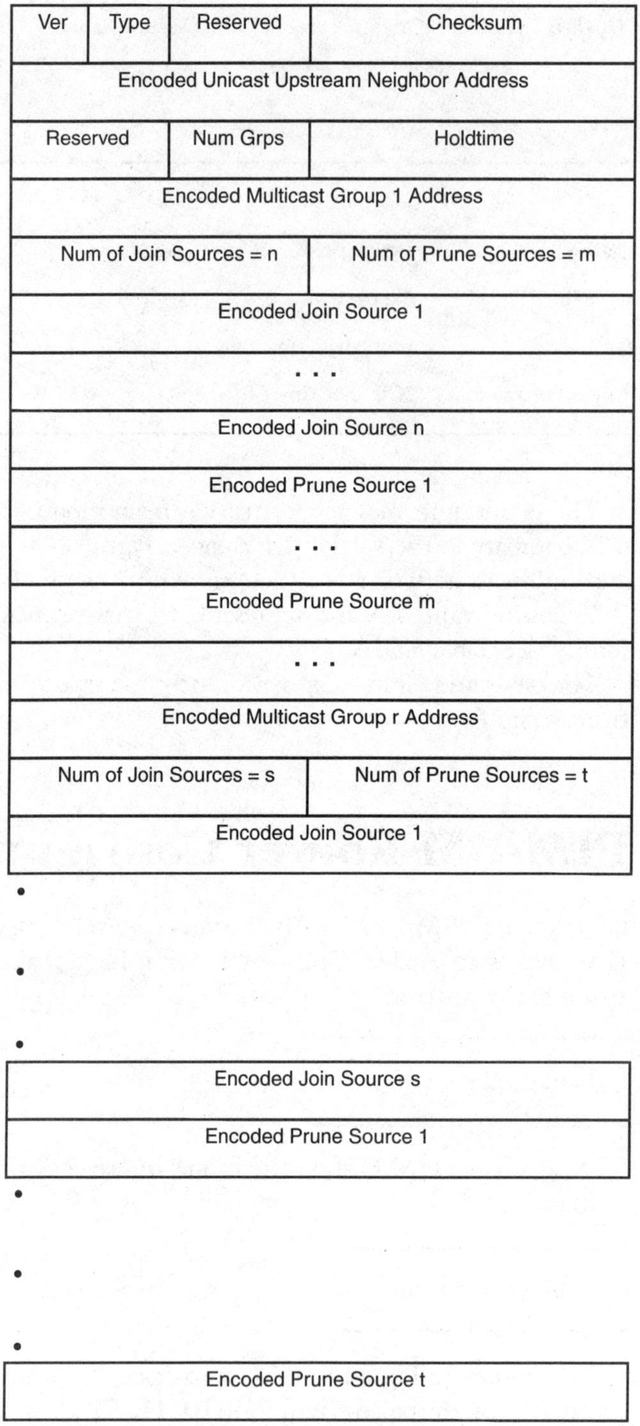

Ver	Type	Reserved	Checksum
Encoded Unicast Upstream Neighbor Address			
Reserved	Num Grps		Holdtime
Encoded Multicast Group 1 Address			
Num of Join Sources = n		Num of Prune Sources = m	
Encoded Join Source 1			
. . .			
Encoded Join Source n			
Encoded Prune Source 1			
. . .			
Encoded Prune Source m			
. . .			
Encoded Multicast Group r Address			
Num of Join Sources = s		Num of Prune Sources = t	
Encoded Join Source 1			

•

•

•

Encoded Join Source s
Encoded Prune Source 1

•

•

•

Encoded Prune Source t

Figure 6-28
PIM version 2 encoded unicast address format

Addr Family	Encoding	Unicast Address

Figure 6-29
Encoded group address format

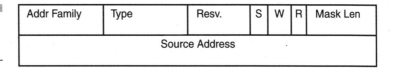

Figure 6-30
Encoded source address

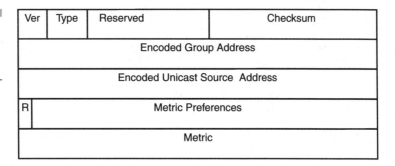

Figure 6-31
PIM-DM version 2 Assert message format

Ver	Type	Reserved	Checksum
Encoded Group Address			
Encoded Unicast Source Address			
R Metric Preferences			
Metric			

The PIM version can be configured using the interface configuration command:

```
ip pim version [1 | 2]
```

If an interface is configured for version 2 (the default) and a PIM version 1 neighbor is discovered on the interface, the router will automatically switch to PIM version 1. If the PIM version 1 neighbors somehow go away, the router will switch the interface back to PIM version 2.

The default interval for PIM query messages is 30 seconds. This can be adjusted using the interface command:

TABLE 6-6

Address family assignments

Number	Description
0	Reserved
1	IP Version 4
2	IP Version 6
3	NSAP
4	HDLC ('-bit multidrop)
5	BBN 1822
6	802
7	E.163
8	E.164 (SMDS, Frame Relay, ATM)
9	F.69 (Telex)
10	X.121 (X.25, Frame Relay)
11	IPX
12	Appletalk
13	Decnet IV
14	Banyan Vines
15	E.164 with NSAP format subaddress

Figure 6-32
Basic PIM-DM router configuration

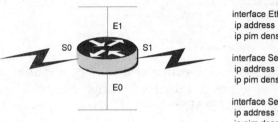

```
ip multicast-routing

interface Ethernet 0
 ip add 172.16.1.1 255.255.255.0
 ip pim dense-mode

interface Ethernet 1
 ip address 172.16.2.1 255.255.255.0
 ip pim dense-mode

interface Serial 0
 ip address 172.16.3.1 255.255.255.252
 ip pim dense-mode

interface Serial 1
 ip address 172.16.3.5 255.255.255.252
 ip pim dense-mode

router eigrp 100
 network 172.16.0.0
```

```
ip pim query-interval seconds
```

seconds   1–65535 seconds

The following command changes the PIM query interval to 60 seconds.

```
interface Serial 0
 ip pim query-interval 60
```

Monitoring and Debugging PIM Dense Mode

The network in Figure 6-33 is configured with PIM-DM and will be used to demonstrate the PIM show and debug commands. The configurations for the routers in Figure 6-33 are listed on the following page.

Figure 6-33
The network used to demonstrate PIM-DM show and debug commands

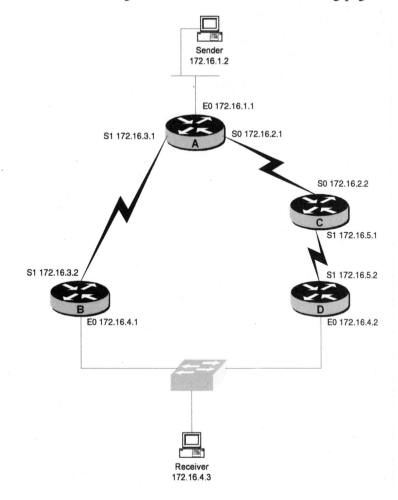

Sender
172.16.1.2

E0 172.16.1.1

S1 172.16.3.1   S0 172.16.2.1
            A

S0 172.16.2.2
        C
S1 172.16.5.1

S1 172.16.3.2   S1 172.16.5.2
       B   D
E0 172.16.4.1   E0 172.16.4.2

Receiver
172.16.4.3

```
Router A
ip multicast-routing
interface Ethernet 0
  ip address 172.16.1.1 255.255.255.0
  ip pim dense-mode
interface Serial 0
  ip address 172.16.2.1 255.255.255.0
  clock rate 1540000
  ip pim dense-mode
interface Serial 1
  ip address 172.16.3.1 255.255.255.0
  clock rate 1540000
  ip pim dense-mode
router eigrp 100
  network 172.16.0.0
```

```
Router C
ip multicast-routing
interface Serial 0
  ip address 172.16.2.2 255.255.255.0
  ip pim dense-mode
interface Serial 1
  ip address 172.16.5.1 255.255.255.0
  clock rate 1540000
ip pim dense-mode
router eigrp 100
  network 172.16.0.0
```

```
Router B
ip multicast-routing
interface Ethernet 0
  ip address 172.16.4.1 255.255.255.0
  ip pim dense-mode
interface Serial 1
  ip address 172.16.3.2 255.255.255.0
  clock rate 1540000
  ip pim dense-mode
router eigrp 100
  network 172.16.0.0
```

```
Router D
ip multicast-routing
interface Ethernet 0
  ip address 172.16.4.2 255.255.255.0
  ip pim dense-mode
interface Serial 1
  ip address 176.16.5.2 255.255.255.0
  clock rate 1540000
  ip pim dense-mode
router eigrp 100
  network 172.16.0.0
```

Use the EXEC command `show ip pim neighbor` to view the state of the PIM interfaces on the routers.

```
B#show ip pim neighbor
```

PIM Neighbor Table

Neighbor Address	Interface	Uptime	Expires	Ver	Mode
172.16.3.1	Serial 1	00:09:40	00:01:35	v2	Dense
172.16.4.2	Ethernet0	00:41:57	00:01:19	v2	Dense (DR)

The fields in the neighbor address are described below.

Neighbor address	IP Address of the PIM neighbor.
Interface	Interface on which the neighbor is attached.
Uptime	How long in hours, minutes, and seconds the neighbor has been in the PIM neighbor table.

Expires	Time to elapse before the neighbor is removed from the table in hours, minutes, and seconds.
Mode	PIM mode of the interface.
(DR)	The neighbor is the designated router on a multi-access network.

The state of a PIM interface can be displayed using the `show ip pim interface` command.

---

show ip pim interface [*interface-type interface-number*] [**count**]

---

interface-type *interface-number*	Optional. Type and number of the interface (Ethernet 0, Serial 1, etc.)
count	Optional. Number of packets that have been sent and received on the interface

```
B4#show ip pim interface
```

Address	Interface	Version/Mode	Nbr Count	Query Intvl	DR
172.16.4.2	Ethernet0	v2/Dense	1	30	172.16.4.1
172.16.3.1	Serial1	v2/Dense	1	30	0.0.0.0

Address	IP address of the next hop router.
Interface	PIM interface type and number.
Version/Mode	Configured PIM mode and version number for the interface.
Neighbor Count	Number of discovered PIM neighbors on this interface.
Query Intvl	Configured PIM query interval.
DR	Address of the designated router. Serial interfaces do not have a designated router so this field is set to 0.0.0.0.

```
B#show ip pim interface count
```

Address	Interface	FS	Mpackets In/Out
172.16.4.2	Ethernet0	•	686/0
172.16.3.1	Serial1	•	738/0

FS	• indicates that fast switching is enabled

Mpackets In/Out   Number of multicast packets sent or received on the interface.

The operation of PIM can be verified by executing the `debug ip pim` command:

```
B#debug ip pim
```

PIM debugging is on:

```
B#
08:18:03: PIM: Send v2 Hello on Ethernet0
08:18:06: PIM: Received v2 Hello on Ethernet0 from 172.16.4.2
08:18:10: PIM: Received v2 Hello on Serial1 from 172.16.3.1
08:18:16: PIM: Send v2 Hello on Serial1
08:18:33: PIM: Send v2 Hello on Ethernet0
08:18:36: PIM: Received v2 Hello on Ethernet0 from 172.16.4.2
08:18:40: PIM: Received v2 Hello on Serial1 from 172.16.3.1
08:18:46: PIM: Send v2 Hello on Serial1
```

Notice that PIM queries to or from a particular neighbor are 30 seconds apart. This is the default query interval for PIM.

REFERENCES ▪ ▪ ▪ ▪ ▪ ▪ ▪ ▪ ▪ ▪

IETF draft, "Protocol Independent Multicast Version 2 Dense Mode Specification," S. Deering et. al., 1998, draft-ietf-pim-v2-dm-01.txt

Protocol Independent Multicast-Sparse Mode

Protocol Independent Multicast-Sparse Mode (PIM-SM) is similar to PIM-DM in that both protocols depend on the underlying unicast routing protocol for determining RPF interfaces. A sparse mode protocol is assumed to operate in an environment where the multicast sources and multicast receivers are not closely located, so the distribution of PIM-SM nodes is sparse. This does not imply that PIM-SM cannot be used in a LAN environment but implies that sparse mode protocols operate more efficiently over *Wide Area Networks* (WAN). Dense mode protocols, on the other hand, use a broadcast and prune methodology, whereas multicast routers assume everyone wants to receive multicast traffic. Under this model, traffic from a multicast source is sent on all downstream interfaces until an interface is pruned from the multicast tree. An interface has a limited prune time, after which the interface is grafted back onto the multicast delivery tree and multicast traffic is again flooded onto the network.

Sparse mode protocols use an explicit join model in which multicast traffic is only forwarded onto an interface if receivers downstream have joined the group. Dense mode protocols, however, use source trees that are dynamically created for each source using the *Reverse Path Forwarding* (RPF) technique. PIM-SM uses shared trees for the delivery of multicast traffic. A shared tree contains a central point to which all senders of a particular multicast group send their traffic (see Figure 7-1). Each sender routes traffic along the shortest path to the central point, which then distributes the traffic to all receivers of the group along the shortest path. The group central

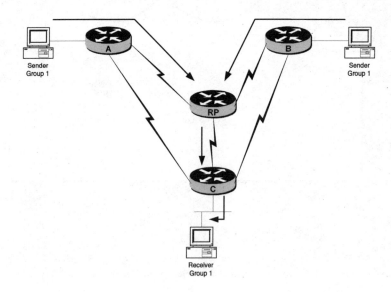

Figure 7-1
PIM-Sparse Mode
shared delivery tree

point in PIM-SM is referred to as the *Rendezvous Point* (RP). Multiple RPs can exist in a network, but there should only be one RP for a particular multicast group.

Figure 7-2 actually contains three source-based trees, depending on how you look at it. Assume the RP is the receiver of the multicast traffic; the paths from routers A and B are the source-based trees because the traffic flows along the shortest path given by the RPF interfaces. Now assume the RP is the sender of the multicast traffic. The path to every receiver in the group from the RP is again the shortest path tree. When these three trees are combined, you have the shared tree of PIM-SM. The combination of these trees is not necessarily the shortest path between the senders and the receivers, as can be seen in Figure 7-2. In the figure, we have the same network topology as in Figure 7-1, except now we are running PIM-DM instead of PIM-SM. Thus, two source trees follow the shortest path from each sender to each receiver.

You may be thinking, what's the point? Why not use the source-based trees instead of the shared tree because the shared tree is not the optimum path? This question can be answered in two ways. The first answer is that PIM-SM has a mechanism that allows the last hop router, the one with directly attached receivers, to join the source tree and leave the shared tree. This process is called *shortest path tree* (SPT) switchover. The decision to switchover is based on configured thresholds that we will examine later in the chapter. The second answer is sparse mode routers do not maintain as

Figure 7-2
PIM-Dense Mode
source delivery trees

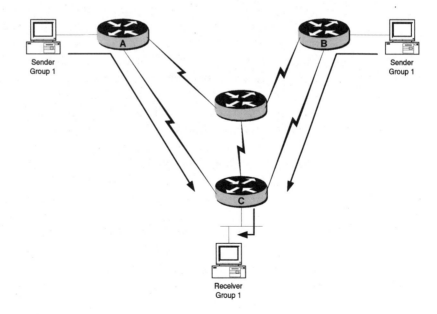

Sender
Group 1

Sender
Group 1

Receiver
Group 1

much state information as dense mode routers, making the maintenance of state more efficient.

Another question that has probably come to mind concerns the RP. How do the routers know where the RP is? A brief answer is that there are three ways for routers to know the location of the RP. The first way is to manually configure the address of the RP on each router that is running PIM-SM. The other two ways are dynamic and depend on the version of PIM-SM that is being employed in the network. PIM-SM version one has a mechanism called Auto-RP and PIM-SM version 2 uses candidate RP advertisements. We will see later how to configure all three methods. For now, we will assume that all the PIM-SM routers know the location of the RP. As with PIM-DM, the trees are constructed by using the routes in the unicast routing table. As we have seen in the previous chapter, the shared tree may not always be the same for a different unicast routing protocol.

PIM-SM—Protocol Operation and Neighbor Discovery

PIM-SM version 1 packets are encapsulated in IGMP packets, as shown in Figure 7-3. PIM-SM packets have a common header that contains a code identifying the PIM-SM message type and the PIM mode: dense, sparse, or sparse-dense (see Figure 7-4). The message types are listed in Table 7-1 and neighbor discovery or router query messages are identified as type 0 (see Figure 7-5); the modes for PIM query messages are displayed in Table 7-2. Router query messages are used to discover neighbors that are attached to a common network. Discover may be a misleading term, however, because there is not an explicit neighbor list section comparable to a DVMRP neighbor discovery message.

A better name for a router query message could be a neighbor inform message or a PIM Hello message. When a neighbor receives a query message, the IP address of the neighbor is recorded, but there is no explicit mechanism to acknowledge that the query was received. Instead, the receiving router simply transmits its own query message that has the effect of informing other PIM-SM routers on the network of its existence.

When a query message is received from a neighbor, will the interface be added to the outgoing interface list as it was in PIM-DM? The answer is no. PIM-SM uses an explicit join model; having a PIM-SM neighbor on

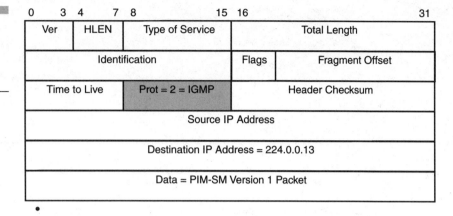

0 3	4 7	8 15	16 31
Ver	HLEN	Type of Service	Total Length
Identification		Flags	Fragment Offset
Time to Live	Prot = 2 = IGMP	Header Checksum	
Source IP Address			
Destination IP Address = 224.0.0.13			
Data = PIM-SM Version 1 Packet			

•

•

•

Type = 0x14	Code	Checksum
Ver	Reserved	

TABLE 7-1

Code	Message Type
0	Router Query
1	Register
2	Register-Stop
3	Join/Prune
4	RP Reachability
5	Assert

Code	Mode
0	Dense Mode
1	Sparse
2	Sparse-Dense

Figure 7-5
PIM-SM version 1
Query Message
packet format

Type = 0x14	Code = 0	Checksum
Ver		Reserved
Mode	Reserved	Holdtime

Figure 7-6
PIM-SM router query
and DR election

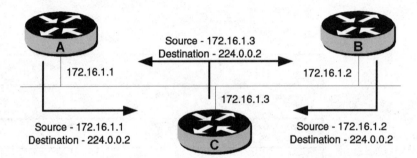

an interface is not sufficient for adding the interface to the output inter-face list. A downstream receiver must join a group before traffic is forwarded on the interface. For a multi-access network, such as an ethernet, the query message is sent to the all-routers multicast address, 224.0.0.2, and serves as the *Designated Router* (DR) election mechanism. For sparse mode PIM, the designated router only has a function if IGMP version 1 is being used. In this case, the DR becomes the IGMP querier for the network (refer to Chapter 3, "Internet Group Management Protocol"). The elected DR is the PIM-SM enabled router with the highest IP address. The query process and DR election is shown in Figure 7-6. For this scenario, router C would be elected DR because it has the highest IP address on the multi-access network.

The holdtime parameter in the router query message indicates how much time will elapse before this neighbor is declared dead. Subsequent router queries from a neighbor will reset this time, so the query interval must be less than the holdtime interval. The router queries act as a keep-alive mechanism to inform neighboring routers that this router is still alive and well. If PIM-SM is disabled on the interface or the router becomes disabled, then the holdtime for this router will expire on the neighboring routers. If the holdtime expires for a neighbor that was elected DR for the multi-access network, then a new DR will need to be elected.

PIM-SM Packet Forwarding

When a PIM-SM router receives the initial multicast packet from a source, the packet is flooded onto all interfaces in the *output interface list* (oilist). Recall that the oilist is populated with those interfaces that lead to downstream receivers which have indicated their desire to receive the traffic using IGMP. In PIM-DM, there is only one RPF interface for a particular source. With PIM-SM, there can be two RPF possibilities for a particular source, depending on whether the traffic is flowing down the shared tree or down the source tree (see Figure 7-7).

Packet forwarding is similar to PIM-DM. If the group is in the oilist and it is not in the prune state, then the packet will be forwarded. One major difference between PIM-DM forwarding and PIM-SM forwarding is that in PIM-DM an interface is added to the oilist if a PIM-DM neighbor has been

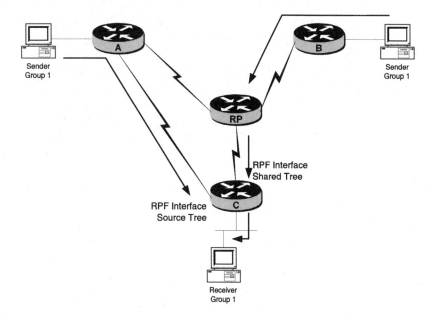

Figure 7-7
PIM-SM RPF check depends on the tree used.

discovered on the interface or if a join has been received or forwarded from a neighbor. In PIM-SM, the interface will only be put in the list if the downstream neighbor has sent a join to this router, if there is a directly attached receiver for the group and a join has been received, or if the interface has been manually configured to join the group.

PIM-SM JOINING   A leaf router will send a (*,G) Join message toward the RP if the leaf router has received a Join from a directly attached receiver or from a downstream neighbor. The router will forward the join to the RP along the unicast route, and each router along the path to the RP will process the Join. If a router does not have (*,G) state, then the state will be created and the Join will be sent toward the RP. If the router does have the state, then the Join message has reached the shared tree and the router does not have to do anything.

PIM-SM REGISTERING   When a PIM-SM-enabled router initially receives a multicast packet from a sender, the router may or may not have the state for this source and group. A sender does not have to join the group it is sending to use IGMP. The router only needs to register with the RP using a PIM-SM register packet (see Figure 7-8).

The Register packet is then sent as a unicast packet to the RP. The multicast packets that are received by the router directly attached to the source are encapsulated in Register messages, one per message. When the RP receives the Register message, the multicast packet will be extracted and sent down the shared tree toward the receivers. The RP will also send a (S,G) Join back toward the source in order to build the shortest path tree back to the source.

Once the path is established from the source to the RP, the source leaf router will begin to send multicast packets toward the RP as normal IP multicast packets. The source will also send the multicast packets encapsulated in Register messages, so the RP will receive them twice. When the RP detects that multicast packets from the source are being received as

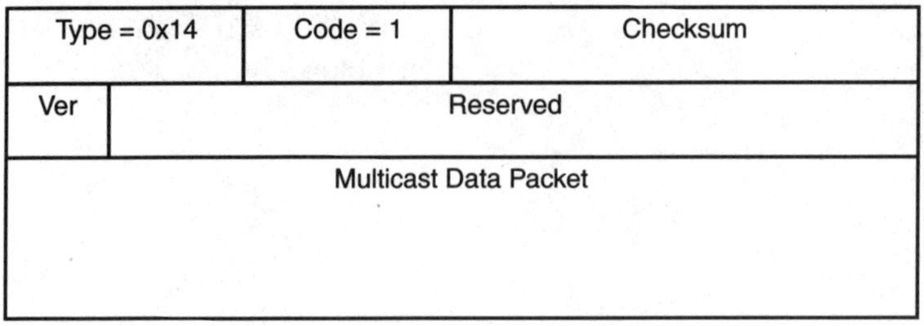

Figure 7-8
PIM Sparse-Mode
Register Packet
Format

Type = 0x14	Code = 1	Checksum	
Ver	Reserved		
Multicast Data Packet			

normal IP multicast packets, the RP sends a Register-Stop packet to the router directly attached to the source (see Figure 7-9).

Upon reception of the Register-Stop message, the first-hop router will quit encapsulating the multicast traffic in Register messages and only send them to the RP as normal IP multicast packets. Figure 7-10 illustrates the registering process.

Figure 7-9
PIM-Sparse Mode
Register-Stop Packets

Type = 0x14	Code = 2	Checksum
Ver	Reserved	
Group Address		
Source Address		

Figure 7-10
The PIM-SM RP
Registration Process

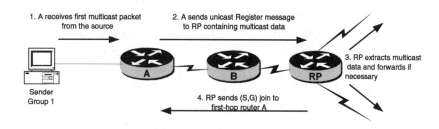

1. A receives first multicast packet from the source
2. A sends unicast Register message to RP containing multicast data
3. RP extracts multicast data and forwards if necessary
4. RP sends (S,G) join to first-hop router A

Sender
Group 1

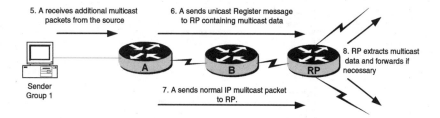

5. A receives additional multicast packets from the source
6. A sends unicast Register message to RP containing multicast data
7. A sends normal IP mulitcast packet to RP.
8. RP extracts multicast data and forwards if necessary

Sender
Group 1

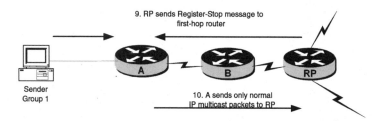

9. RP sends Register-Stop message to first-hop router
10. A sends only normal IP multicast packets to RP

Sender
Group 1

PIM-SM Interface Pruning

When the last receiver for a group on an interface sends a version 2 IGMP Leave message or simply times out in IGMP version 1, then the router IGMP state for the group is deleted. Additionally, the interface is removed from the (*,G) and (S,G) entries on the oilist for the group G.

If the (*,G) state has been removed from every interface in the oilist, then a Prune message is sent up the shared tree towards the RP. If upstream routers do not have the state for the group, except on the interface on which the prune is received, then the Prune message is forwarded towards the RP. If the Prune message arrives at a router on the shared tree that still has receivers for the group on a different interface, the Prune message stops and is not forwarded toward the RP. The same procedure occurs if the router is receiving traffic on the source-based tree, instead of the shared tree. The format of the Prune/Join message is contained in Figure 7-11.

The Upstream Neighbor Address is the address to which the Join/Prune packet is being sent. Its holdtime value indicates the lifetime of the Join/Prune. When a Prune is received, traffic from the source/group indicated in the Prune message is no longer forwarded onto the interface, while Join messages can be used to add a pruned interface to the oilist.

No Graft messages exist in PIM-SM because it is an explicit join model; Grafts instead are used in PIM-DM to add an interface back to the oilist

Figure 7-11
PIM Join/Prune
packet format

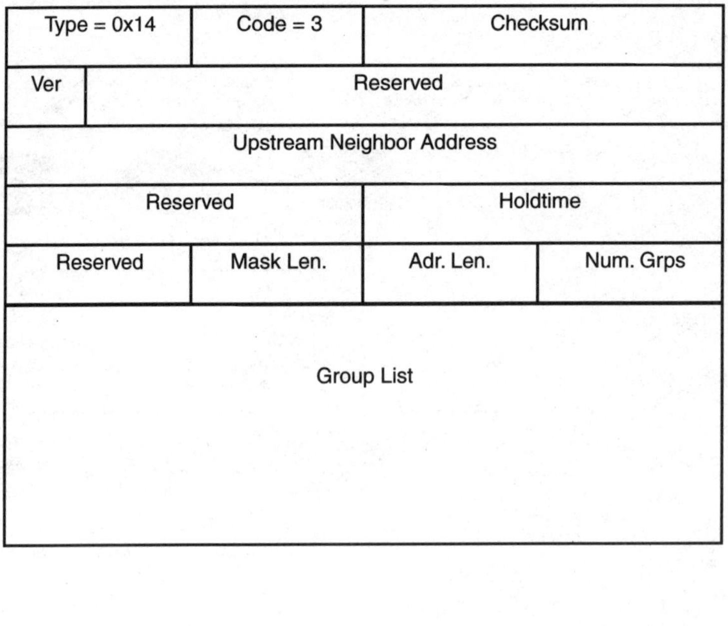

Type = 0x14	Code = 3	Checksum	
Ver	Reserved		
Upstream Neighbor Address			
Reserved		Holdtime	
Reserved	Mask Len.	Adr. Len.	Num. Grps
Group List			

if the interface is in the Prune state (in PIM-DM, Prune states expire and traffic is reflooded). Grafts can add an interface back in the oilist before the Prune state expires.

In PIM-SM, when an interface is pruned, the only way to add it back to the oilist is to use a Join message. The *Mask Length* (mask len) and *Address Length* (adr len) fields indicate the length in bytes of the mask and address for the group(s) to be pruned from the source-based delivery tree. Either the Prune list or the Join list may be empty, but a Join/Prune packet should never be sent when both the Join and Prune lists are empty. The format for the Group list is shown in Figure 7-12. The number of groups in the Group list is determined by the Number of Groups parameter in Figure 7-11.

Each group is identified by the address and mask of the group to be pruned or joined. Following the Address and Mask Pair is the number of Join and Prune sources for the group. Join sources are listed first, followed by the Prune sources, and they are represented by the encoded format of Figure 7-13.

The S bit in the encoded source address format indicates whether or not this is a Sparse Mode group and should be set to 1 for Sparse Mode groups. The W bit is the wildcard bit and indicates whether the entry applies to a specific source/group (S,G), where W equals 0, or if the entry applies to all sources of the group (*,G), where W equals 1. The R bit applies to PIM-SM. Recall that in PIM-SM there can be either a source-based tree or a shared tree. The R bit indicates whether the packet is being sent toward the source (R = 0) or toward the RP (R = 1). The Len filed is the length of the source mask in bits and the source address is the IP address of the source to be joined or pruned.

PIM-SM Assert Message

To avoid duplicate multicast packets from traversing multi-access networks, PIM-SM uses the Assert message to determine a designated forwarding router for a multi-access network. Figure 7-14 demonstrates the situation that would warrant the Assert mechanism. The steps taken are as follows:

1. Router A receives multicast traffic.

2. Routers B and C are PIM-SM neighbors, so the multicast traffic is forwarded to routers B and C.

Figure 7-12
Group list format

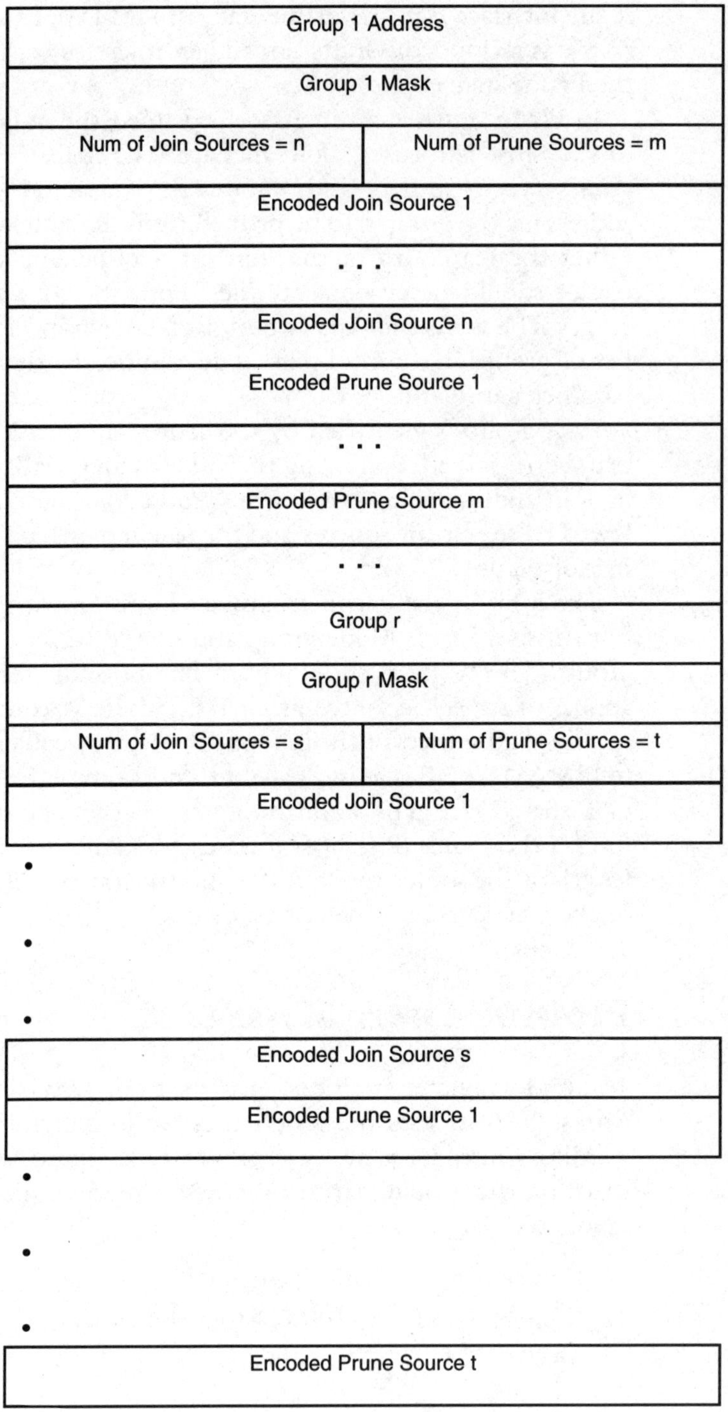

Group 1 Address
Group 1 Mask

Num of Join Sources = n	Num of Prune Sources = m

Encoded Join Source 1
. . .
Encoded Join Source n
Encoded Prune Source 1
. . .
Encoded Prune Source m
. . .
Group r
Group r Mask

Num of Join Sources = s	Num of Prune Sources = t

Encoded Join Source 1

•

•

•

Encoded Join Source s
Encoded Prune Source 1

•

•

•

Encoded Prune Source t

Figure 7-13
Encoded Source
Address format

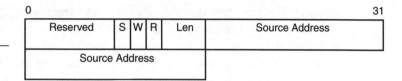

0						31
Reserved	S	W	R	Len	Source Address	
Source Address						

Figure 7-14
Assert messages are
used to prevent
multiple copies of
multicast traffic on a
multi-access network.

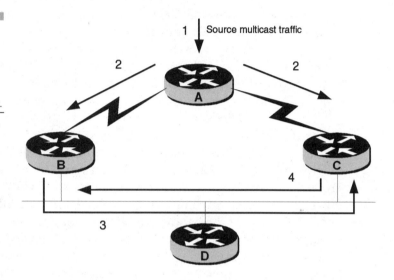

3. Router D is a PIM-SM neighbor, so routers B and C forward the traffic onto the ethernet LAN. Assume router B transmits first. Router C receives the multicast packet on an interface that has this group in the oilist. This alerts router C to the fact that a PIM-SM neighbor on the ethernet LAN has forwarded traffic for the group.

4. Router C forwards the multicast packet to routers B and D. B notices that the packet has arrived on an output interface for the group. Router D really doesn't care because this router is not forwarding traffic for the group onto the ethernet LAN. Router D has received the same multicast packet twice, a situation that needs to be eliminated.

If a router receives a multicast packet for which it has a state, either (S,G) or (*,G) on an outgoing interface, then the router knows that there is another router forwarding packets onto the network. For example, the serial interfaces for both routers B and C are the RPF interfaces back to the multicast source. When router A receives a packet from the source, the packet is forwarded to both routers B and C. With no other mechanism in place, both routers B and C will forward the traffic to router D, creating duplicate packets on the network. Assert messages are used to avoid this situation.

An Assert message also contains the group address and mask for the multicast source and the router's metric back to the source (see Figure 7-15). If both routers have an equal metric back to the source, then the router with the highest IP address becomes the forwarder for the network. The router that is not the forwarder prunes the interface.

Back in Figure 7-14, even though router D does not send Assert messages, it must listen to the Assert messages and determine which router is the designated router for the LAN. This information is necessary so that router D knows where to send Prune and Join messages for the group.

The Assert process is straightforward if both routers are running the same IP routing protocol. Recall that PIM-SM uses whatever protocol has been configured on the router to determine the RPF interface and the metric for the RPF interface. For the configuration in Figure 7-16, both routers on the multi-access network are running OSPF and the metrics back to the source are comparable. The OSPF metric is calculated by dividing 100,000,000 by the bandwidth of the link. The metric for the T1 link is approximately 67 and for the 28.8K link the metric is 3472. By comparing the metrics of the two links back to the source, we can easily choose the T1 link because it has a smaller metric than the 28.8K link. If different routing protocols are being utilized, then the metrics cannot be compared.

In Figure 7-17, router B is running OSPF and router C is running RIP. Comparing the metric back to the source for the two routers is like comparing apples and oranges. OSPF uses the speed of the interface to determine the metric and RIP uses a simple hop count. In this case, the metric

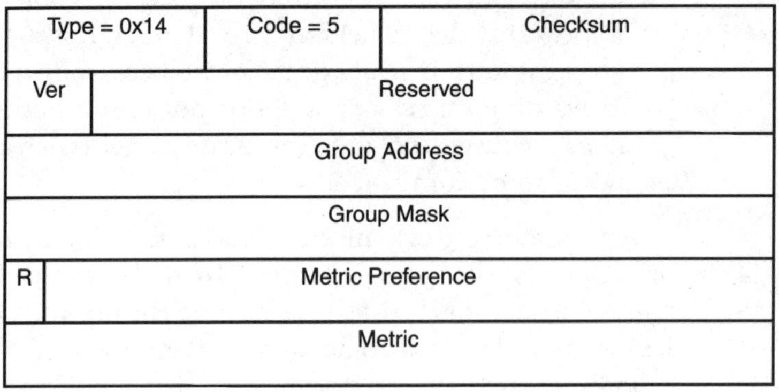

Figure 7-15
PIM Assert
packet format

Type = 0x14		Code = 5		Checksum	
Ver		Reserved			
Group Address					
Group Mask					
R	Metric Preference				
Metric					

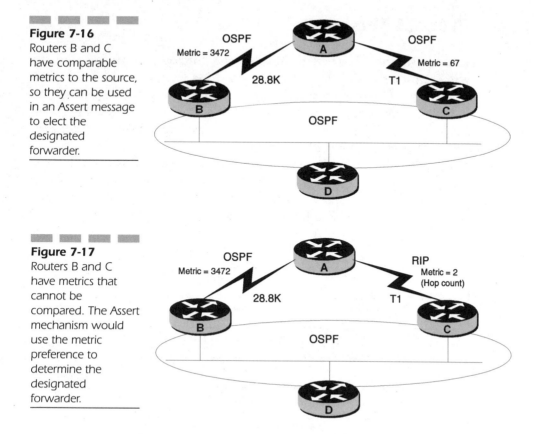

Figure 7-16
Routers B and C have comparable metrics to the source, so they can be used in an Assert message to elect the designated forwarder.

Figure 7-17
Routers B and C have metrics that cannot be compared. The Assert mechanism would use the metric preference to determine the designated forwarder.

preference value in the assert packet is used to determine which router will forward traffic and which router will prune the interface. Metric preference is analogous to an administrative distance for a unicast routing protocol. For example, the default administrative distance for RIP is 120 and for OSPF it is 110. Using the defaults always causes an OSPF route to be preferred over a RIP route.

Metric preferences can also be configured for each unicast-routing protocol. When PIM-SM receives an Assert message for a group, the metric preference is compared to its own metric preference. If they are equal, then the metrics can be compared to determine which router will forward traffic. If the metric preference values are different, then the router with the lowest metric preference is selected as the forwarder on the network. If we assign a lower metric value for OSPF than for RIP, then the routers on the multi-access network in Figure 7-17 will select the OSPF router to forward traffic, and the RIP router will prune its interface for the group.

PIM-SM Version 2

PIM-SM version 2 is specified in RFC 2362, June 1998. In this section, we will examine the differences between PIM-SM versions 1 and 2. The first major change is that version 2 messages are no longer encapsulated in IGMP messages but are encapsulated in IP packets with protocol number 103 (see Figure 7-18). PIM-SM version 2 messages are sent to the multicast group 224.0.0.13, ALL-PIM-ROUTERS.

The PIM-SM version 2 packet header has been modified from the version 1 packet header (see Figure 7-19). The types of messages identified in the packet header, along with the version 1 types, are listed in Table 7-3. As you can see, there have been a few modifications from Table 7-1.

Figure 7-18
Encapsulation of a PIM-SM version 2 packet in an IP datagram

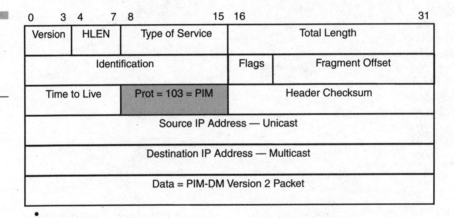

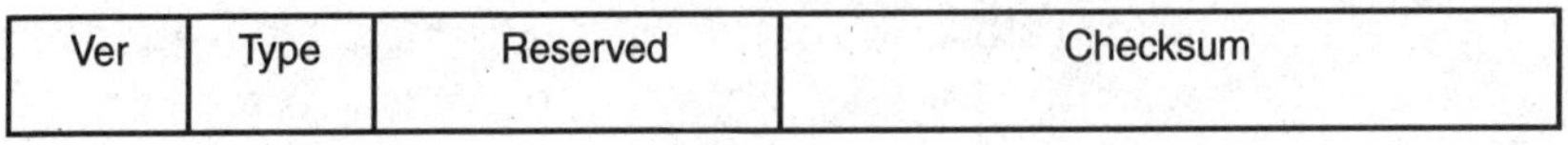

Figure 7-19
PIM-SM version 2 packet header format

| Ver | Type | Reserved | Checksum |

TABLE 7-3

PIM versions 1 and
2 message types

Type	Description Version 2	Description Version 1
0	Hello	Router query
1	Register (Sparse mode)	Same
2	Register-Stop (Sparse mode)	Same
3	Join/Prune	Same
4	Bootstrap (Sparse mode)	RP Reachability (Sparse mode)
5	Assert	Same
6	Graft (Dense mode)	Same
7	Graft-Ack (Dense mode)	Same
8	Candidate RP advertisement	Type not used

Figure 7-20
PIM-SM Version 2
Hello message
format

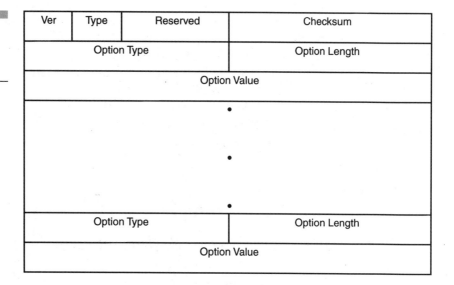

The router query message that was used as the Neighbor Discovery mechanism in version 1 has been replaced by the Hello message, shown in Figure 7-20.

The Option fields for the Hello message are listed in Table 7-4 and the values of the holdtime in Table 7-5.

A timeout value of 0xFFFF means that the neighbor never expires. This value has the affect of preventing periodic Hello messages being sent and is useful on a tariff connection, such as ISDN. Periodic Hellos would keep

TABLE 7-4

Hello message
Option fields

Option Type	Option Length	Option Value
1	2	Hold time
2–16	Reserved	Reserved

TABLE 7-5

Hello message
holdtime values

Value	Description
0xFFFF	No time out
0	Immediate time out
Any other value	Neighbor time out value

the link active, even in the absence of user data traffic, but you may not be happy receiving an ISDN bill for nothing more than periodic Hello traffic. A holdtime of zero signifies that the neighbor should immediately time out.

The Prune/Join message format has been modified, as shown in Figure 7-21. The encoded unicast and multicast address formats are shown in Figures 7-22 and 7-23.

Encoding value is 0 and represents the native encoding for the address family (see Table 7-6). Further encoded address examples are shown in Figures 7-23 and 7-24. Figure 7-25 displays the PIM-SM version 2 Assert message format.

The Rendezvous Point—Where Is It?

We assumed in all of the previous examples that the RP was configured and that the routers knew where it was. In this section, we will look at how this is accomplished. There are three methods that can be used to configure the RP. The first method is a static method and it requires configuring each leaf-designated router with the address of the RP for a group or range of groups. Leaf routers are those routers that have directly connected multicast sources or receivers (see Figure 7-26).

If the static RP method and one of the two dynamic RP methods are utilized simultaneously, the dynamic method takes precedence unless the static method is configured to take precedence, as we shall see when we look at the actual router configuration commands. Routers that may become designated routers in case the primary designated router fails

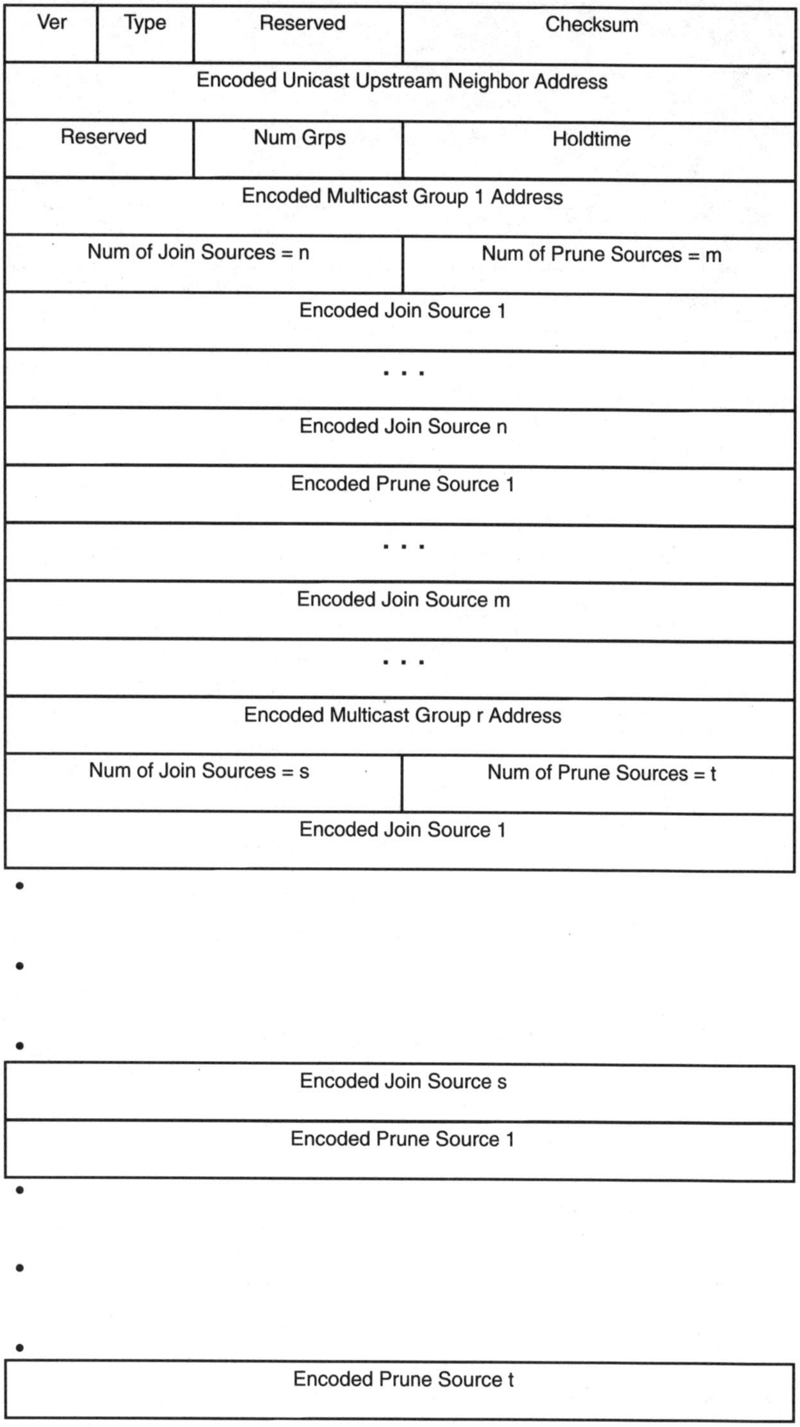

Figure 7-21
PIM version 2
Join/Prune packet
format

Ver	Type	Reserved	Checksum

Encoded Unicast Upstream Neighbor Address		

Reserved	Num Grps	Holdtime

Encoded Multicast Group 1 Address

Num of Join Sources = n	Num of Prune Sources = m

Encoded Join Source 1

. . .

Encoded Join Source n

Encoded Prune Source 1

. . .

Encoded Join Source m

. . .

Encoded Multicast Group r Address

Num of Join Sources = s	Num of Prune Sources = t

Encoded Join Source 1

Encoded Join Source s

Encoded Prune Source 1

Encoded Prune Source t

Figure 7-22
PIM version 2
encoded unicast
address format

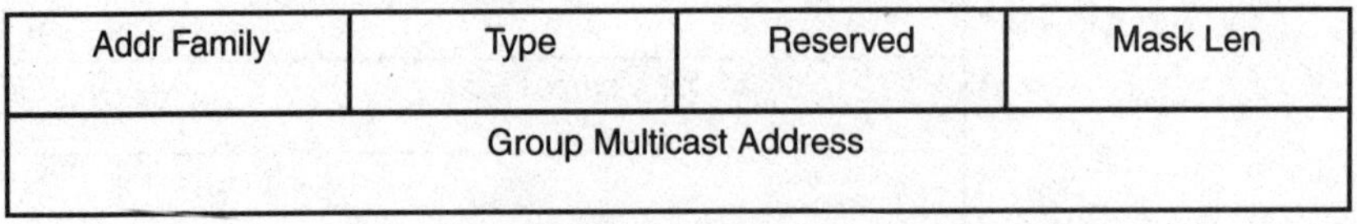

Encoded Prune Source t

Figure 7-23
Encoded Group
address format

Addr Family	Type	Reserved	Mask Len
Group Multicast Address			

TABLE 7-6

Address Family
Assignments

Number	Description
0	Reserved
1	IP Version 4
2	IP Version 6
3	NSAP
4	HDLC ('-bit multidrop)
5	BBN 1822
6	802
7	E.163
8	E.164 (SMDS, Frame Relay, ATM)
9	E.69 (Telex)
10	X.121 (X.25, Frame Relay)
11	IPX
12	AppleTalk
13	DECnet IV
14	Banyan Vines
15	E.164 with NSAP format subaddress

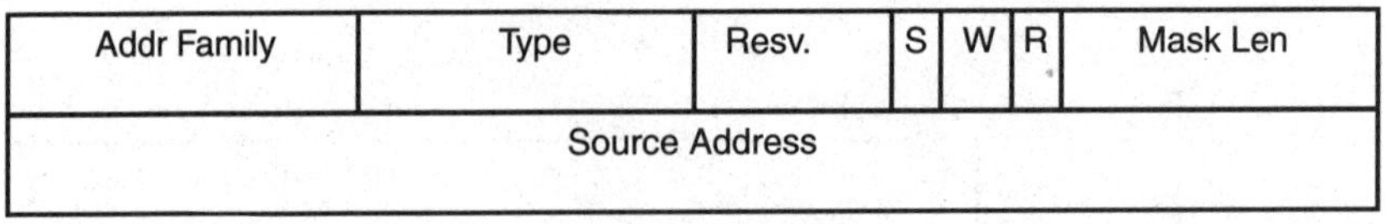

Figure 7–24
Encoded Source
address

Addr Family	Type	Resv.	S	W	R	Mask Len
Source Address						

Figure 7-25
PIM-SM version 2
Assert message
format

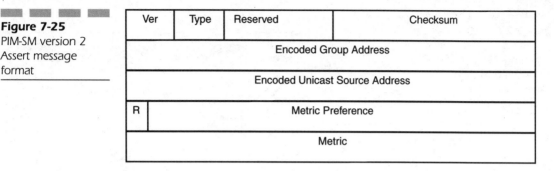

Figure 7-25
PIM-SM version 2
Assert message
format

Ver	Type	Reserved	Checksum
Encoded Group Address			
Encoded Unicast Source Address			
R	Metric Preference		
Metric			

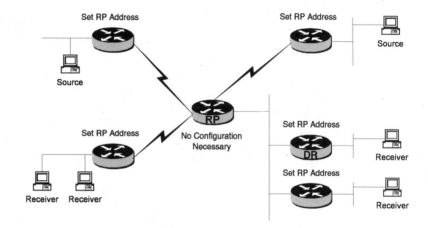

Figure 7-26
Static RP assignment.
Only leaf routers
need to be
configured with the
address of the RP.

need to be configured with the RP address. All the leaf routers in the PIM-SM domain are told where the RP is except for the RP itself! The RP is expected to deduce that it is the RP.

PIM version 1 uses a dynamic technique developed by Cisco called Auto-RP. Although one or more routers are statically configured as RPs, non-RP routers do not need to be configured with the address of the RPs. Configured RPs send RP announcements through all PIM-enabled interfaces with a configured TTL value that limits the scope of the announcement. These announcements are sent to the CISCO-RP-ANNOUNCE multicast group with address 224.0.1.39 and are received by an RP mapping agent, shown in Figure 7-27, which can also be the RP. This agent then sends the RP-to-group mappings to the group CISCO-RP-DISCOVERY (224.0.1.40). PIM-SM enabled routers listen to this group to determine the RP-to-group mappings (see Figure 7-28).

The mapping agent does not seem to be necessary when there is only one RP in the PIM-SM domain, but if there are multiple RPs and the

Figure 7-27
Rendezvous
points send RP
announcements that
are received by the
mapping agent.

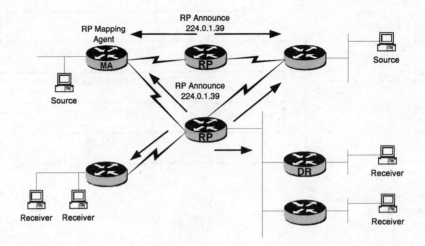

Figure 7-28
Mapping agents
send RP-to-group
mappings that are
received by PIM-SM-
enabled routers.

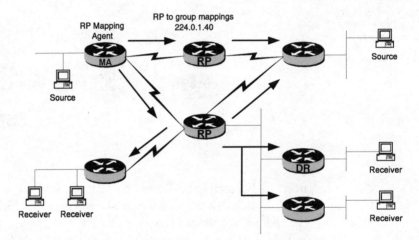

groups are announcing overlap, the mapping agent determines which router will be the RP for which groups. The mapping agent then distributes this information throughout the PIM-SM domain.

In PIM version 2 RP, information is disseminated using Bootstrap messages (see Figure 7-29).

Fragment Tag   A randomly generated number that is used to identify
                   fragments. Fragment tags with the same value are from the
                   same Bootstrap message.

HML   Hash Mask Length. The length of the mask to use in the
                   Hash function.

BSR-priority   The *Bootstrap router* (BSR) priority of the included BSR.

Figure 7-29
PIM-SM Version 2
Bootstrap message
format

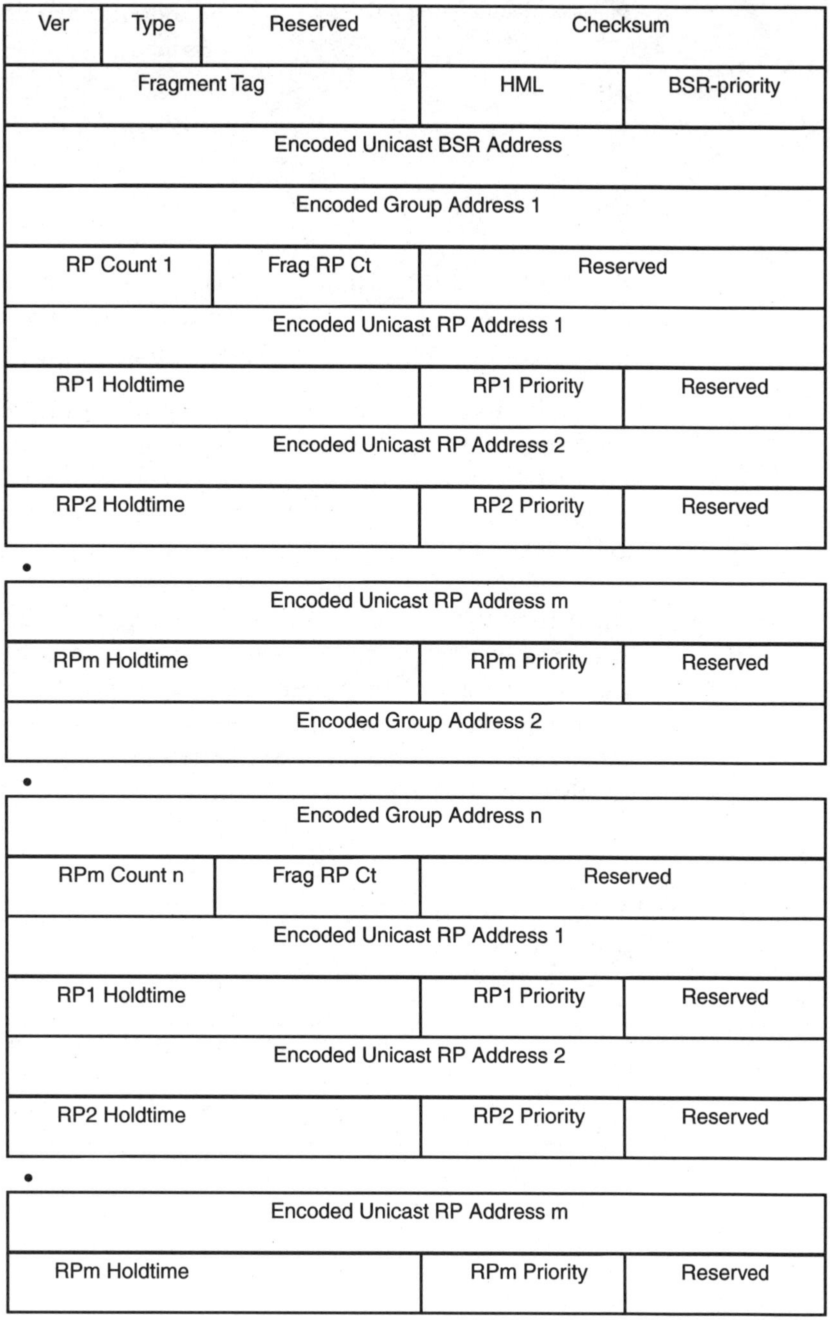

Ver	Type	Reserved	Checksum	
Fragment Tag			HML	BSR-priority
Encoded Unicast BSR Address				
Encoded Group Address 1				
RP Count 1		Frag RP Ct	Reserved	
Encoded Unicast RP Address 1				
RP1 Holdtime			RP1 Priority	Reserved
Encoded Unicast RP Address 2				
RP2 Holdtime			RP2 Priority	Reserved

•

Encoded Unicast RP Address m				
RPm Holdtime			RPm Priority	Reserved
Encoded Group Address 2				

•

Encoded Group Address n				
RPm Count n		Frag RP Ct	Reserved	
Encoded Unicast RP Address 1				
RP1 Holdtime			RP1 Priority	Reserved
Encoded Unicast RP Address 2				
RP2 Holdtime			RP2 Priority	Reserved

•

Encoded Unicast RP Address m				
RPm Holdtime			RPm Priority	Reserved

Encoded Unicast BSR Address	The address of the Bootstrap router for the domain.
RP Count	The number of candidate RP addresses in the message for the corresponding group prefix.
Frag RP Ct	The number of candidate RP addresses in this fragment.
Encoded Unicast RP Address	The address of the candidate RPs for the corresponding group prefix.
RP Priority	The priority if the RP. Highest is 0.

The PIM-SM domain has a bootstrap router responsible for originating bootstrap messages. These messages are used to elect a BSR if needed (see Figure 7-30) and to distribute RP information that is sent to the multicast group ALL PIM ROUTERS (224.0.0.13). One or more routers are configured as candidate BSRs and the BSR candidate with the highest configured priority will be elected as the *Bootstrap router* (BSR). If all the priorities are equal, then the candidate BSR with the highest IP address will be elected, while another set of routers will be configured as candidate RPs. Usually the routers that are configured as candidate BSRs are also configured as candidate RPs, which will periodically send Candidate RP Advertisement messages to the elected BSR (see Figure 7-31). Candidate RP Advertisements are also sent to the BSR unicast address (see Figure 7-32).

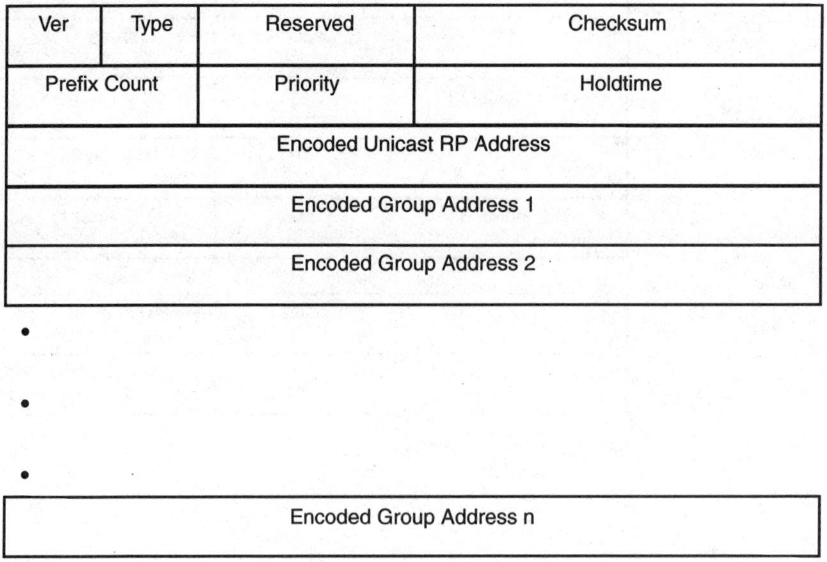

Figure 7-30
Each candidate BSR sends Bootstrap messages that are used to elect the BSR.

Ver	Type	Reserved	Checksum
Prefix Count		Priority	Holdtime
Encoded Unicast RP Address			
Encoded Group Address 1			
Encoded Group Address 2			

•

•

•

Encoded Group Address n

Bootstrap Messages
224.0.0.13

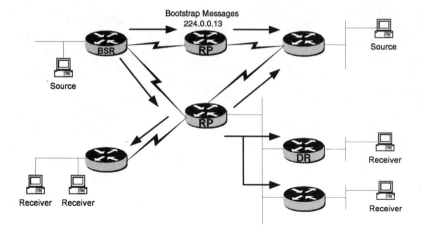

Figure 7-31
Candidate RPs send
RP announcements
to the Bootstrap
router.

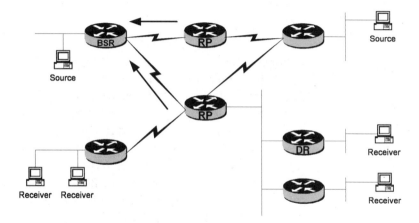

Figure 7-32
PIM-SM version 2
Candidate RP
advertisement

Prefix Count	Number of encoded group addresses in the message.
Priority	The priority of the RP for the encoded group address. Zero is highest.
Holdtime	The amount of time this advertisement is valid.
Encoded Unicast RP Address	The address of the candidate RP.

The Candidate RP advertisements contain the address of the Advertising Candidate RP as well as the groups that can be serviced by the candidate RP. The BSR periodically transmits this information throughout the domain and the PIM-SM routers receive and store it (see Figure 7-33). When a receiver joins a group using IGMP, the router maps the group address to one of the RPs and each candidate BSR sends Bootstrap messages that are used to elect the BSR.

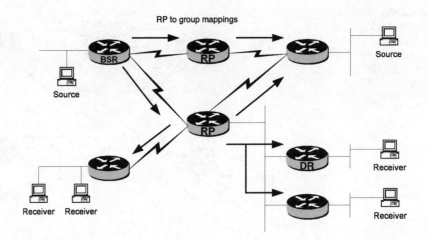

SPT Switchover

A threshold on a leaf router can be configured that, when exceeded, will cause the router to switch from the shared tree through the RP to the source tree. When PIM-SM is enabled, the default threshold is 0 kbps. This means that when the first packet is received from a multicast source, the router switches from the shared tree to the source tree. The threshold can be configured from 0 to infinity. A setting of infinity prevents the router from ever switching to the source tree.

The traffic for the group G from any source S is measured once each second. If the threshold is exceeded, then set a flag for (*,G) to remember that the threshold was exceeded. When the next packet for G arrives from any source, if the threshold exceeded flag is set, then clear the flag in (*,G), set the flag in (S,G), and switch to the source tree for that particular source. Again, every second the state of the flag is in (S,G) will be checked and if the traffic rate is less than the threshold, then switch back to the shared tree. The advantages of switching to the source tree is that traffic is being received on the shortest path tree. The shortest path tree will generally have a lower latency than the shared tree. The disadvantage is that (S,G) state will have to be maintained in the router. In other words, there is more detail that has to be maintained.

PIM-SM Router Configuration Commands

PIM-SM is more complicated to configure than PIM-DM because an RP is required for each group. One RP can handle all groups, which can be spread across multiple RPs. The first step is to enable multicast routing in Global Configuration mode using the command

```
ip multicast-routing
```

Next, enable PIM-SM on the router interfaces using the interface command

```
ip pim sparse-mode
```

or

```
ip pim sparse-dense-mode
```

PIM-Sparse-Dense-Mode is used when there are groups with no RP. In this case, groups with an assigned RP are treated as Sparse Mode groups, and groups without an RP are treated as Dense Mode groups.

Rendezvous Point Configuration and Static RP Configuration

There is not a default RP and one or more must be configured using one of the three methods. For the static case, the RP does not need to be configured, only the leaf routers. To configure the static RP, use the global configuration command

```
ip pim rp-address ip-address [access-list-number] [override]
```

ip-address	ip address of the RP
group-access-list-number	Optional. Standard IP access list number, 1–100. If no access list is used, then the RP can handle all groups. Use an access list to limit the groups that the RP will service.
override	Optional. If there is a conflict between the static RP and one configured using Auto-RP, then the static RP takes precedence.

For example, to configure an RP that handles all groups, use

ip pim rp-address 172.16.1.1

where 172.16.1.1 is the address of the RP. If we want the RP to only handle a subset of multicast groups, then an access list is needed. If the RP is to handle only group 239.252.1.1, then we would use the following commands:

ip pim rp-address 172.16.1.1 1
access-list 1 permit 239.252.1.1 0.0.0.0

If the RP is to service the groups 239.252.1.0 through 239.252.1.255, then the access list would contain

access-list 1 permit 239.252.1.0 0.0.0.255.

Auto-RP Configuration

For Auto-RP, the RPs and a mapping agent need to be configured. The RPs are configured using the Global Configuration command:

```
ip pim send-rp-announce interface-type interface-number scope ttl
group-list access-list-number
```

interface-type interface-number	The address of the specified interface is used to identify the RP.
scope	TTL value of the announcements. Limits the distance an RP announcement can travel.
access-list-number	An access-list determines the groups that the RP is announcing that it can service.

The router sends RP announcements on all PIM-enabled interfaces for a maximum number of hops specified by the scope parameter. The announcements are sent to the group CISCO-RP-ANNOUNCE (224.0.1.39). To enable the RP to announce all multicast groups, use the command below.

```
ip pim send-rp-announce ethernet 0 scope 30 group-list 2
access-list 2 permit 224.0.0.0 15.255.255.255
```

The next step in configuring Auto-RP is to configure the RP mapping agent using the global command

```
ip pim send-rp-discovery scope ttl
```

scope   TTL of the Discovery messages. Used to
                                          limit the scope of the message.

The router configured as a mapping agent will listen for RP announcements to group CISCO-RP-ANNOUNCE (224.0.1.39). The RP mapping agent then sends the RP-to-group mappings to the group CISCO-RP-DISCOVERY (224.0.1.40), and PIM routers get their RP information from the Discovery messages.

PIM-SM Version 2 RP Selection

One or more BSRs need to be configured in the domain using the global configuration command:

```
ip pim bsr-candidate interface-type interface-number hash-mask-length [priority]
```

interface-type interface-number   The address of the specified interface will
                                          be used to identify the BSR.

hash-mask-length   Length of the mask (32 bits maximum) that
                                          is ANDed with the group address before
                                          the hash function is called. All groups with
                                          the same seed correspond to the same RP.
                                          If the value is 24, then only the first 24 bits
                                          of the group address are used. Therefore,
                                          one RP can have multiple groups.

priority   Optional. Value from 0 to 255. The BSR
                                            candidate with the largest priority is
                                            preferred. If BSR candidates have the same
                                            priority, the one with the highest IP
                                            address is elected as the BSR.

This command causes the router to send Bootstrap messages to PIM neighbors. When a Bootstrap message is received, the priority and address of the message are compared to the previous message. If they are the same, then the message is forwarded. If the received message has a lower priority, or if the priority is the same but the IP address is lower, the message is discarded. Otherwise, the address and priority are cached and the message is forwarded.

After the bootstrap router(s) are configured, then the RP routers are configured using the global command:

---

ip pim rp-candidate *interface-type interface-number* [**group-list** *access-list-number*]

---

interface-type interface-number   The address of the specified interface will
                                            be used to identify the candidate RP.

group-list *access-list number*   Optional. Standard IP access list used to
                                            determine the groups that the candidate
                                            RP advertises

To configure a candidate RP that will advertise any multicast group starting with 227, the following command can be used:

```
ip pim rp-candidate serial 1 group-list 51
access-list 51 permit 227.0.0.0 0.255.255.255
```

The PIM-SM domain can be divided into BSR subdomains with their own configured BSRs. If you do not want BSR messages to cross domains, use the interface configuration command

---

ip pim border

When this command is used, no Bootstrap messages can pass through the router in either direction, but other PIM messages can pass through the router.

By default, a router will accept all Join and Prune messages. A router can be configured to accept Joins or Prunes for specified groups for a specified RP. The command used to accomplish this filtering is the global command:

---
ip pim accept-rp {*address* | **auto-rp**} [*access-list-number*]

---

address	Address of the RP.
auto-rp	Messages are accepted only for RPs that are in the Auto-RP cache.
access-list-number	Optional. Defines the groups that are allowed.

This command causes the router to accept only Join and Prune messages destined for the specified RP. If an access list is used, then the group must also be allowed by the list. If the address in the command is an address on the receiving router, then the router is the RP and it will accept messages only for the groups specified. If the group is not allowed by the access list, then the router will respond immediately to Register messages with Register-Stop messages. For example, to configure a router to accept Join and Prune messages for the RP whose ID is 172.16.1.1 related to groups 225.0.0.0 through 225.255.255.255, use the command

```
ip pim accept-rp 172.16.1.1 8
access-list 8 permit 225.0.0.0 0.255.255.255
```

RP mapping agents can be configured to filter Auto-RP announcements using the global configuration command:

---
ip pim rp-announce-filter rp-*list* *access-list-number* **group-list** *access-list-number*

---

rp-list *access-list-number*	Standard access list of RP addresses from which Auto-RP announcements will be accepted.
group-list *access-list-number*	Standard access list of group addresses that will be accepted.

For example, to configure an RP mapping agent to accept Auto-RP announcements from the RP with address 172.16.1.1 for all multicast groups, use

```
ip pim rp-announce-filter rplist 12 group-list 13
access-list 12 permit 172.16.1.1
access-list 13 permit 224.0.0.0 15.255.255.255
```

The PIM version can be configured using the interface configuration command

```
ip pim version [1 | 2]
```

If an interface is configured for version 2 (the default) and a PIM version 1 neighbor is discovered on the interface, then the router automatically switches to PIM version 1. If the PIM version 1 neighbors somehow vanish, the router switches the interface back to PIM version 2.

The default interval for PIM query messages is 30 seconds. This can be adjusted using the interface command:

```
ip pim query-interval seconds
```

seconds   1–65535 seconds

The following command changes the PIM query interval to 60 seconds:

```
interface Serial 0
ip pim query-interval 60
```

PIM-SM SPT-Switchover is controlled by the global configuration command:

```
ip pim spt-threshold {kbps | infinity} [group-list access-list-number]
```

kbps   Traffic rate in kilobits per second.

infinity   The specified groups will use the shared-tree.

group-list *access-list-number*   Optional. Determines which groups to apply the threshold.

By default, a PIM-SM router sends periodic Join/Prune messages every 60 seconds. To alter this interval, use the global configuration command

```
ip pim message-interval seconds
```

seconds   Value in the range 1 to 65535

All PIM-SM-enabled routers should be configured with the same message interval time. A router will be pruned from a group if a Join message is not received in the message interval. The default value is three minutes.

Example of an PIM-SM Network

The networks that follow will be configured for PIM-SM and each of the RP configuration methods (see Figure 7-34). This network will be used to illustrate complete router configurations and the information that can be gathered using PIM Show and Debug commands.

Figure 7-34
Example network for static RP configuration. Only the leaf routers need to be configured with the address of the RP.

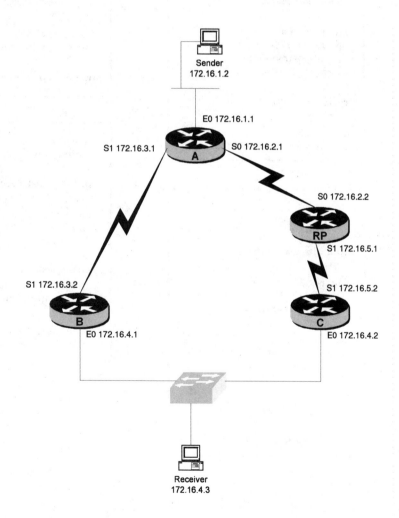

NETWORK 1—STATIC RP ROUTER CONFIGURATIONS

Router A
hostname A

ip multicast-routing

interface Ethernet 0
ip address 172.16.1.1 255.255.255.0
ip pim sparse-mode

interface Serial 0
ip address 172.16.2.1 255.255.255.0
ip pim sparse-mode
clock rate 1540000

interface Serial 1
ip address 172.16.3.1 255.255.255.0
ip pim sparse-mode
clock rate 1540000

router eigrp 100
 network 172.16.0.0

ip pim rp-address 172.16.2.2

Router C
hostname C

ip multicast-routing

interface Ethernet 0
ip address 172.16.4.2 255.255.255.0
ip pim sparse-mode

interface Serial 1
ip address 172.16.5.2 255.255.255.0
ip pim sparse-mode
clock rate 1540000

router eigrp 100
 network 172.16.0.0

ip pim rp-address 172.16.2.2

Router RP
hostname RP

ip multicast-routing

interface Serial 0
ip address 172.16.2.2 255.255.255.0
ip pim sparse-mode

interface Serial 1
ip address 172.16.5.1 255.255.255.0
ip pim sparse-mode

router eigrp 100
 network 172.16.0.0

Router B
hostname B

ip multicast-routing

interface Ethernet 0
ip address 172.16.4.1 255.255.255.0
ip pim sparse-mode

interface Serial 1
ip address 172.16.3.2 255.255.255.0
ip pim sparse-mode

router eigrp 100
 network 172.16.0.0

ip pim rp-address 172.16.2.2

Use the command `show ip pim rp` to verify that the routers have learned the location of the RP.

show ip pim rp [*group-name* | *group-address* | **mapping**]

group-name   Optional. Show RPs for the named group.

group-address   Optional. Show RPs for the group with the entered group address.

mapping   Optional. Display all group to RP mappings.

```
A#show ip pim rp
Group: 224.0.1.40, RP: 172.16.2.2, next RP-reachable in 00:01:11
```

The operation of PIM can be verified and monitored using the debug command, `debug ip pim`.

```
A#debug ip pim
PIM debugging is on
```

```
08:31:16: PIM: Received v2 Hello on Serial1 from 172.16.2.1
08:31:16: PIM: Received v2 Hello on Serial0 from 172.16.5.2
08:31:16: PIM: Send v2 Hello on Serial0
08:31:26: PIM: Send v2 Hello on Serial1
08:31:30: PIM: Received v2 Join/Prune on Serial1 from 172.16.2.1, to us
08:31:30: PIM: Join-list: (', 224.0.1.40) RP 172.16.2.2, RPT-bit set, WC-bit set, S-bit set
08:31:30: PIM: Add Serial1/172 .16.2.1 to (', 224.0.1.40), Forward state
08:31:39: PIM: Received v2 Join/Prune on Serial0 from 172.16.5.2, to us
08:31:39: PIM: Join-list: (', 224.0.1.40) RP 172.16.2.2, RPT-bit set, WC-bit set, S-bit set
08:31:39: PIM: Add Serial0/172 .16.5.2 to (', 224.0.1.40), Forward state
08:31:40: PIM: Building Join/Prune message for 224.0.1.40
08:31:46: PIM: Received v2 Hello on Serial1 from 172.16.2.1
08:31:46: PIM: Received v2 Hello on Serial0 from 172.16.5.2
08:31:46: PIM: Send v2 Hello on Serial0
08:31:56: PIM: Send v2 Hello on Serial1
08:32:16: PIM: Received v2 Hello on Serial1 from 172.16.2.1
08:32:16: PIM: Received v2 Hello on Serial0 from 172.16.5.2
08:32:16: PIM: Send v2 Hello on Serial0
```

NETWORK 2—AUTO-RP CONFIGURATION

AUTO-RP Router Configurations

Router MA

hostname MA

ip multicast-routing

interface Ethernet 0
ip address 172.16.1.1 255.255.255.0
ip pim sparse-mode

interface Serial 0
ip address 172.16.2.1 255.255.255.0
ip pim sparse-mode
clock rate 1540000

interface Serial 1
ip address 172.16.3.1 255.255.255.0
ip pim sparse-mode
clock rate 1540000

router eigrp 100
network 172.16.0.0

ip pim send-rp-announce

Router B

hostname B

ip multicast-routing

interface Ethernet 0
ip address 172.16.4.1 255.255.255.0
ip pim sparse-mode

interface Serial 1
ip address 172.16.3.2 255.255.255.0
ip pim sparse-mode

router eigrp 100
network 172.16.0.0

Router C

hostname C

ip multicast-routing

interface Ethernet 0
ip address 172.16.4.2 255.255.255.0
ip pim sparse-mode

interface Serial 1
ip address 172.16.5.2 255.255.255.0
ip pim sparse-mode
clock rate 1540000

router eigrp 100
network 172.16.0.0

Router RP

hostname RP

ip multicast-routing

interface Serial 0
ip address 172.16.2.2 255.255.255.0
ip pim sparse-mode

interface Serial 1
ip address 172.16.5.1 255.255.255.0
ip pim sparse-mode

router eigrp 100
network 172.16.0.0
ip pim send-rp-announce scope
16 group-list 1
access-list 1 permit 224.0.0.0 15.255.255.255

For the network of Figure 7-35, show the RP mappings on the mapping agent and on the RP router.

```
MA#show ip pim rp mapping
PIM Group-to-RP Mappings
This system is an RP-mapping agent

Group(s) 224.0.0.0/4
 RP 172.16.5.1 (?), v2v1
  Info source: 172.16.5.1 (?), via Auto-RP
  Uptime: 00:15:06, expires: 00:02:53
```

```
RP#show ip pim rp mapping
PIM Group-to-RP Mappings
This system is an RP (Auto-RP)

Group(s) 224.0.0.0/4
 RP 172.16.5.1 (?), v2v1
  Info source: 172.16.2.1 (?), via Auto-RP
  Uptime: 00:17:18, expires: 00:02:33
```

Verify the Auto-RP operation with the `debug ip pim`:

```
RP#debug ip pim auto-rp
PIM Auto-RP debugging is on

08:46:19: Auto-RP: Received RP-discovery, from 172.16.2.1, RP_cnt 1, holdtime 18
0 secs
08:46:19: Auto-RP: update (224.0.0.0/4 , RP:172.16.5.1), PIMv2 v1
08:46:19: Auto-RP: Build RP-Announce packet for 172.16.5.1, PIMv2/v1
08:46:19: Auto-RP: Build announce entry for (224.0.0.0/4 )
08:46:19: Auto-RP: Send RP-Announce packet, IP source 172.16.5.1, ttl 16 holdtime 181
secs
08:47:19: Auto-RP: Received RP-discovery, from 172.16.2.1, RP_cnt 1, holdtime 180 secs
08:47:19: Auto-RP: update (224.0.0.0/4 , RP:172.16.5.1), PIMv2 v1
08:47:19: Auto-RP: Build RP-Announce packet for 172.16.5.1, PIMv2/v1
08:47:19: Auto-RP: Build announce entry for (224.0.0.0/4 )
08:47:19: Auto-RP: Send RP-Announce packet, IP source 172.16.5.1, ttl 16 holdtime 181
secs
```

```
MA#debug ip pim auto-rp
PIM Auto-RP debugging is on

08:47:53: Auto-RP: Build RP-Discovery packet
08:47:53: Auto-RP: Build mapping (224.0.0.0/4 , RP:172.16.5.1), PIMv2 v1,
08:47:53: Auto-RP: Send RP-discovery packet (1 RP entries)
08:47:53: Auto-RP: Received RP-discovery, from ourselves (172.16.1.1), ignored
08:47:53: Auto-RP: Received RP-announce, from 172.16.5.1, RP_cnt 1, holdtime 181 secs
```

Figure 7-35
PIM-SM using
Auto-RP.

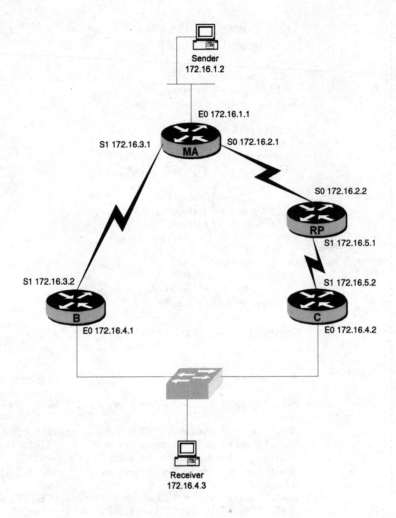

08:47:53: Auto-RP: update (224.0.0.0/4 , RP:172.16.5.1), PIMv2 v1
08:48:52: Auto-RP: Build RP-Discovery packet
08:48:52: Auto-RP: Build mapping (224.0.0.0/4 , RP:172.16.5.1), PIMv2 v1,
08:48:52: Auto-RP: Send RP-discovery packet (1 RP entries)
08:48:52: Auto-RP: Received RP-discovery, from ourselves (172.16.1.1), ignored
08:48:53: Auto-RP: Received RP-announce, from 172.16.5.1, RP_cnt 1, holdtime 181 secs
08:48:53: Auto-RP: update (224.0.0.0/4 , RP:172.16.5.1), PIMv2 v1

NETWORK 3—USING BOOTSTRAP ROUTERS

BSR-RP Router Configurations

```
Router BSR1
hostname BSR1
ip multicast-routing

interface Ethernet 0
ip address 172.16.1.1 255.255.255.0
ip pim sparse-mode

interface Serial 0
ip address 172.16.2.1 255.255.255.0
ip pim sparse-mode
clock rate 1540000

interface Serial 1
ip address 172.16.3.1 255.255.255.0
ip pim sparse-mode
clock rate 1540000

router eigrp 100
 network 172.16.0.0
ip pim bsr-candidate serial 0 24 8
```

```
Router BSR2
hostname BSR2
ip multicast-routing

interface Ethernet 0
ip address 172.16.4.2 255.255.255.0
ip pim sparse-mode

interface Serial 1
ip address 172.16.5.2 255.255.255.0
ip pim sparse-mode
clock rate 1540000

router eigrp 100
 network 172.16.0.0
ip pim bsr-candidate ethernet 0 24 8
```

```
Router RP2
hostname RP2
ip multicast-routing

interface Serial 0
ip address 172.16.2.2 255.255.255.0
ip pim sparse-mode

interface Serial 1
ip address 172.16.5.1 255.255.255.0
ip pim sparse-mode

router eigrp 100
 network 172.16.0.0
ip pim rp-candidate serial 0
```

```
Router RP1
hostname RP1
ip multicast-routing

interface Ethernet 0
ip address 172.16.4.1 255.255.255.0
ip pim sparse-mode

interface Serial 1
ip address 172.16.3.2 255.255.255.0
ip pim sparse-mode

router eigrp 100
 network 172.16.0.0
ip pim rp-candidate ethernet 0
```

Two candidate Bootstrap routers have been configured in the network of Figure 7-36. Router BSR2 should be elected for this because its IP address is higher than BSR2. To view the BSR, use the `show ip pim bsr` command.

```
rp1#show ip pim bsr-router
PIMv2 Bootstrap information
 BSR address:       172.16.4.2 (?)
 Uptime:            00:06:46, BSR Priority: 8, Hash mask length: 24
 Expires:           00:01:43
 Next Cand_RP_advertisement in 00:00:35
 RP: 172.16.5.1(Serial0)
```

PIM-SM BOOTSTRAP BORDER ROUTER   A PIM-SM network can be divided into regions that are serviced by a regional Bootstrap router. Bootstrap messages can then be confined to a region by configuring a border router that does not allow Bootstrap messages from passing through the router, but the router will forward all other PIM traffic. The interface command used to configure a Bootstrap border router is

```
ip pim border
```

An example of the use of the border command is shown in Figure 7-37.

```
Border Configuration
interface Serial 0
 ip pim sparse-mode
 ip pim border

interface Serial 1
 ip pim sparse-mode
 ip pim border
```

REFERENCES

RFC 2362, "Protocol Independent Multicast-Sparse Mode (PIM-SM): Protocol Specification," D. Estrin, D. Farinacci, A. Helmy, D. Thaler, S. Deering, M. Handley, V. Jacobson, C. Liu, P. Sharma, L. Wei, 1998

RFC 2117, "Protocol Independent Multicast-Sparse Mode (PIM-SM): Protocol Specification," D. Estrin, D. Farinacci, A. Helmy, D. Thaler, S. Deering, M. Handley, V. Jacobson, C. Liu, P. Sharma, L. Wei, 1997

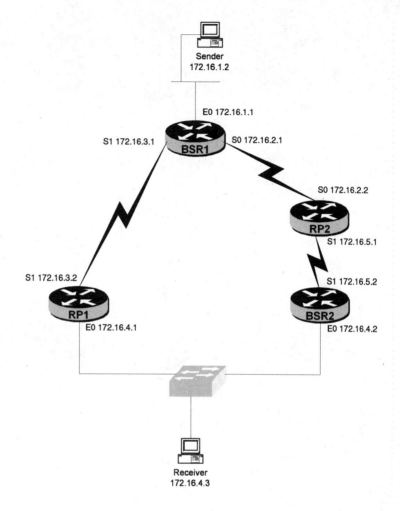

Figure 7-36
PIM-SM RP selection using Bootstrap routers.

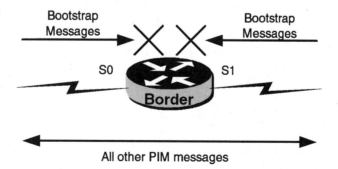

Figure 7-37
PIM-SM Bootstrap border router

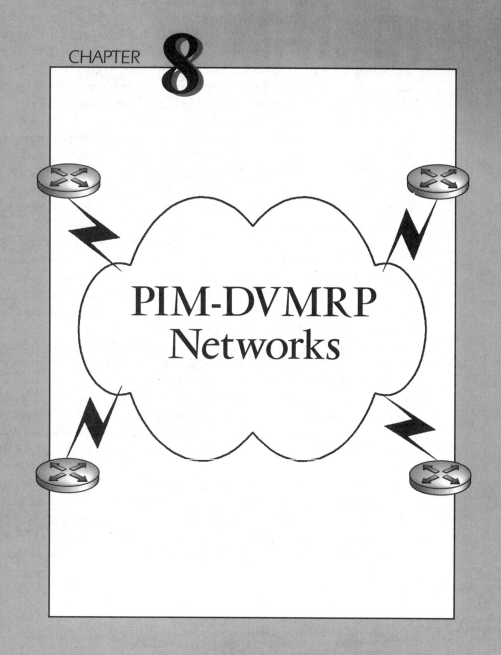

PIM-DVMRP
Networks

Consider these facts. Approximately 80 percent of the Internet routers are Cisco routers, and the *Multicast Backbone* (MBONE) runs on top of the Internet. The multicast protocol that is used on the MBONE is DVMRP and Cisco does not support a full implementation of DVMRP. So how do we get MBONE multicast traffic into a Cisco network? Very easily. Cisco routers interoperate with DVMRP routers for route exchange.

At the outset of this chapter, it is important to clarify the distinction between a *routing* protocol and a *routed* protocol. OSPF, for example, is a routing protocol. Routing protocols are used to determine a path to the destination for a routed protocol. Routed protocols include IP, IPX, AppleTalk and DECNet. Routed protocols carry their data inside of specific packets. If we are using OSPF, then we are routing IP packets, which do not travel inside of OSPF packets; they travel inside of IP packets. The same argument can be made for IP multicast data, which travels inside of IP packets. The packet does not care how it gets routed to the destination as long as it gets there. It makes no difference if the network is running DVMRP, PIM-DM, or PIM-SM. Therefore, if a mechanism exists so that PIM and DVMRP can exchange routes, then MBONE packets can be delivered to non-DVMRP networks.

No configuration commands can enable PIM-DVMRP interoperability; thus, no commands are needed because PIM-DVMRP interaction on a Cisco router is automatic. In the network of Figure 8-1, we have a Cisco router connected to an MBONE router running mrouted. When the DVMRP router sends a periodic neighbor probe message on the common interface between the two routers, the Cisco router realizes that a DVMRP router is out there and PIM-DVMRP interoperability will be automatically enabled.

The interaction between the two domains depends on the type of connection between them. In a tunnel connection, the PIM router does not respond to the neighbor probe, but other information is exchanged. When the PIM router receives a DVMRP route report, the DVMRP routes are installed in a separate DVMRP routing table on the PIM router. The

Figure 8-1
PIM router discovery of a DVMRP neighbor

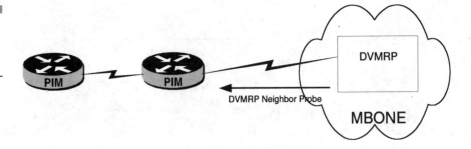

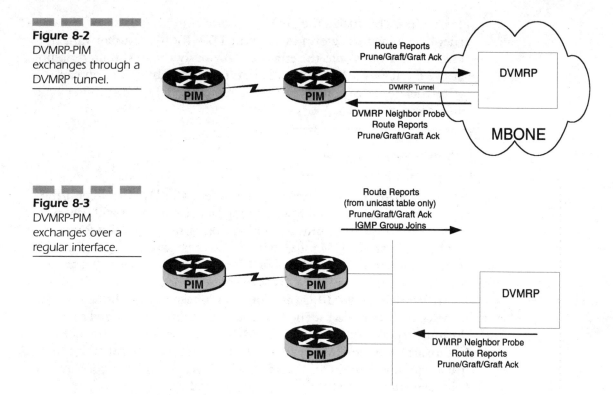

Figure 8-2
DVMRP-PIM exchanges through a DVMRP tunnel.

Figure 8-3
DVMRP-PIM exchanges over a regular interface.

PIM router then poison-reverses the appropriate routes learned from the DVMRP router and sends a route report to the DVMRP neighbor. Selected routes from the unicast routing table are also advertised in the route report, while DVMRP probes and grafts are exchanged between the PIM and DVMRP routers over the DVMRP tunnel (see Figure 8-2).

For a non-tunnel connection, such as ethernet, the information exchange is modified slightly from the tunnel case (see Figure 8-3). Again, DVMRP probes are not sent by the PIM router. If the PIM routers in Figure 8-3 send a DVMRP neighbor probe onto the ethernet network, then the other PIM neighbor would receive them and think that the other PIM router is a DVMRP router.

The route report only contains selected routes from the unicast routing table and does not contain poison-reversed DVRMP routes, as in the tunnel case. Received DVRMP route reports are actually ignored by the PIM routers. Although Prunes, Grafts, and Graft Acknowledgments are also exchanged, Prunes from the DVMRP neighbor are also ignored. The PIM routers sends IGMP joins for any group that has IGMP state on the

PIM routers. This makes the DVMRP router think that hosts on the ethernet have joined the group, causing the DVMRP router to forward traffic for these groups onto the ethernet. Obviously, the PIM routers do not act like a true DVMRP router. An interface command that you can use to instruct the PIM routers to behave more like a DVMRP router on a multi-access network is

```
ip dvmrp unicast-routing
```

The interface command causes routes received in DVMRP Report messages to be cached in the DVMRP routing table; these routes will have preference over routes in the unicast routing table. Also, IGMP Joins for groups that have state on the PIM router will no longer be sent (see Figure 8-4). This command is not used to enable DVMRP between Cisco routers but to force the router to act more like a DVMRP router when there is a non-Cisco DVMRP neighbor. IGMP Group Joins no longer need to be sent to the DVMRP neighbor because the PIM router sends poison-reversed routes in the route report that inform the DVMRP neighbor which traffic needs to be forwarded to the PIM neighbor. The Cisco router now functions more like a true DVMRP router, except that DVMRP neighbor probes are not being sent and received Prunes are still ignored.

Figure 8-4
PIM routers configured to exchange DVMRP route reports

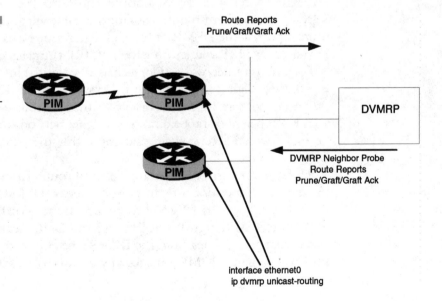

Route Exchange

Which unicast routes from the local routing table are reported to the DVMRP neighbor? By default, only the directly connected routes are reported. For example, in Figure 8-5, we have a PIM-DM-enabled router connected through a DVMRP tunnel to an MBONE DVMRP router. The configuration for the PIM router is given below.

```
interface Ethernet 0
 ip address 10.1.1.1 255.255.255.0
 ip pim dense mode

interface Serial 0
 ip address 10.1.2.1 255.255.255.0
 ip pim dense mode

interface Tunnel 0
 ip unnumbered Ethernet 0
 ip pim dense-mode
 tunnel source Ethernet 0
 tunnel destination 10.1.1.2
 tunnel mode dvmrp
```

The routing table for the PIM router contains the directly connected routes and any routes learned through a dynamic unicast IP routing protocol. Assume that for now the unicast routing table contains only the directly connected routes and that the DVMRP route advertises two routes:

144.223.136.0/24   Metric = 5

156.26.31.0/24   Metric = 7

Figure 8-5
Connecting to the
MBONE with a
DVMRP tunnel

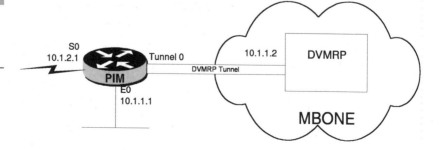

When the PIM router receives the routes, the metric is increased by one and the routes are placed in the local DVMRP routing table, which contains

144.223.136.0/24   Metric = 6

156.26.31.0/24   metric = 8

These routes are then reported back to the DVMRP router and are poisoned-reversed. The routes from the local DVMRP table sent in the route report are

144.223.136.0/24   metric 38

156.26.31.0/24   metric 40

The routes that are reported from the unicast routing table to the DVMRP router are

10.1.1.0/24   Metric = 1

10.1.2.0/24   Metric = 1

Notice that a default metric of one hop is used for the routes reported from the unicast routing table. How do we advertise non-connected networks from the unicast routing table? The answer is with the following interface command on the tunnel interface:

---

ip dvmrp metric *metric* [**list** *access-list*] {[*protocol process-id]* | **dvmrp**]
ip dvmrp metric *metric* **route-map** *map-name*

---

metric	Metric to be used for the routes in the DVMRP route report. The value can be between 0 and 32. A value of 0 prevents a route or routes from being advertised. A value of 32 indicates infinity or unreachable.
list *access list*	Optional. A standard IP access list can be used to control which routes are reported.
protocol	Optional. Unicast routing protocol name (rip, igrp, eigrp, ospf, bgp, isis, static, or dvmrp).
process-id	Optional. Unicast routing protocol process ID.
dvrmp	Optional. Allows routes in the DVMRP routing table to be filtered or have their metric adjusted.
route-map	Filter the unicast routes that are reported using a route map.

map-name
```
ip dvmrp metric <metric>
```

The configuration for the DVMRP tunnel would be

```
interface Tunnel 0
 ip unnumbered Ethernet 0
 ip pim dense-mode
 ip dvmrp metric 1
 tunnel source Ethernet 0
 tunnel destination 10.1.1.2
 tunnel mode dvmrp
```

What we have done is make a very serious mistake. The dvmrp metric command applies to every route in the unicast routing table. This is not too serious, however, if the unicast routing table is small. If the table is large, on the order of thousands of routes, then all these routes will be injected in the DVMRP router and the MBONE. When something like this occurs, we usually need a rule to remind us not to do it:

When using the command **ip dvmrp metric**, always use an access list.

Another good rule when connecting PIM and DVMRP is to always use a tunnel, because a tunnel gives us the maximum DVMRP capability.

If we have the routes 172.16.1.0/24 and 202.5.6.0/24 in our routing table, for example, and we only want to advertise the 172.16.1.0 network, then we could use the access list shown below:

```
access-list 1 permit 172.16.1.0 0.0.0.255
access-list 1 deny any
```

The modified tunnel configuration would now contain

```
interface Tunnel 0
 ip unnumbered Ethernet 0
 ip pim dense-mode
 ip dvmrp metric 1 list 1
 tunnel source Ethernet 0
 tunnel destination 10.1.1.2
 tunnel mode dvmrp

access-list 1 permit 172.16.1.0 0.0.0.255
access-list 1 deny any
```

If the value of the metric is 0, then this means the indicated routes will not be advertised. Let's look at some examples to illustrate some of the permutations of this command.

ip dvmrp metric 0	Do not advertise any of the routes in the unicast routing table. The same effect can be achieved by not even using this command.
ip dvmrp metric 0 list 1	Denies routes in list 1 but advertises others with a metric of one.
ip dvmrp metric 1 eigrp 100	Advertises EIGRP routes in the routing table with a metric of one.
ip dvmrp metric 0 dvmrp	If your network has more than one PIM-DVMRP boundary router, then you may want to prevent DVRMP routes learned from one border from being advertised back into the MBONE by another boundary router. This form of the command will prevent that from happening.

Route Selection

In the PIM-DVMRP network, there now exist many routes that have been learned from possibly many sources. Dynamic unicast routing protocols, unicast static routes, multicast static routes, and DVMRP can all be sources of routing information. When performing the RPF check for a particular multicast source, the route will be selected according to the following rules:

1. If the route is contained in both the unicast table and the DVMRP table, then use the route with the lowest administrative distance.

   The administrative distance is used to select a route when the route has been learned from routing sources with metrics that cannot be compared. A route learned from RIP, for example, has a hop count metric. The same route learned from OSPF has a metric that is related to the speed of the link. Therefore, the RIP and OSPF metrics are not comparable. The administrative distance is then used in determining the "better" route. The Administrative distance for RIP is 120 and for OSPF it is 110. The lowest administrative distance indicates a better route, so in this case the OSPF route would be selected over the RIP route. The default administrative distance for DVMRP routes is 0, meaning that

DVMRP routes take precedence when determining the RPF interface for a particular multicast source. The administrative distance for DVMRP routes reported by a DVMRP neighbor can be adjusted using the interface command:

---

ip dvmrp accept-filter *access-list-number* [*distance*] **neighbor-list** *access-list-number*

---

access-list-number	IP standard access list number (0–99). If 0, then all sources are accepted with the value of *distance*.
distance	Optional. The administrative distance of the reported route.
neighbor-list *access-list-number*	Reports are only accepted from neighbors in the list.

For example, if the DVMRP neighbor is reporting the routes

144.223.136.0/24	Metric = 5
156.26.31.0/24	Metric = 7

and we wish to set the administrative distance of the 156.26.31.0 network to 130 but leave the administrative distance for network 144.223.136.0 set to the default of 0, we could use the following configuration:

```
interface Tunnel 0
 ip unnumbered Ethernet 0
 ip pim dense-mode
 ip dvmrp accept-filter 1 130
 tunnel source Ethernet 0
 tunnel destination 10.1.1.2
 tunnel mode dvmrp
 access-list 1 permit 156.26.31.0 0.0.0.255
```

2. Use the DVMRP route if the administrative distances are equal.

3. If there is a static multicast route (mroute) and the administrative distance of the static mroute is less than or equal to the DVMRP route, use the static mroute.

4. If there are multiple routes in the selected table to the destination, use the longest match. For example, assume the two routes to the 156.26.0.0 network in the DVMRP table are

156.26.0.0/16
156.26.31.0/24

Each route contains the source address 156.26.31.1, but the route given by 156.26.31.0 in the DVMRP table would be preferred.

Any time routes from different routing tables are compared, things can go wrong. Unicast and multicast traffic on the Internet and MBONE typically do not follow the same path due to the tunnels that connect DVMRP areas through non-DVMRP areas. In Figure 8-6, we have the following situation. Router B has a logical connection through a tunnel to the DVMRP router. Logically, when multicast traffic is sent by the source, the path the packets take is from the source to the DVMRP router, from the DVMRP router through the tunnel to router B, and then to the S1 interface of router A. Router A has a unicast route table but no DVMRP route table because router A has no DVMRP neighbors. When the packet arrives from router B, it does not pass the RPF test and therefore is discarded. Router A also has a unicast route to the source through the S0 interface, so the S0 interface is the RPF interface for the source.

The problem is illustrated differently in Figure 8-7. Here the actual physical path the multicast traffic takes from the source is displayed. The packet arrives at the DVMRP router and is encapsulated in an IP unicast packet. The packet is then sent to router A, which forwards the packet to router B. Router B removes the encapsulated multicast packet and checks the RPF interface. Because the packet is received on the tunnel interface, the RPF check passes and the packet is forwarded to router A, where we have already seen the RPF check fail, so the packet is discarded.

Figure 8-6
Logical path for
multicast traffic

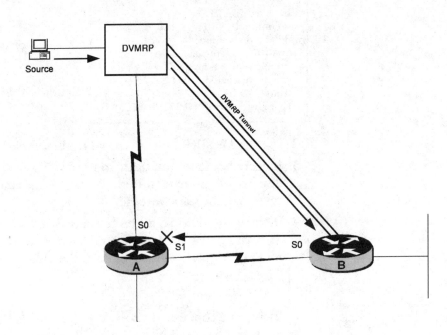

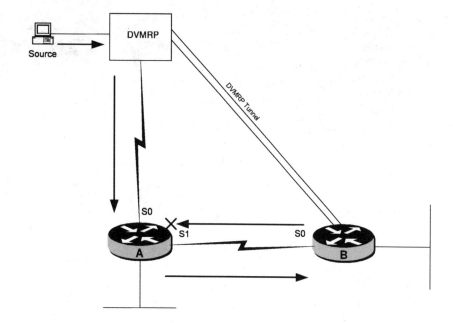

Figure 8-7

Physical path for tunnel-encapsulated multicast traffic

The solution to this problem is to avoid such situations. Whenever possible, the physical and logical paths should be the same. Stated differently, the unicast and multicast paths from the source to the receivers should be the same. This is not always possible, but it is a good goal to keep in mind.

Another solution is to advertise the DVMRP table on router B to router A. This can be accomplished by using the interface command, `ip dvmrp unicast-routing`, on the serial interfaces connecting the two routers. Router B sends its DVRMP routing table to A, but router A does not poison-reverse the DVMRP routes and sends them back. In this case, split horizon is used on the link. If router A has the DVMRP table, then the RPF check succeeds because DVMRP routes take precedence over routes in the unicast routing table.

Another situation arises when hooking a PIM-SM domain to a DVMRP domain and you have a sender in the PIM-SM domain and a receiver in the DVMRP domain. In Figure 8-8, the RP and the PIM-DVMRP border router are not the same router.

Recall from Chapter 7, "Protocol Independent Multicast—Sparse Mode," that PIM-SM can be thought of as having two distinct trees. One tree is from the source to the RP and the other tree is from the RP to the receivers. Senders and receivers register to the RP and, in this case, the receiver's Join does not get propagated to the RP. When the sender sends

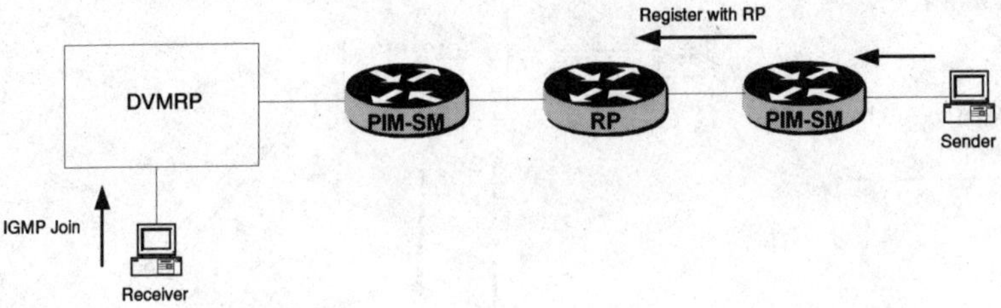

Figure 8-8
When the border
router and RP are
different, multicast
traffic cannot be
forwarded to the
DVMRP receiver.

Figure 8-8
When the border
router and RP are
different, multicast
traffic cannot be
forwarded to the
DVMRP receiver.

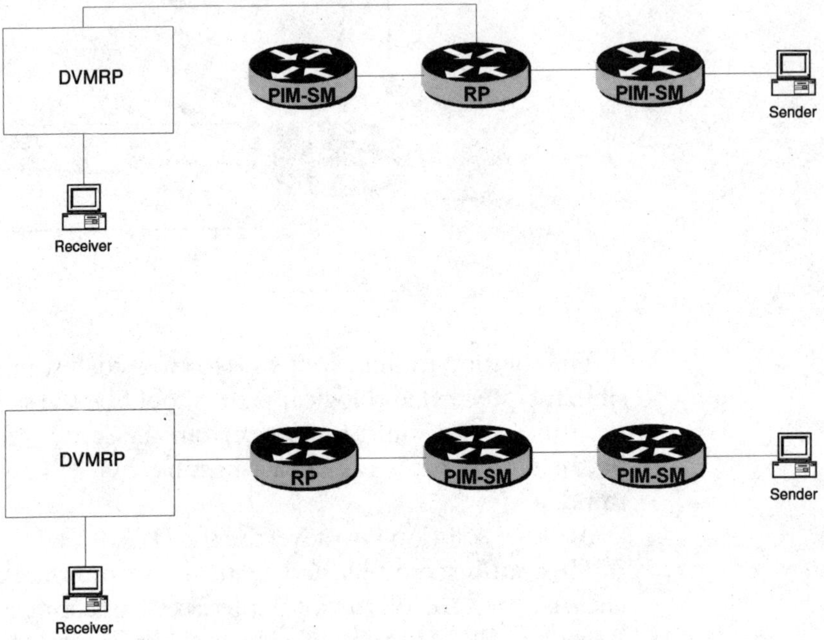

Figure 8-9
When connecting to
the MBONE, make
the RP the border
router.

the first multicast packet, the directly attached router registers with the
RP-creating state (S,G) in the RP. The receiver joins by sending an IGMP
Join to the DVMRP router and the DVMRP router creates a (*,G) state.
Because the RP does not know to forward packets to the receiver in the
DVMRP domain, the packets never reach it. An easy solution for this
problem is to make the RP the border router by either attaching it
directly to the DVMRP router or by making it the current border router
(see Figure 8-9).

DVMRP Configuration Commands

We have already seen some of the commands that can be used to configure the route exchange process between a DVMRP and a PIM router. This section will present the rest of the commands that can be used to fine-tune this process.

---

ip dvmrp metric-offset [in | out] *increment*

---

in   Optional. The value of *increment* is added to routes in incoming DVMRP route reports. The default *increment* for **in** is 1.

out   Optional. The value of the *increment* is added to routes in outgoing DVMRP reports. The default *increment* for **out** is 0.

increment Value added to the routes in a DVMRP route report.

Use this interface command to adjust the metric of DVMRP routes being received on an *interface* (in) or reported to a *neighbor* (out). The default value when applied to incoming routes is 1 and the default value applied to outgoing routes is 0. But be careful, this command adds the same metric to all incoming or outgoing routes.

---

ip dvmrp output-report-delay *delay-time* [*burst*]

---

delay-time Number of milliseconds between DVMRP route reports.

burst   Optional. Number of packets in a set of route reports. The default value is 2.

Use this interface command to send the route reports to a neighbor. DVMRP typically runs as mrouted on UNIX machines, and if the Cisco router has a large DVMRP routing table, then it is possible for the route reports to overload the DVMRP router, preventing some of the routes from being received. Any missed routes consequently expire and are placed in hold-down. Subsequent reports may fix this problem for the routes missed in previous route reports, but other routes may be dropped in subsequent reports, causing route flapping to occur. The delay-time parameter is the time to wait between sending route report packets to the neighbor and the Burst parameter indicates how many reports to send. For example, if we use

---

ip dvmrp output-report-delay 300 3

---

and nine reports must be sent, then the sequence listed on the following page will be executed.

1. Send three reports.
2. Wait 300 milliseconds.
3. Send three reports.
4. Wait 300 milliseconds.
5. Send three reports.

The default value for delay-time is 100 milliseconds and the default value of burst is 2.

---

ip dvmrp route-limit *count*

---

count   Number of DVMRP routes that can be advertised. The default value is 7000.

This global command limits the number of routes that can be advertised on an interface that has DVMRP enabled. When the first interface is configured with `ip dvmrp unicast-routing`, when a DVMRP tunnel is configured, or when a PIM interface hears a DVMRP neighbor, this command is automatically configured with a default limit of 7000 routes. This prevents flooding routes into DVMRP when the `ip dvmrp metric` command is accidentally misused.

---

ip dvmrp route-hog-notification *count*

---

count   Number of routes allowed before a syslog message is sent. Default is 10,000 routes.

This global command places a limit on the number of routes that can be advertised over a DVMRP-enabled interface, including tunnels during a one-minute interval. If the number is exceeded, a syslog message is sent. This is another method for determining if a misconfigured router is injecting too many routes. The default value is 10,000.

---

ip dvmrp reject-non-pruners

This is an interface command that prevents peering with a DVMRP neighbor that does not support pruning and grafting.

---

ip dvmrp default-information {originate | only}

---

originate   Routes more specific than the default route (0.0.0.0) can be advertised

only   Only the default route (0.0.0.0) is advertised

Here we have an interface command used to advertise the default network 0.0.0.0. to the DVMRP neighbor on the interface. The **originate** option allows more specific routes to be advertised. The **only** keyword prevents other routes from being advertised. Do not use this command to inject a default route into the MBONE.

---

ip dvmrp auto-summary

This interface command is enabled by default. Auto-summarization is when subnets are advertised as a classful network number. To turn off this feature, use the **no** form of the command.

---

ip dvmrp summary-address *address mask* [**metric** *value*]

---

address   The summary IP address that is advertised.

mask   The mask for the summary address.

metric *value*   Optional. The metric that is advertised for the summary address. The default metric is 1.

This command is used on an interface to summarize addresses in a route report. The summarization applies only to routes in the unicast routing table, not the DVMRP routing table, and the default metric assigned to the summarized route is one of the unicast routing table routes. This command can be used multiple times on an interface.

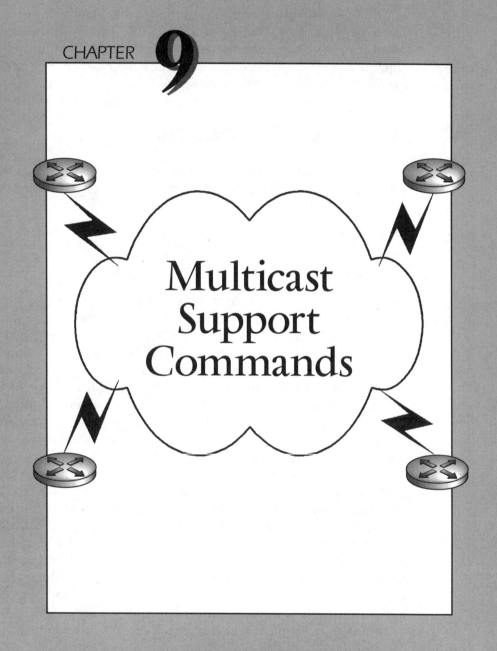

CHAPTER 9

Multicast
Support
Commands

The previous chapters have covered the operation and configuration of Cisco-supported IP multicast protocols. In this chapter, we will look at a number of multicast scenarios and multicast support commands. The support commands are not specific to any multicast routing protocols but are used to fine-tune your network.

Multicast Boundaries

The unicast IP address allocation reserved three sets of IP addresses for private use. An address block was reserved in each of the IP classes A, B, and C, as shown.

10.0.0.0	—	10.255.255.255
172.16.0.0	—	172.31.255.255
192.168.0.0	—	192.168.255.255

If these networks are used in a private intranet, then care must be taken not to advertise these networks on the Internet. Because multiple intranets may be using the same private IP address space, advertising them globally would cause confusion (see Figure 9-1). To prevent such confusion, private addresses should not be advertised outside the local intranet. Company A and Company B in Figure 9-1 would have to use Network Address Translation on their border routers to allow internal users Internet access. What has effectively been done is to form a boundary around the private addressed networks to prevent these addresses from being accessed through the Internet.

The multicast address space has a block of addresses assigned that are analogous to the private IP unicast address blocks. The block of Class D addresses from 239.0.0.0 to 239.255.255.255 are referred to as administratively scoped; the block is further subdivided, as shown in Table 9-1. Assume that in your company each department (finance, engineering, and marketing) wants to deploy multicasting, but they do not want to receive multicast traffic from the other departments. For this scenario, a multicast boundary will need to be set up around each department to prevent multicast traffic from crossing departmental boundaries (see Figure 9-2).

To configure a multicast boundary, use the interface command

```
ip multicast boundary access-list-number
no ip multicast boundary access-list-number
```

access-list-number   Standard IP access-list (1–99).

Figure 9-1

If private IP addresses are advertised over the Internet, then routing confusion can occur. For this reason, private IP addresses should not be advertised globally.

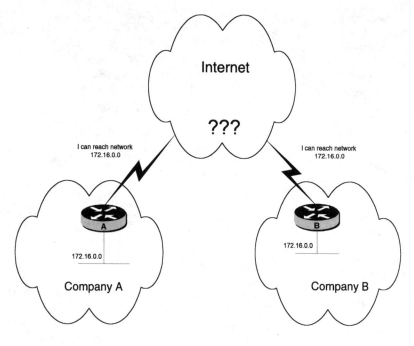

TABLE 9-1

Administratively Scoped Multicast Address Block

239.0.0.0–239.255.255.255	Administratively Scoped
239.0.0.0–239.63.255.255	Reserved
239.64.0.0–239.127.255.255	Reserved
239.128.0.0–239.191.255.255	Reserved
239.192.0.0–239.251.255.255	Organization–Local Scope
239.252.0.0–239.252.255.255	Site-Local Scope (Reserved)
239.253.0.0–239.253.255.255	Site-Local Scope (Reserved)
239.254.255.255–239.254.255.255	Site-Local Scope (Reserved)
239.255.0.0–239.255.255.255	Site-Local Scope

When configured on an interface, the **ip multicast border** command prevents multicast packets identified by the access list from flowing into or out of the interface. Each of the interfaces that connect border routers in Figure 9-2 would have the configuration as shown on the following page.

Figure 9-2
Multicast boundaries need to be established on the department border routers.

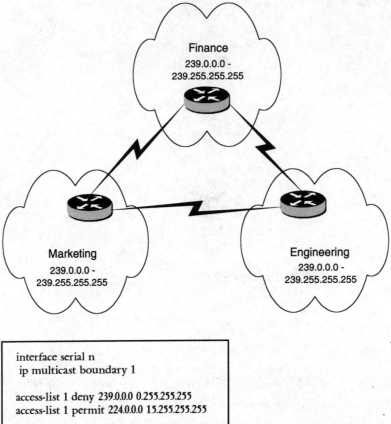

```
interface serial n
 ip multicast boundary 1

access-list 1 deny 239.0.0.0 0.255.255.255
access-list 1 permit 224.0.0.0 15.255.255.255
```

The permit statement in the access list is required because every access list has an implicit **deny any** at the end of the list. In Chapter 7, we used the interface command **ip pim border** to prevent Bootstrap messages from passing through the interface, but allowed all other multicast traffic to pass. The **ip multicast border** command can be used in the same manner with regards to Auto-RP.

```
interface serial n
 ip multicast boundary 1

access-list 1 deny 224.0.1.39
list 1 deny 224.0.1.40
access-list 1 permit 224.0.0.0 15.255.255.255
```

The ip multicast border command blocks Auto-RP and Mapping Agent messages from crossing the interface but allows all other multicast traffic. Although the ip multicast boundary command is usually used in conjunction with the administratively scoped block of multicast addresses, it can be used to block any multicast address on an interface.

Broadcast/Multicast Conversion

Assume that you have an application on a host that does not support IP multicast, only IP unicast and broadcast. Further assume that the application wants to send to a receiver or multiple receivers on a different subnet. We have seen in Chapter 2, "Internet Protocol (IP) Addresses," that this is not possible, at least not yet. Using IP unicast only allows the sender to send to one host, and IP broadcast only allows the sender to send to hosts on the same subnet. What we need is a way to turn a broadcast into a multicast for delivery to the receivers. Now if the receivers cannot receive multicast traffic, then the multicast stream would need to be converted back to a broadcast stream on the receiving subnet (see Figure 9-3).

To enable the broadcast-to-multicast conversion and the multicast-to-broadcast conversion, use the following interface configuration command on the router attached to the sender, or first hop router:

```
ip multicast helper-map broadcast multicast-address extended-acl
```

broadcast	Specifies the traffic is being converted from broadcast to multicast.
multicast-address	Multicast group address of the traffic that is to be converted to broadcast traffic.
extended-acl	IP extended access list used to determine which broadcast packets are to be converted to multicast. Based on the UDP port number.

Use the following form of the command on the router attached to the receiver or last hop router:

Figure 9-3
A broadcast-to-multicast-to-broadcast conversion is needed to enable a non-mulitcast sender to send to a non-multicast receiver.

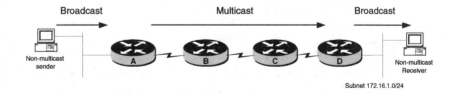

Broadcast　　Multicast　　Broadcast

Non-multicast sender　　A　　B　　C　　D　　Non-multicast Receiver

Subnet 172.16.1.0/24

> **ip multicast helper-map** *group-address IP-broadcast-address extended-acl*

group-address   Multicast group address of traffic to be converted to
                           broadcast traffic.

IP-broadcast-address   IP broadcast address to which broadcast traffic is sent.

extended-acl   IP extended access list used to determine which
                           multicast packets are to be converted to broadcast.
                           Based on the UDP port number.

For the network in Figure 9-3, the first hop and last hop routers would
have the configuration listed below:

```
Router A–First Hop Router.

interface Ethernet 0
 ip directed-broadcast
 ip multicast helper-map broadcast 239.1.2.3 100
 ip pim dense-mode

access-list 100 permit any any udp 2000
access-list 100 deny any any udp

ip forward-protocol udp 2000
```

```
Router D Last Hop Router

interface ethernet 0
 ip directed-broadcast
 ip igmp join-group 239.1.2.3
 ip multicast helper-map 239.1.2.3 172.16.1.255 100
 ip pim dense-mode

access-list 100 permit any any udp 2000
access-list 100 deny any any udp

ip forward-protocol udp 2000
```

As configured, router A translates broadcasts to udp port 2000 to the multicast address 239.1.2.3, while router D translates traffic for multicast group
239.1.2.3 to the IP broadcast address for the subnet. The command **ip igmp
join-group** on the last hop router is automatically configured when the **ip
multicast helper-map** command is used. The **ip forward-protocol** command is necessary to disable fast-switching, which does not perform the conversion from broadcast to multicast and multicast to broadcast.

Session Directory

Session Directory (SDR) is an MBONE scheduling system used to announce and schedule multimedia conferences. SDR uses the *Session Directory Announcement Protocol* (SDAP) that will periodically multicast a session announcement packet describing a particular session. SDAP announcement packets can be received by a multicast receiver by joining the well-known group 224.2.127.254. A user can then select to receive traffic for a multicast group using the SDR tool (see Figure 9-4).

To enable the reception of Session Directory Protocol announcements on an interface, use the interface command

> **ip sdr listen**

This command enables the router to accept SDAP packets on the interface, and the router joins the multicast group 224.2.127.254. SDR entries are cached on the router and the time that an SDR remains in the cache is configured using the global configuration command:

> **ip sdr cache-timeout** *minutes*

minutes   The amount of time an SDR cache entry stays active in the cache. A value of 0 indicates the entry will never time-out. The default value is 24 hours.

The remaining commands pertaining to SDR are listed below.

Figure 9-4
Sample output for
the Session Directory

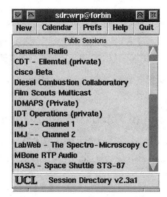

```
debug ip sdr
```

The above command enables logging of received SDR announcements.

```
show ip sdr [group | "session-name" | detail]
```

no parameters given   A sorted list of cached sessions names are displayed.

group   Detailed information is displayed for the multicast group.

detail   Displays sessions in detailed format.

This command displays the entries in the SDR cache if the router is configured to listen to SDR announcements.

```
clear ip sdr [group-address | "session-name"]
```

no parameters   Clears the SDR cache.

group-address   Clears all sessions associated with the given group-address.

session-name   Clears the cache entry for the given session name.

IP Multicast Rate Limiting

The amount of bandwidth that multicast traffic uses on a link can be controlled using the interface command.

```
ip multicast rate-limit in | out [video] | [whiteboard] [group-list access-list]
[source-list access-list] [kbps]
```

in   Only packets at the rate of kbps or slower are accepted on the interface.

out   Only a maximum of kbps is transmitted on the interface.

video   Optional. Rate-limiting is performed based on the UDP port number used by video traffic, which is identified by consulting the SDR cache.

whiteboard Optional. Rate limiting is performed based on the UDP port number used by whiteboard traffic, which is identified by consulting the SDR cache.

group-list Optional. An access list that is used to determine which
access-list multicast groups will be constrained by the rate limit.

source-list Optional. An access list that is used to determine which senders
access-list will be constrained by the rate limit.

kbps Rate limit in kilobits per second. Packets sent at a rate greater than *kbps* are discarded. If no value is given, then the default rate is 0 kilobits per seconds. In this case, no multicast traffic is permitted.

This command requires that **ip sdr listen** be enabled so port numbers can be obtained from the SDR cache. If SDR is not enabled, then no limiting occurs.

Stub Multicast Routing

Networks that have remote sites connected in a hub and spoke arrangement over lower speed links can benefit by configuring the spoke routers as stub networks (see Figure 9-5). If PIM-Dense or Sparse-Dense mode is configured on the main campus network, then without additional configuration, multicast traffic would periodically be flooded to the stub network. PIM-Dense mode can also flood multicast traffic on links where a PIM neighbor has been discovered. To prevent this periodic flooding of traffic, the PIM neighbor relationship must be prevented and an IGMP proxy needs to be configured. If PIM-Sparse mode is being employed on the campus, a stub network would not need to know RP-group mappings.

The configurations for the routers in Figure 9-5 that are needed to create a stub network are listed below:

```
Router A

ip multicast-routing

interface serial 0
 ip address 172.16.1.1 255.255.255.0
 ip pim dense-mode
 ip pim neighbor-filter 5

access-list 5 deny host 172.16.1.2
```

Figure 9-5
A stub multicast
network is
configured with an
IGMP proxy because
the PIM neighbor
relationship has been
prevented from
forming.

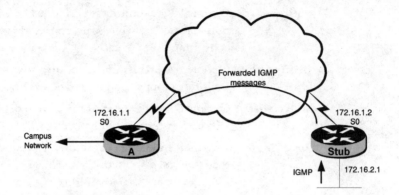

```
Router stub

ip multicast-routing

interface e0
  ip address 172.16.2.1 255.255.255.0
  ip pim dense-mode
  ip igmp helper-address 172.16.1.1

interface serial 0
  ip address 172.16.1.2 255.255.255.0
  ip pim dense-mode
```

The stub router forwards IGMP messages from hosts on the ethernet
network to router A, which has an access list that blocks the PIM neighbor relationship from forming between the two routers. Only multicast
traffic for a group that has been joined on the stub router is forwarded
by router A, reducing the multicast traffic on the link.

Load Balancing

When two equal cost paths exist for a destination, an IP unicast routing
protocol, such as OSPF, will load-balance unicast traffic over the two links.
Load-balancing, without additional configuration, is not possible with
multicast routing protocols. The reason that load-balancing does not
occur for multicast traffic over equal cost links is because of the selection
of the RPF interface. Only one RPF interface can be selected for a multicast source and therefore all multicast traffic must flow over that link.
Multicast traffic flowing on the other link will be rejected because it
does not arrive on the RPF interface (see Figure 9-6).

In order to achieve multicast load-balancing, we need to configure a tunnel between routers A and B in Figure 9-6. All multicast traffic will flow across the tunnel and the unicast routing protocols will load-balance across the actual physical links (see Figure 9-7). Load-balancing occurs because we are encapsulating the multicast traffic in unicast IP packets. Multicasting needs to be disabled on the physical interfaces and enabled on the tunnel interface.

The configurations for routers A and B are listed below:

```
Router A

interface ethernet 0
 ip address 172.16.2.1 255.255.255.0

interface serial 0
 ip address 172.16.1.1 255.255.255.252
 bandwidth 200
 clock rate 200000

interface serial 1
 ip address 172.16.1.5 255.255.255.252
 bandwidth 200
 clock rate 200000

interface tunnel 0
 ip unnumbered ethernet 0
 ip pim dense-mode (or sparse or sparse-dense mode)
 tunnel source ethernet 0
 tunnel destination 172.16.3.1
```

Figure 9-6
Multicast traffic is only accepted on one link.

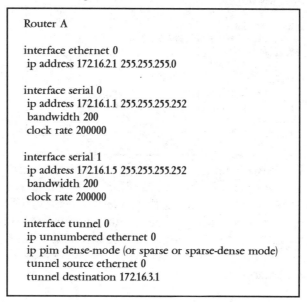

Figure 9-7
Load-balancing multicast traffic using a tunnel.

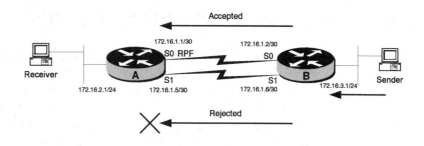

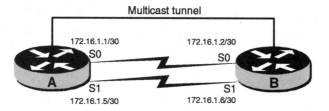

```
Router B

interface ethernet 0
 ip address 172.16.3.1 255.255.255.0

interface serial 0
 ip address 172.16.1.2 255.255.255.252
 bandwidth 200

interface serial 1
 ip address 172.16.1.6 255.255.255.252
 bandwidth 200

interface tunnel 0
 ip unnumbered ethernet 0
 ip pim dense-mode (or sparse or sparse-dense mode)
 tunnel source ethernet 0
 tunnel destination 172.16.2.1
```

Load-balancing will now occur over the two serial links, but the mechanisms will be different, depending on whether the routers are process-switching or fast-switching. For process-switching, the load-balancing occurs with each packet using a round-robin method. Also, the packet counts on each link will be the same. For fast-switching, load-balancing occurs with each multicast flow because an (S,G) flow will be assigned to one of the physical interfaces.

Multicast Static Routes

When using PIM, unicast and multicast routes are congruent. In other words, the unicast and multicast packets follow the same path. This makes sense because PIM uses the unicast routing table to make multicast routing decisions. Occasions can arise where you may want the unicast and multicast routing tables to diverge. For whatever reason, to accomplish this route divergence, use a static *multicast route* (mroute).

```
ip mroute source mask [protocol process-number] rpf-address | interface [distance]
```

source   IP address/mask of the multicast source.
mask

protocol	Optional. The unicast routing (OSPF, EIGRP, and so on).
process-number	Optional. The process number of the routing protocol that is being used.
rpf-address	The incoming interface for the mroute. If the Reverse Path Forwarding address, rpf-address, is a PIM neighbor, PIM Joins, Grafts, and Prunes are sent.
interface	The interface type and number for the mroute (ethernet 0, serial 1, and so on).
distance	Optional. This determines whether a unicast route, a DVMRP route, or a static mroute should be used for the RPF lookup. The lower distances have better preference. If the static mroute has the same distance as the other two RPF sources, the static mroute takes precedence. The default is 0.

Static multicast routes are not exported or redistributed; they are local to the router on which they were configured. The first example of a static mroute is in a network in which a tunnel is used to maneuver around a non-multicast capable router (see Figure 9-8).

Routers A and C would be configured with an mroute that directs multicast traffic to the tunnel.

ip mroute 0.0.0.0 0.0.0.0 tunnel 0

The next example involves a tunnel that drops multicast traffic right in the middle of your network from an external source (see Figure 9-9).

When the RPF check is made, routes are looked up in the unicast and the static mroute tables. If we use a simple default mroute like we did in the last example, all RPF checks would point to the tunnel. We may also have internal multicast sources in our network and we would want the RPF interface to be determined from the unicast routing table and not the static mroute table. The way to accomplish this is with the following router commands:

```
ip mroute 172.16.0.0 255.255.0.0 null0 255
ip mroute 0.0.0.0 0.0.0.0 tunnel 0
```

Figure 9-8

A static mroute is needed to direct multicast traffic over the tunnel.

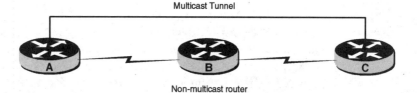

Multicast Tunnel

Non-multicast router

Figure 9-9
Static mroute needed
for multicast traffic
not originating in the
internal network

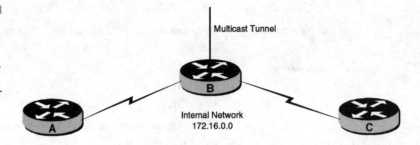

For sources in the 172.16.0.0 network, we will have an RPF route from the unicast routing table and the mroute table. The administrative distance for the mroute is greater than that for the unicast routing table, so the unicast route will be used as the RPF. Because there is a match in the mroute table, there is no need to check any other mroutes, so the default mroute will not take affect.

For external sources, there is no route in the unicast routing table and the first mroute does not match, so the default mroute will be used. This technique is a bit strange, but it does come in handy. If you only wanted to check a particular unicast (OSPF, EIGRP, IGRP, RIP) routing protocol, use the following form:

```
ip mroute 0.0.0.0 0.0.0.0 ospf 100 null0 255
ip mroute 0.0.0.0 0.0.0.0 tunnel 0.
```

Be careful, because if you reverse the order of the `ip mroute` statements, then the default route will always be taken.

Multicasting and Non-Broadcast Multi-Access Networks

A *non-broadcast multi-access* (NBMA) network, such as frame relay, needs special consideration in regards to multicast traffic. The network in Figure 9-10 is a partially meshed frame relay network configured as a hub and spoke arrangement.

If the hub router needs to send a broadcast to every spoke router, then the broadcast packet needs to be replicated and sent four times, once to each spoke router. This is not a problem with an occasional broadcast packet, yet with multicast traffic this method of operation can dramatically affect the bandwidth utilization on the frame relay network. For

Figure 9-10
Partially meshed
Non-Broadcast Multi-
Access (NBMA)
network

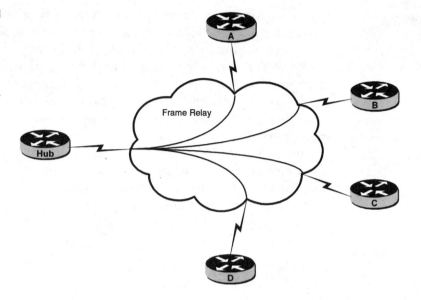

example, assume the hub router receives multicast traffic for groups that only router B and C have joined. The multicast traffic would be replicated and sent to routers A, B, C, and D, even though A and D do not have receivers. We also assume here that all four spoke routers are running PIM. To override this behavior, configure the interface in NBMA mode.

```
interface serial 0
 ip pim nbma-mode
 ip pim sparse-mode
```

When the hub router receives a Join from one of the spoke routers, the router records the group and the address of the joiner. Therefore, when the hub router receives a multicast packet to be forwarded over the frame relay network, the packet is only sent to the spoke routers that have joined the group. When a spoke router sends a Prune to leave the group, the forwarding entry is then deleted on the hub router. This command only works with PIM-Sparse Mode.

Multicast over ATM

If the frame relay network in Figure 9-10 is replaced by an ATM network, then we can use multipoint *virtual circuits* (VC) to limit the replication of multicast packets. By default, PIM establishes a static multipoint VC that provides a connection to each PIM neighbor. If the hub receives a multicast packet that only one PIM neighbor needs, it is sent to all PIM neighbors.

Let's say, for instance, we would like to modify this behavior so that the multicast packet is only forwarded to those neighbors that want to receive it. Assume the routers in the network are all running PIM Sparse-Mode and the Hub router is the RP. When router A sends a Join for a multicast group to the hub, the hub router sets up a multipoint VC for the group. If another spoke router joins the same group, the hub router just adds the spoke router to the multipoint VC. When traffic for the group is received by the hub, the router only needs to send one copy on the multipoint VC that was established for the group. Then the ATM switches between the hub and spoke routers are responsible for replicating and delivering the packets. This feature is configured using the interface command:

```
ip pim multipoint-signaling
```

This command can only be used on an ATM interface. To limit the maximum number of VCs that PIM can open for multicast traffic, use the interface command

```
ip pim vc-count number
```

number Maximum number of VCs PIM can open. Default value is 200.

If the router needs to open another VC that causes the router to exceed the configured maximum VC count, then the VC with the least amount of activity is deleted. If there are multiple VCs with the same minimum amount of activity, then the VC that is connected to the fewest neighbors is deleted first. The activity level is measured in packets per second and by default all activity levels are considered when a VC needs to be deleted. To configure the activity level that determines whether VCs will be considered for deletion, use the interface command

```
ip pim minimum-vc-rate pps
```

pps Set the minimum packets per second rate to the value given by pps.

If the number of VCs open already equals the maximum number allowed, then packets for new groups are sent over the static multicast VC.

Resource Reservation Protocol

The Resource **ReSerVation Protocol** (RSVP) is an Internet control protocol that is used by unicast and multicast receivers to request a specific *quality of service* (QoS) for the data flow from a unicast or multicast source. RSVP would typically be used to establish a bandwidth reservation for real-time traffic, such as voice or video, as opposed to data traffic, such as a file transfer. RSVP can prevent a data application from depleting the bandwidth available for real-time traffic. Without a guaranteed bandwidth along the path from sender to receiver, real-time traffic can suffer from jitter or delay inconsistencies.

RSVP is also used by routers to forward QoS requests on the path from the receiver to the source. RSVP is not a routing protocol but is a transport layer control protocol used to establish a QoS along a routed path. RSVP interoperates with unicast and multicast routing protocols to determine the path along which QoS reservations need to be made. If available, resources are reserved in each router along the selected path from the receiver to the source. QoS Reservations are unidirectional, typically from the source to the receiver (see Figure 10-1).

The RSVP request will flow along the source-based or shared multicast tree depending on which multicast routing protocol has been enabled. The RSVP requests are forwarded towards the source by examining the routing table and determining the next hop toward the source. The functional components of RSVP run as a background process in parallel with the data path as shown in Figure 10-2.

Figure 10-1
RSVP request flows along the shared or source-based multicast tree

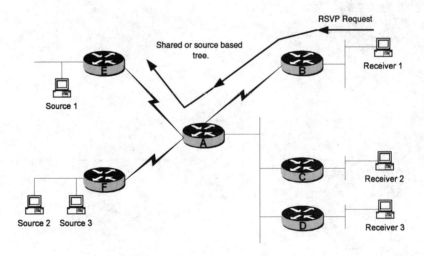

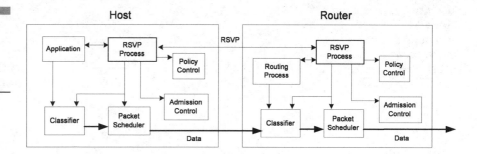

When a resource reservation request is initiated, the request is sent to the policy and admission control modules. The admission control module will check to see if the node can satisfy the request. The policy control module determines if the entity requesting the reservation has the required privileges to do so. If either of these checks is unsuccessful, the application will be notified of the failure. If no failures occur, the classifier and the packet scheduler establish the requested reservation. Multicast membership is usually dynamic. Hosts can join or leave a multicast group at any time. To accommodate the dynamic nature of multicast data flows, RSVP will periodically send refresh messages along the data flow path in order to maintain the established reservation. When refresh messages stop being sent, the reservation will timeout, releasing the resources back to the system.

RSVP Reservation Model

An RSVP reservation request is referred to as a *flow descriptor*. The flow descriptor consists of two elements. The first element is the *flowspec*, which specifies the QoS and is used in conjunction with the packet scheduler. The second element is the *filter spec,* which is used to determine which packets in the flow will receive the QoS that has been reserved at the node. The filter spec is used to inform the packet classifier of the parameters that will be checked to determine if a packet is a candidate for the QoS reservation. The RSVP specification currently has a basic filter specification consisting of the sender's IP address and the UDP/TCP source port number. Figure 10-3 shows the relationship between the flow descriptor and the RSVP functional model.

Figure 10-3
Flow descriptor and
RSVP functional
model relationships

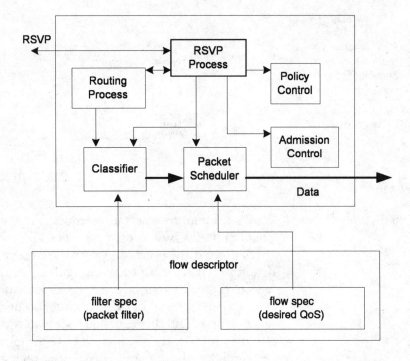

Figure 10-3
Flow descriptor and
RSVP functional
model relationships

TABLE 10-1

RSVP Reservation
Styles

Sender Selection	Distinct Reservation	Shared Reservation
Explicit	Fixed-Filter (FF) style	Shared-Explicit (SE) style
Wildcard	(None Defined)	Wildcard-Filter (WF) style

Reservation Styles

A *style* refers to a reservation request and the set of options pertaining to that request. Reservations can be distinct or shared. A distinct reservation is one in which a specific reservation is established for each sender to a particular multicast group. A shared reservation is one where all senders for a session share a reservation. For both styles the selection of the sender can either be explicitly referenced in the request or not referenced at all. The not referenced case is referred to as the wildcard case in which every sender is automatically selected. For the explicit sender case, each filter specification will match only one sender. The wildcard case would not need a sender filter specification. Table 10-1 lists the various styles that can be used when setting up a resource reservation.

Wildcard-Filter (WF) Style

The WF style is a shared reservation style with implicit sender selection. Since all reservations are sharing the same resource allocation, the amount of resource that needs to be reserved is equal to the largest value of the resource requested by all receivers. The WF style is represented by the equation

$$WF(*\{Q\})$$

with the asterisk signifying a wildcard sender selection and Q signifying the flowspec. The symbol Q, or flowspec, is essentially the QoS or amount of bandwidth requested by the receiver. The network in Figure 10-4 shows a WF scenario. The receivers are requesting bandwidth for a particular session that is supported by sources 1,2, and 3. The receivers don't care from which source the data arrives so all are using the wildcard specification WF(*{Q}). Receiver 1 is requesting 500K and sends a WF(*{500K}) RSVP request to router A.

Router A receives only one WF request and attempts to allocate the bandwidth on the input interface, E0, and the output interface, S0. For reservation requests, input and output interfaces refer to the direction of the reservation request flow. The data flow from the sources will reverse the direction of these interfaces. For the following examples, assume the routers have the resources to satisfy reservation requests. Since the request is a shared reservation request, router A will allocate the largest of the

Figure 10-4
WF(*{Q}) reservation style example

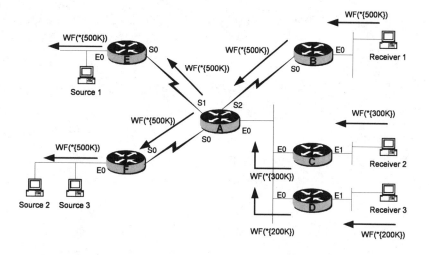

requested allocations. With only one request, the allocation will equal what receiver 1 requested. The same argument applies to routers C and D and receivers 2 and 3. Router C will allocate 300K on the E0 and E1 interfaces, while router D will allocate 200K on the E0 and E1 interfaces. Router A will receive one reservation request on interface S2 for 500K and two reservation requests for 200K and 300K on interface E0. Router A will allocate 500K on interface S2. The largest of the two requests, 300K, is received on interface E0. On interfaces S0 and S1, Router A has to be able to handle the largest of the three requests received. For this case, a 500K allocation is reserved on the S0 and S1 interfaces and the reservation is forwarded toward the sources. Routers E and F only receive an RSVP request for 500K. This amount will be allocated on all interfaces between the sources and the receivers. The bandwidth allocations for the WF example network in Figure 10-4 are listed in Table 10-2.

Fixed-Filter (FF) Style

Fixed-filter reservations have distinct reservations with explicit sender selection. For each FF reservation established, the router must allocate bandwidth for each request. The total bandwidth allocated is the sum of the bandwidths requested by each FF request for a distinct source. If two or more receivers request a resource and specify the same sender, the allocated resource will be shared by the receivers for that sender. The FF style can be represented by

$$FF(S\{Q\})$$

where S is the specific sender and Q is the flowspec. The FF style is contained in Figure 10-5 with the total bandwidth allocations shown in Table 10-3.

TABLE 10-2

Bandwidth Allocations for the Wildcard-Filter Style Example

Router	Interface E0	Interface E1	Interface S0	Interface S1	Interface S2
A	300K		500K	500K	500K
B	500K		500K		
C	300K	300K			
D	200K	200K			
E	500K		500K		
F	500K		500K		

Figure 10-5
Fixed Filter FF(S{Q})
reservation style
example

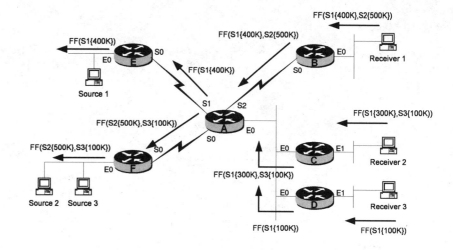

TABLE 10-3

Bandwidth
Allocations for the
Fixed-Filter Style
Example

Router	Interface E0	Interface E1	Interface S0	Interface S1	Interface S2
A	400K		600K	400K	900K
B	900K		900K		
C	400K	400K			
D	100K	100K			
E	400K		400K		
F	600K		600K		

Shared Explicit (SE) Style

Shared Explicit style reservations are characterized by a shared reservation and an explicit sender, creating a reservation that is shared by specific senders. The SE style is represented by

$$SE((S1,S2,\dots Sn)\{Q\})$$

indicating that the list of senders shares the reservation Q. SE style type reservations are illustrated in Figure 10-6 with the bandwidth allocations listed in Table 10-4.

Figure 10-6
Shared Explicit
SE(S{Q}) reservation
style example

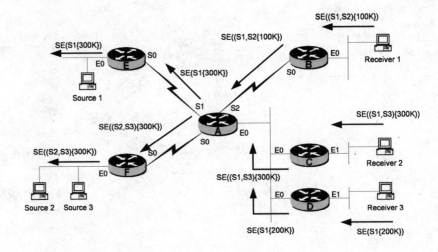

TABLE 10-4

Bandwidth
Allocations for the
Shared-Explicit (SE)
Style Example

Router	Interface E0	Interface E1	Interface S0	Interface S1	Interface S2
A	300K		300K	300K	100K
B	100K		100K		
C	300K	300K			
D	200K	200K			
E	300K		300K		
F	300K		300K		

When router A in Figure 10-6 receives the requests

$$SE(S1\{\{200K\}\}) + SE((S1,S3)\{300K\})$$

from routers C and D, the filter specs are combined and the flow spec is set to the largest flow spec received. The resulting flow descriptor will be ((S1,S2,S3){300K}).

Reservation Style Summary

The three RSVP styles and the actions a router will take when merging requests are summarized in Figures 10-7 through 10-10.

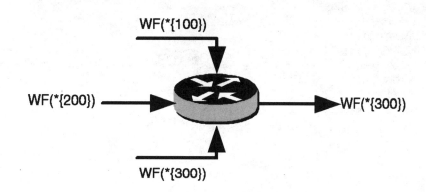

Figure 10-7
The merging of WF style RSVP requests. The size of the resource allocated is equal to the largest, regardless of the senders.

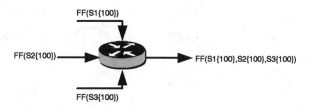

████ ████ ████ ████
Figure 10-8
The merging of FF style RSVP requests for distinct sources is shown. For each distinct source allocated, the requested resource is shown also. For a common source allocated, the largest of the resource is requested. The allocated bandwidth equals 300.

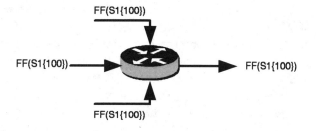

████ ████ ████ ████
Figure 10-9
The merging of FF style RSVP requests for a common source. For a common source, allocate the largest of the resources requested. The allocated bandwidth equals 100.

Figure 10-10
The merging of SE style RSVP requests. Merge all sources and allocate the largest of the requested resource for all specified sources. The total bandwidth allocated equals 300.

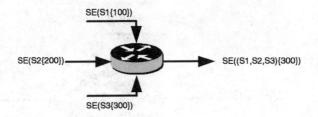

Figure 10-11
RSVP terminology

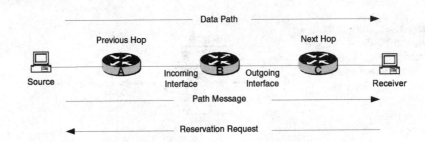

RSVP Protocol Messages

When discussing RSVP messages we need to agree on the definition of terms. Figure 10-11 illustrates some fundamental terms used in discussing RSVP messages. The incoming and outgoing interfaces, as well as the next and previous hops, are from the point of view of the data flow. RSVP utilizes two types of messages for resource reservation. The first message is a *reservation request* (RESV) message that is sent from receivers to senders. The RESV messages will traverse the network from the receiver to the sources in the messages along the RPF interfaces as discussed in previous chapters. A reservation state will be established in each router along the path.

Each source that implements RSVP will transmit Path messages along the route that the data will follow. At each node along the path, the path state is stored. The path state is used to route the reservation messages. A fundamental component of the path state is the IP address of the previous hop. In Figure 10-11, the previous hop for router B is router A, as shown. The path message contains other required components and possibly optional components for the establishment of the path state. The two required components are the Sender Template and the Sender Tspec. Sender Template contains a description of the structure of the packets that the source sends in the form of a filter spec. This implies that the sender template will contain the IP address of the source and possibly the UDP port the source is using. The Sender Tspec defines the characteristics of the traffic the source will originate in order to prevent over-reservation. An optional component of a path message is the Adspec. An Adspec carries *One Pass With Advertising* (OPWA) information. As the Path message travels towards the receiver, information is collected at each node so the receiver is able to predict the end-to-end service. This information is referred to as an advertisement, hence, the name Adspec. When the path message arrives at a node, the Adspec is passed to the local traffic control module. The local traffic control module updates the Adspec which is sent in a path message to the next downstream node.

The state that is established along the path from the source to receiver is a dynamic, or soft, state. It is refreshed by periodic path and reservation messages. If there are any changes in the reservation request, they are contained in the request updating the soft state in the routers. The state maintains a cleanup timeout timer whose expiration causes the state to be deleted. A state may also be deleted by the reception of a teardown message. Teardown messages will remove reservation of path state upon reception of the message. Two types of states are established—path and reservation— so two teardown messages—ResvTear and PathTear— are also established.

RSVP uses two messages to report errors. For path errors, the PathErr message is used. PathErr messages are sent upstream toward the source that was the cause of the error. Intermediate nodes the PathErr message crosses won't have its path state modified. For reservation errors, the ResvErr message is used. When a reservation request is denied by the admission control module, existing reservations are unaffected and the error is reported to all affected receivers. ResvErr messages create a new state in the nodes the error message traverses. This state is called the blockade state and prevents the flowspec that caused the error to be omitted from the flowspec merging process.

RSVP confirmation messages (ResvConf) are used to signal the requesting receiver that the reservation was successful. When a reservation request reaches a merge point and the request is smaller than or equal to an existing reservation, the reservation has succeeded. At this point, if the receiver requested a confirmation, then a ResvConf message will be sent back to the receiver.

There may be situations where RSVP reservation and path messages may be routed through routers that are not RSVP capable (see Figure 10-12).

A path message from the source will be forwarded towards the destination by both the RSVP capable and non-RSVP capable routers and allow

Figure 10-12
A non-RSVP router in
the path between
the receiver and
source

Source · RSVP Capable · Not RSVP Capable · RSVP Capable · Receiver

Figure 10-13
RSVP message
header format

Vers	Flags	Msg Type	RSVP Checksum
Send TTL		Reserved	RSVP Length

RSVP to operate correctly. Problems may arise because there is no knowledge about the non-RSVP router and whether or not it can handle the reservations that were setup on the RSVP capable routers. In this case RSVP will propagate a non-RSVP flag to the local traffic control module and will be forwarded using Adspecs. Non-RSVP capable routers can cause an RSVP message to arrive at the wrong node or the wrong interface on the correct node. A *Logical Interface Handle* (LIH) is used to handle the case of the wrong interface on the right router. The previous hop information in the path message will contain the IP address of the previous hop and a LIH identifying the interface.

RSVP Message Formats

Every RSVP message begins with a common header (see Figure 10-13).

Version	Four-bit version number. Current version is 1.
Flags	Four-bit number. Not defined.
Msg type	Eight-bit number. 1 = Path
	2 = Resv
	3 = PathErr
	4 = ResvErr
	5 = PathTear
	6 = ResvTear
	7 = ResvConf
RSVP Checksum	16-bit ones complement sum of the RSVP message.

| Send_TTL | Eight-bit original TTL value of the message. |
| RSVP Length | 16-bit total length of the RSVP message. |

Each RSVP message has an object field that follows the common header. The object field has a minimum size of 32-bits, as shown in Figure 10-14.

Length	Sixteen-bit length in bytes of the object. The length must be a multiple of four and the minimum length is four bytes.
C-Type	Identifies the address family. One is for IPv4 and 2 is for IPv6.
Class-Num	Type of object contained in the message. The Class-Num identifiers and their corresponding packet formats and descriptions are contained in Figures 10-15–10-16.

Class-Num identifies one of the following objects.

NULL	NULL objects are ignored and can be anywhere in the message. The object length is a multiple of four bytes.
SESSION	A session object is required in every RSVP message. This object will contain the IP address of the destination, the IP protocol ID and the destination port.
RSVP_HOP	Contains the IP address of the RSVP node that sent the message along with the *Logical Interface Handle* (LIH). For downstream messages, the object is referred to as a *previous hop* (PHOP) object and for next hop or upstream messages it is referred to as a *next hop* (NHOP) object.

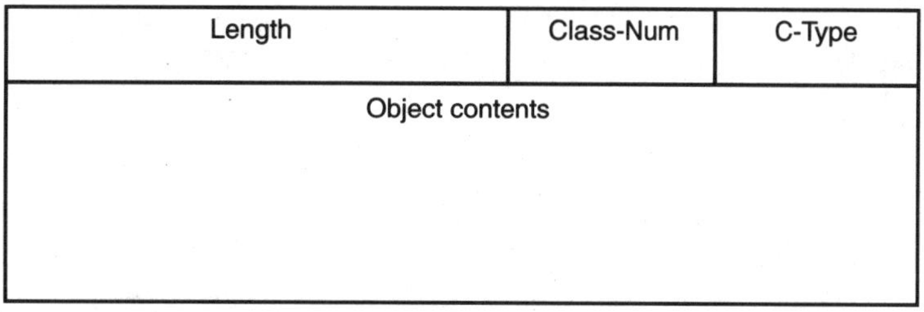

Figure 10-14
RSVP Object format

Length		Class-Num	C-Type
Object contents			

TIME_VALUES

Every Path and RESV message will contain a TIME_VALUES object that contains the refresh period. This object is required in every Resv and Path message.

STYLE

Contains the reservation style, WF, FF, or SE, and style specific information not contained in FLOWSPEC or FILTER_SPEC objects.

FLOWSPEC

Contains the desired QoS. Used in the RESV message.

FILTER_SPEC

Used to identify the data packets in a session that should receive the requested QoS. Used in the RESV message.

SENDER_TEMPLATE

Contains the sender's IP address and is required in the Path message.

ADSPEC

Contains OPWA information and is used in the PATH message.

ERROR_SPEC

Identifies the error that is being returned in a PathErr or ResvErr message. Also used as a confirmation in a ResvConf message.

POLICY_DATA

Not currently specified.

INTEGRITY

Contains cryptographic information to authenticate the originating node and to verify the message.

SCOPE

Contains a list of senders to which the message is forwarded.

RESV_CONFIRM

Contains the IP address of the receiver that requested the confirmation.

The Session class object, shown in Figures 10-15 and 10-16, specifies the session for the objects that follow in the message. The destination address, in conjunction with the UDP destination port field, identifies the session. The destination address can be either a multicast or unicast address.

The RSVP_HOP message (see Figures 10-17 and 10-18) contains the IP address and Logical Interface Handle (LIH) of the RSVP node that forwarded the message.

Figure 10-15
IPv4 UDP Session Object; Class-Num = 1 C-Type = 1

IPv4 Destination Address		
Protocol ID	Flags	UDP Destination Port

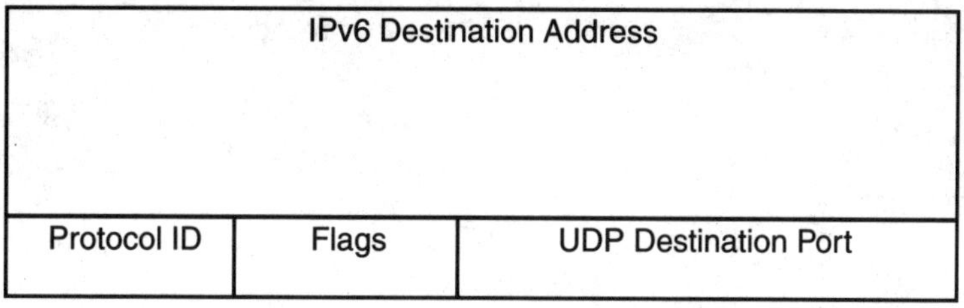

Figure 10-16
IPv6 UDP Session object; Class-Num = 1 C-Type = 2

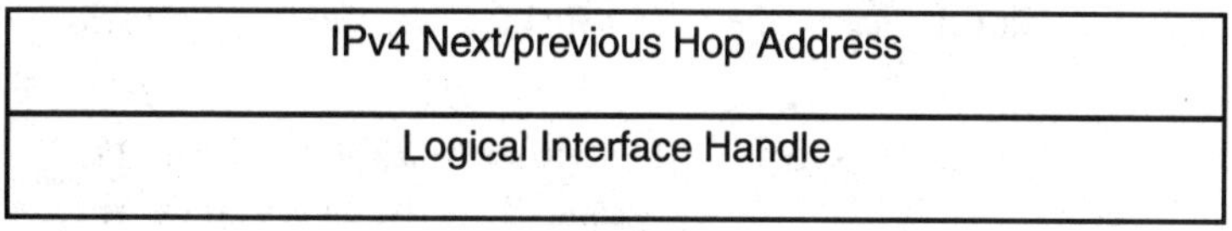

IPv6 Destination Address		
Protocol ID	Flags	UDP Destination Port

Figure 10-17
IPv4 RSVP_HOP object; Class-Num = 3 C-Type = 1

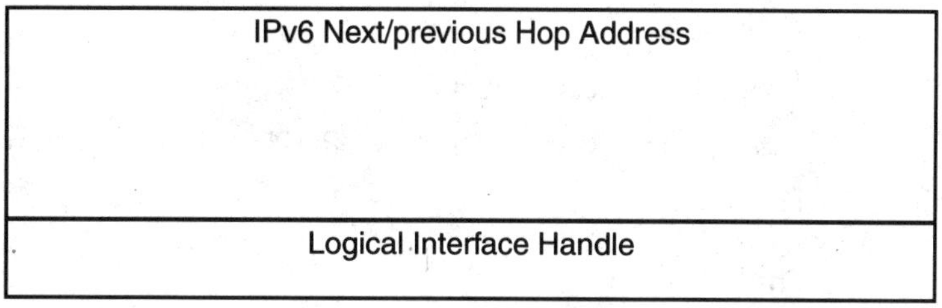

IPv4 Next/previous Hop Address
Logical Interface Handle

Figure 10-18
IPv6 RSVP_HOP object; Class-Num = 3 C-Type = 2

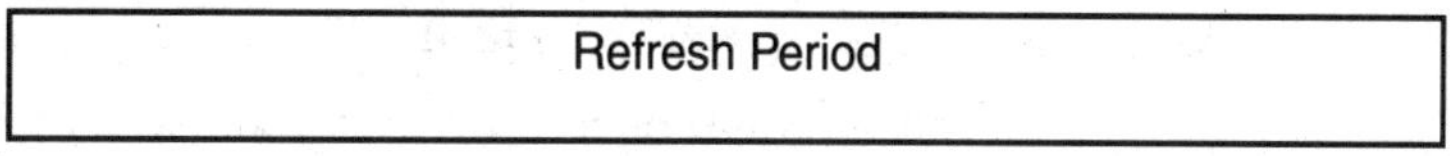

IPv6 Next/previous Hop Address
Logical Interface Handle

Figure 10-19
TIME_VALUES object; Class-Num = 5 C-Type = 1

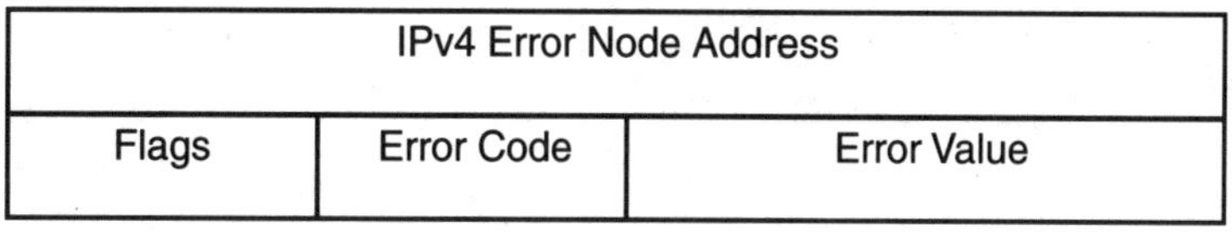

Refresh Period

Figure 10-20
IPv4 ERROR_SPEC object; Class-Num = 6 C-Type = 1

IPv4 Error Node Address		
Flags	Error Code	Error Value

The TIME_VALUE object (see Figure 10-19) contains the refresh period in milliseconds.

The ERROR_SPEC object contains the IP address of the node where the error was detected (see Figure 10-21). The flags field has the values listed on the following page.

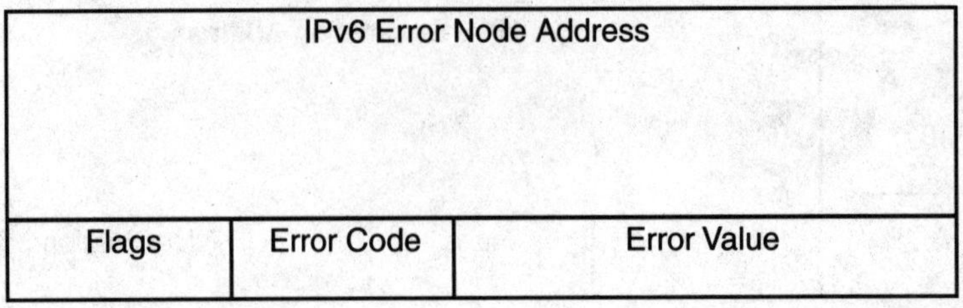

Figure 10-21
IPv6 ERROR_SPEC
object; Class-Num = 6
C-Type = 2

IPv6 Error Node Address		
Flags	Error Code	Error Value

0×01 (InPlace)   If this bit is set then a reservation is in place on the node where the error occurred. Only used in a ResvErr message.

0×02 (NotGuilty)   If set then indicates that the FLOWSPEC that failed was greater than the FLOWSPEC that was requested by the receiver.

Error code 0

Type   Confirmation.

Description   Used in the ERROR_SPEC object in a ResvConf message.

Error Value   0

Error Code 1

Type   Admission Control Failure.

Description   The reservation request failed due to resource(s) not available.

Error Value   The 16 bits of the error value are defined as follows:

15	14	13	12	11	10	9	8	7	6	5	4	3	2	1	0
s	s	u	r	c	c	c	c	c	c	c	c	c	c	c	c

ss = 00

Error Code 2

Type   Policy control failure.

Description   A reservation or path message failed for administrative reasons.

Error Value   Undefined.

Error Code 3

Type   No path state for the session and the resv message cannot be forwarded.

Error value   Undefined.

Error Code 4

Type	No sender information for the Resv message.
Description	A path state exists for the session but the state does not contain a flow descriptor that matches the sender in the Resv message.
Error value	Undefined.

Error Code 5

Type	Conflicting reservation style.
Description	The requested reservation style conflicts with the existing style.
Error Value	Lower order 16-bits of the option vector of the existing style.

Error Code 6

Type	Unknown reservation style.

Error Code 7

Type	Conflicting destination ports.
Description	Sessions for the same destination address and protocol and appeared with both zero and non-zero destination port fields.
Error Value	Undefined.

Error Code 8

Type	Conflicting sender ports.
Description	The sender port is both zero and non-zero in path messages for the same session.

Error Code 9,10,11

Type	Reserved.

Error Code 12

Type	Service preempted.
Description	The service requested by the STYLE object and the flow descriptor has been administratively preempted.
Error value	

Error Code   13

Type   Unknown object class.

Error Value   Contains the Class-Num and C-type of the unknown object.

Error Code   14

Type   Unknown object C-type.

Error Value   Contains the Class-Num and C-type of the unknown object.

Error Code   15, 16, 17, 18, 19, 20

Type   Reserved.

Error Code   21

Type   Traffic control error.

Description   Traffic control call failed due to the format or contents of the
                request.

Error Code   22

Type   Traffic control system error.

Description   A system error was detected and reported by the traffic control
                modules.

Error Value   System specific.

Error Code   23

Type   RSVP system error.

Description   Every RSVP message is rebuilt at every hop and an error in a
                node could cause a malformed message.

Error Value   Implementation dependent.

The SCOPE class object is a list of IP addresses used for routing messages with wildcard scope without loops (see Figures 10-22 and 10-23). The addresses must be listed in ascending order.

The STYLE object identifies the reservation type (see Figure 10-24) and the flags field is not defined. The 24-bit option vector (see Figure 10-25) identifies the style.

The FILTER_SPEC object contains the IP source address for the sender (see Figures 10-26, 10-27, and 10-28). The source port field contains the UDP/TCP port for the sender or 0 to indicate "none."

The SENDER_TEMPLATE object contains the IP source address for the sender (see Figures 10-29, 10-30, and 10-31). The source port field contains the UDP/TCP port for the sender or 0 to indicate "none."

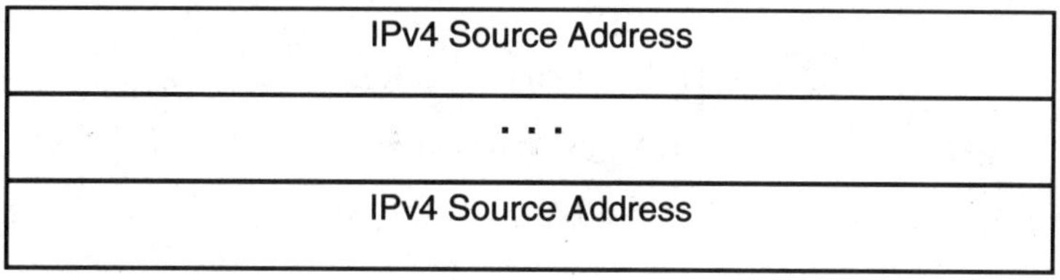

Figure 10-22
IPv4 SCOPE List object; Class-Num = 7 C-Type = 1

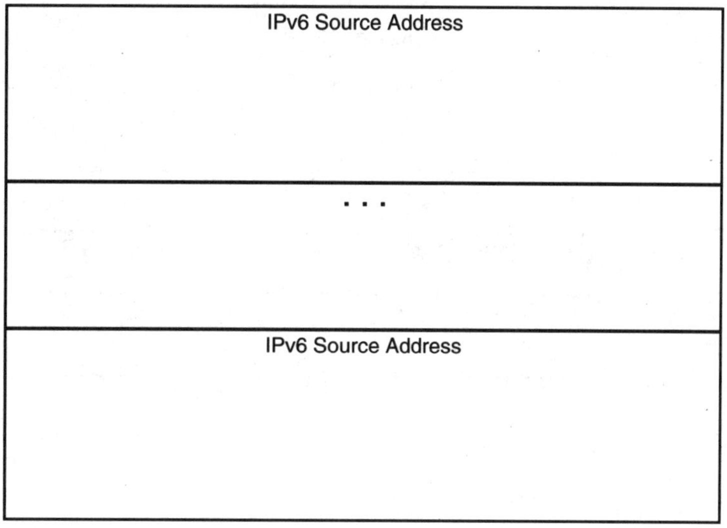

IPv4 Source Address
. . .
IPv4 Source Address

Figure 10-23
IPv6 SCOPE List object; Class-Num = 7 C-Type = 2

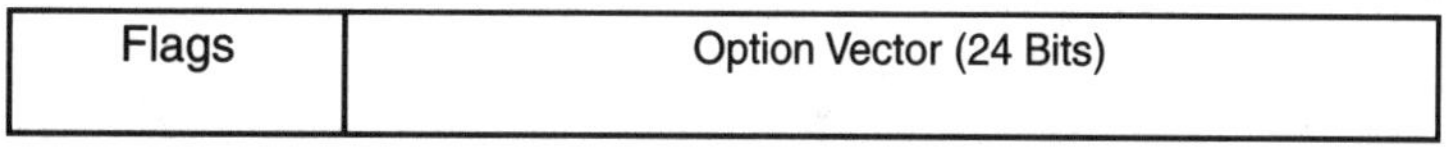

IPv6 Source Address
. . .
IPv6 Source Address

Figure 10-24
STYLE object; Class-Num = 8 C-Type = 1

Flags	Option Vector (24 Bits)

Figure 10-25
Option Vector bit
definitions

23	22	21	20	19	18	17	16	15	14	13	12	11	10	9	8	7	6	5	4	3	2	1	0
R	R	R	R	R	R	R	R	R	R	R	R	R	R	R	R	R	R	R	R	C	C	S	S	S

R = reserved

C = Sharing Control   0x00 – Reserved

                     0x01 – Distinct reservations

                     0x10 – Shared reservations

                     0x11 – Reserved

S = Sender Selection   0x000 – Reserved

                     0x001 – Wildcard

                     0x010 – Explicit

Sharing control and sender selection determine the style.

                     0x10001 – WF

                     0x01010 – FF

                     0x10010 – SE

Figure 10-26
IPv4 FILTER_SPEC
object;
Class-Num = 10
C-Type = 1

IPv4 Source Address		
(Don't Care)	(Don't Care)	Source Port

Figure 10-27
IPv6 FILTER_SPEC
object;
Class-Num = 10
C-Type = 2

IPv6 Source Address		
(Don't Care)	(Don't Care)	Source Port

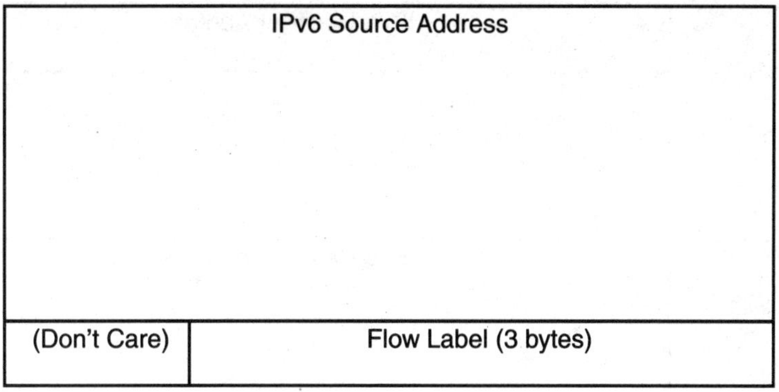

Figure 10-28
IPv6 FILTER_SPEC
object;
Class-Num = 10
C-Type = 3

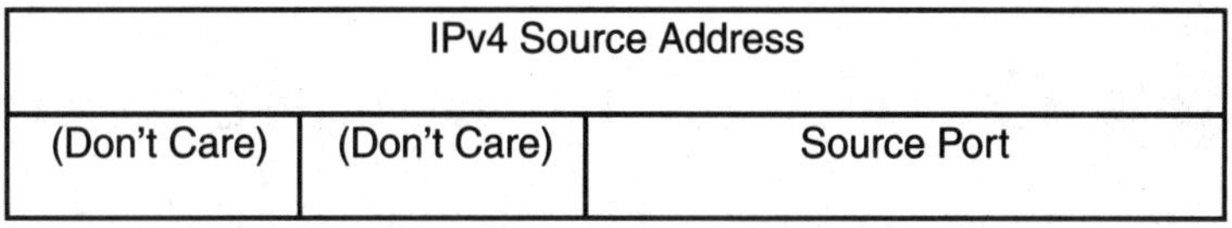

IPv6 Source Address	
(Don't Care)	Flow Label (3 bytes)

Figure 10-29
IPv4
SENDER_TEMPLATE
object;
Class-Num = 11
C-Type = 1

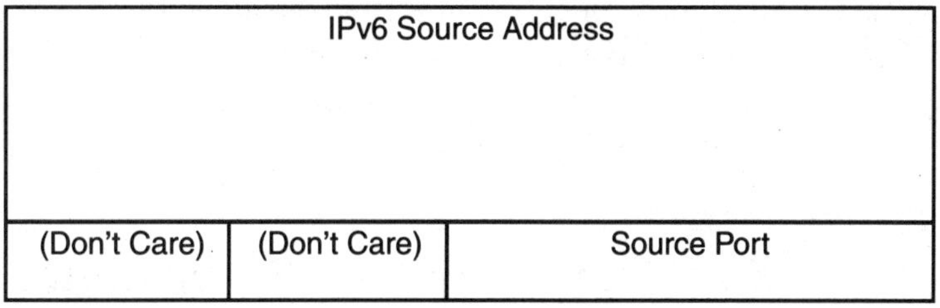

IPv4 Source Address		
(Don't Care)	(Don't Care)	Source Port

Figure 10-30
IPv6
SENDER_TEMPLATE
object;
Class-Num = 11
C-Type = 2

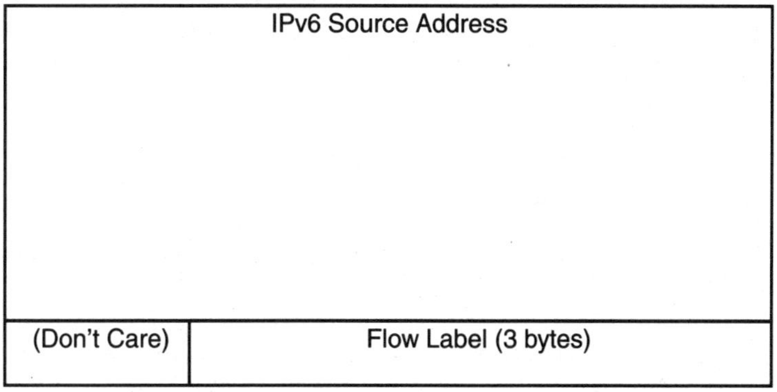

IPv6 Source Address		
(Don't Care)	(Don't Care)	Source Port

Figure 10-31
IPv6
SENDER_TEMPLATE
object;
Class-Num = 11
C-Type = 3

IPv6 Source Address	
(Don't Care)	Flow Label (3 bytes)

Figure 10-32
IPv4 RESV_CONFIRM
object;
Class-Num = 15
C-Type = 1

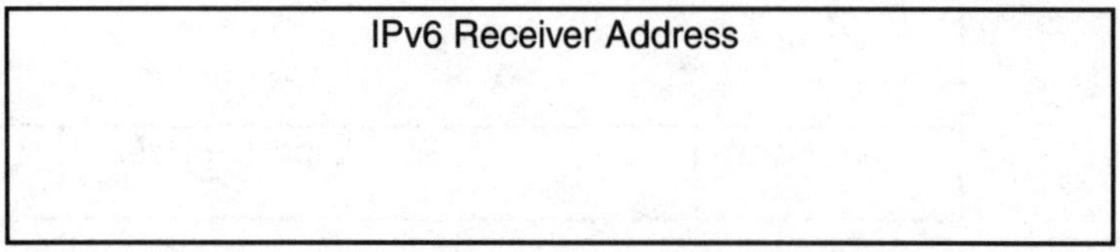

```
┌────────────────────────────────────────────────────┐
│                 IPv4 Receiver Address                │
└────────────────────────────────────────────────────┘
```

Figure 10-33
IPv6 RESV_CONFIRM
object;
Class-Num = 15
C-Type = 2

```
┌────────────────────────────────────────────────────┐
│                 IPv6 Receiver Address                │
│                                                      │
│                                                      │
│                                                      │
└────────────────────────────────────────────────────┘
```

Configuring and Monitoring RSVP

Three types of configuration commands can be used to configure or monitor RSVP. The first type is configuration commands used to enable and configure RSVP. The second type of RSVP command is used to view RSVP configurations and parameters. The third type of RSVP command is used for debugging an RSVP configuration. Each command will be presented and the use of the command will be explained. After the command overview we will examine RSVP scenarios and the use of all three types of RSVP commands.

RSVP Configuration Commands

RSVP is disabled on router interfaces and this is the default interface state. In order for a router to participate in RSVP, RSVP must be enabled on the interfaces using the command

```
ip rsvp bandwidth [interface-kbps] [single-flow-kbps]
```

interface-kbps   Optional parameter. Value can be 1–10,000,000.

single-flow-kbps   Optional parameter. Value can be 1–10,000,000.

The parameters shown in brackets are optional parameters. The first optional parameter is the total amount of bandwidth that will be reserved on the interface for RSVP flows. The second optional parameter is the amount of bandwidth that can be allocated to a single flow. By default 75 percent of the bandwidth on an interface can be reserved.

EXAMPLE

For the router in Figure 10-34, reserve 75 percent of the bandwidth on the ethernet interfaces with a limit of 10 percent of the bandwidth for any one flow.

```
interface Ethernet 0
  ip address 10.1.1.1 255.255.255.0
  ip pim dense-mode
  ip rsvp bandwidth 7500 1000

interface Ethernet 1
  ip address 10.1.1.1 255.255.255.0
  ip pim dense-mode
  ip rsvp bandwidth 7500 1000
```

To disable RSVP on an interface, use the command

> **no ip rsvp bandwidth** *interface-kbps single-flow-kbps*

By default, any neighbor can request a reservation on a router interface. If only selected neighbors are to be permitted to request a reservation using RSVP, we would use the interface command

> **ip rsvp neighbors** *access-list-number*

access-list-number   Integer from 1 to 199. 1 to 99 for a standard access list. 100–199 for an extended access list.

In Figure 10-35, we want to only permit the receiver with IP address 10.1.4.2 to be able to request a reservation. There is an implicit deny any at the end of every access list. Therefore the access list in Figure 10-35 will block all other receivers from requesting reservations. If we wanted to only block 10.1.4.2 from making a reservation but permit any other receiver to request a reservation then we would need the access list shown in Figure 10-36. The permit any is required because of the implicit deny any at the end of the list.

Figure 10-34
Enabling RSVP and reserving bandwidth on router interfaces

Figure 10-35
Allow only sender
10.1.4.2 to request a
reservation

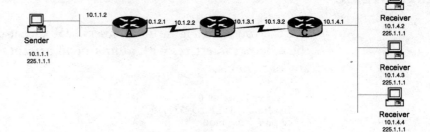

```
Router C
interface Ethernet 0
 ip address 10.1.4.1 255.255.255.0
 ip pim dense-mode
 ip rsvp bandwidth
 ip rsvp neighbors 1

access-list 1 permit host 10.1.4.1
```

Figure 10-36
Deny sender
10.1.4.2 from
requesting a
reservation

```
Router C
interface Ethernet 0
 ip address 10.1.4.1 255.255.255.0
 ip pim dense-mode
 ip rsvp bandwidth
 ip rsvp neighbors 1

access-list 1 deny host 10.1.4.1
access-list 1 permit any
```

To remove an access list for a neighbor, use the interface command

no ip rsvp neighbors *access-list-number*

We have seen that RSVP will periodically send refresh messages for PATH and RESV messages. The refresh messages keep the path and reservation states in place by preventing them from timing out. The router can be configured to behave as though it were receiving reservation or path messages using

```
ip rsvp sender session-ip-address sender-ip-address
[tcp|udp|ip-protocol] session-dport sender-sport
previous-hop-ip-address previous-hop-interface bandwidth burst-size
```

for PATH messages and

```
ip rsvp reservation session-ip-address sender-ip-address
[tcp|udp|ip-protocol] session-dport sender-sport
next-hop-ip-address next-hop-interface
{ff|se|wf} {rate|load} bandwidth burst-size
```

for RESV messages. The explanations of the parameters for the two messages are listed below.

session-ip-address	For a unicast session, this is the address of the receiver. For a multicast session, this is the session IP multicast address.
sender-ip-address	IP address of the sender.
tcp|udp|*ip-protocol*	
session dport	Destination and source port numbers. If one is zero
session sport	then both must be zero.
previous-hop-ip-address	Address of the sender if the sender is connected to the interface or address of the router interface on the path back to the sender.
previous-hop-interface	Interface type of the previous hop. It can be ethernet, loopback, null, or serial.
next-hop-ip-address	Hostname or address of the receiver or the address of the router interface on the path back to the receiver.
next-hop-interface	Interface type of the next hop. Can be ethernet, loopback, null, or serial.
:ff | se | wf	Reservation style: fixed filter, shared explicit, or wild card.
rate | load	QoS: guaranteed bit rate service or controlled load service.

bandwidth   Optional. Average bit rate (kbps) to reserve, up to 75 percent of the interface capacity. Range is 1 to 10,000,000.

burst-size   Optional. Maximum burst size (kilobytes of data in the queue). Range is 1 to 65,535.

To remove the effect these commands, use the form

```
no ip rsvp sender session-ip-address sender-ip-address
[tcp|udp|ip-protocol] session-dport sender-sport
previous-hop-ip-address previous-hop-interface bandwidth burst-size
```

for PATH messages and

```
no ip rsvp reservation session-ip-address sender-ip-address
[tcp|udp|ip-protocol] session-dport sender-sport
next-hop-ip-address next-hop-interface
{ff|se|wf} {rate|load} bandwidth burst-size
```

for RESV messages.

In Figure 10-37, routers A and C are configured so the sender path state and the receivers reservation never time out.

Router A

```
interface Ethernet0
ip address 10.1.1.2 255.255.255.0
ip pim dense-mode
ip rsvp bandwidth
ip rsvp sender 225.1.1.1 10.1.1.1 udp 20 30 10.1.1.1 ethernet0 50 5
```

Figure 10-37
Example of static
RSVP reservations

Router C

```
interface Ethernet0
 ip address 10.1.4.1 255.255.255.0
 ip pim dense-mode
 ip rsvp bandwidth
 ip rsvp reservation 225.1.1.1 10.1.4.2 udp 30 20 10.1.4.2 ethernet0 ff rate 300 60
```

The final RSVP configuration command addresses the encapsulation of the RSVP messages. If the router detects that RSVP neighbors are using UDP encapsulation, the router will automatically generate UDP encapsulated messages. In some situations, a host will not originate a message unless it has heard from the router. To configure the router to generate UDP encapsulated RSVP multicasts, use the command

ip rsvp udp-multicast *multicast-address*

RSVP Scenarios

In this section, various RSVP scenarios are presented to illustrate the use of the RSVP configuration and monitoring commands. Another purpose is to present examples of different combinations of RSVP styles and verify that the router that is the merge point does indeed merge, as presented earlier in the chapter. The first scenarios involve one receiver and one sender, with the receiver requesting either a WF, FF, or SE style reservation. The configurations used do not need any actual multicast senders or receivers. These configurations are meant for you to configure in your own lab for the purpose of practicing and understanding the commands. Senders and receivers will be simulated using the IP_RSVP_SENDER and IP_RSVP_RESERVATION commands. The initial configuration for the network in Figure 10-38 is shown in Listings 10-1 through 10-3.

The initial configurations for routers A, B, and C do not contain any RSVP configuration commands. Initially ip multicast routing and PIM-DM has been configured. Also, the simulated sender and receiver will be located on the loopback interfaces. Since both RSVP and PIM-DM relay on the ip unicast routing table, EIGRP has been enabled on all routers. The first RSVP configuration step is to enable RSVP on all interfaces using the command

ip rsvp bandwidth *interface-kbps single-flow-kbps*

Figure 10-38

Network for RSVP configuration examples containing a single source and a single reservation

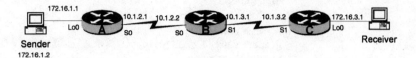

LISTING 10-1

Initial configuration for single server single reservation scenarios— router A

```
hostname A
!
ip multicast-routing
ip dvmrp route-limit 7000
!
interface Loopback0
 ip address 172.16.1.1 255.255.255.0
 ip pim dense-mode
!
interface Serial0
 ip address 10.1.2.1 255.255.255.0
 ip pim dense-mode
!
router eigrp 100
 network 10.0.0.0
 network 172.16.0.0
```

LISTING 10-2

Initial configuration for single server single reservation scenarios— router B

```
hostname B
!
ip multicast-routing
ip dvmrp route-limit 7000
!
interface Loopback0
 ip address 172.16.2.1 255.255.255.0
 ip pim dense-mode
!
interface Serial0
 ip address 10.1.2.2 255.255.255.0
 ip pim dense-mode
 clockrate 1544000
!
interface Serial1
 ip address 10.1.3.1 255.255.255.0
 ip pim dense-mode
 clockrate 15440000
!
router eigrp 100
 network 10.0.0.0
```

LISTING 10-3

Initial configuration
for single server
single reservation
scenarios—
router C

```
hostname C
ip multicast-routing
ip dvmrp route-limit 7000
!
interface Loopback0
 ip address 172.16.3.1 255.255.255.0
 ip pim dense-mode
 ip igmp join-group 224.250.250.1
!
interface Serial1
 ip address 10.1.3.2 255.255.255.0
 ip pim dense-mode
 bandwidth 1544
 no fair-queue
!
router eigrp 100
 network 10.0.0.0
 network 172.16.0.0
```

For these examples we will not use the optional parameters so the form of the command is

ip rsvp bandwidth <CR>

When we use this command on each interface and then list the configuration we can see that the default bandwidth reserved for RSVP is 75 percent of the interface bandwidth. The serial interfaces have been configured for T1 bandwidth, 1.544 Mbits, and 75 percent of 1.544 Mbits is 1.158 Mbit as shown in Listing 10-4. The next step is to simulate the sender on router A with the command

ip rsvp sender 224.250.250.1 172.16.1.2 UDP 20 30 172.16.1.2 Lo0 50 10.

To verify that RSVP Path messages are being sent by router A use the command `show ip rsvp sender` on routers A, B, and C as shown.

```
A#sh ip rsvp sender

To            From         Pro    Dport    Sport    Prev Hop      I/F    BPS    Bytes
224.250.250.1 172.16.1.2   UDP    20       30       172.16.1.2    Lo0    50K    10K
```

```
B#show ip rsvp sender

To            From         Pro    Dport    Sport    Prev Hop     I/F    BPS    Bytes
224.250.250.1 172.16.1.2   UDP    20       30       10.1.2.1     Se0    50K    10K
```

```
C#show ip rsvp sender

To              From        Pro     Dport   Sport   Prev Hop    I/F    BPS    Bytes
224.250.250.1   172.16.1.2  UDP     20      30      10.1.3.1    Se1    50K    10K
```

LISTING 10-4

Enabling RSVP
on the router inter-
faces

```
hostname A
!
interface Loopback0
 ip address 172.16.1.1 255.255.255.0
 ip pim dense-mode
 ip rsvp bandwidth 1705033 1705033

interface Serial0
 ip address 10.1.2.1 255.255.255.0
 ip pim dense-mode
 ip rsvp bandwidth 1158 1158
 fair-queue 64 256 1000

hostname B
!
interface Serial0
 ip address 10.1.2.2 255.255.255.0
 ip pim dense-mode
 ip rsvp bandwidth 1158 1158
 fair-queue 64 256 1000
 clockrate 1544000
!
interface Serial1
 ip address 10.1.3.1 255.255.255.0
 ip pim dense-mode
 ip rsvp bandwidth 1158 1158
 fair-queue 64 256 1000
 clockrate 1544000

hostname C
!
interface Loopback0
 ip address 172.16.3.1 255.255.255.0
 ip pim dense-mode
 ip rsvp bandwidth 1705033 1705033
 ip igmp join-group 224.250.250.1

interface Serial1
 ip address 10.1.3.2 255.255.255.0
 ip pim dense-mode
 ip rsvp bandwidth 1500 1500
 bandwidth 1544
 no fair-queue
```

where

To	IP addresses of the receiver
From	IP Address of the sender
Pro	Protocol code
Dport	Destination port number
Sport	Source port number
Prev Hop	IP address of the previous hop
I/F	Interface of the previous hop
BPS	Reservation rate in bits per second the sender is advertising it might achieve
Bytes	Bytes of the burst size the sender is advertising it might achieve

The final step for the single sender single receiver scenarios is to simulate RSVP Resv messages from the receiver attached to router C using the global command

```
ip rsvp reservation 224.250.250.1 172.16.1.2 UDP 20 30 172.16.3.4
Lo0 WF RATE 100 200
```

The first scenario requests a WF style reservation. The effect of this command can be seen by using the commands show ip rsvp reservation and show ip rsvp request on routers A, B, and C.

```
A#sh ip rsvp request

To            From     Pro    Dport   Sport   Next Hop      I/F    Fi    Serv    BPS    Bytes
224.250.250.1  0.0.0.0  UDP    20      0       172.16.1.2    Lo0    WF    RATE    100K   200K

A#sh ip rsvp reservation

To            From     Pro    Dport   Sport   Next Hop      I/F    Fi    Serv    BPS    Bytes
224.250.250.1  0.0.0.0  UDP    20      0       10.1.2.2      Se0    WF    RATE    100K   200K
```

```
B#sh ip rsvp request

To            From     Pro    Dport   Sport   Next Hop      I/F    Fi    Serv    BPS    Bytes
224.250.250.1  0.0.0.0  UDP    20      0       10.1.2.1      Se0    WF    RATE    100K   200K

B#sh ip rsvp reservation

To            From     Pro    Dport   Sport   Next Hop      I/F    Fi    Serv    BPS    Bytes
224.250.250.1  0.0.0.0  UDP    20      0       10.1.3.2      Se1    WF    RATE    100K   200K
```

```
C#show ip rsvp request

To           From      Pro    Dport   Sport   Next Hop   I/F   Fi   Serv   BPS    Bytes
224.250.250.1 0.0.0.0  UDP    20      0       10.1.3.1   Se1   WF   RATE   100K   200K


C#show ip rsvp reservation

To           From      Pro    Dport   Sport   Next Hop   I/F   Fi   Serv   BPS    Bytes
224.250.250.1 0.0.0.0  UDP    20      0       172.16.3.4 Lo0   WF   RATE   100K   200K
```

The second scenario for the single sender single receiver group is when the receiver requests a FF style reservation. First, remove the WF reservation from router C using the command

no ip rsvp reservation 224.250.250.1 172.16.1.2 UDP 20 30 172.16.3.4 Lo0 WF RATE 100 200

Install the FF Style Reservation on Router C with the Global Command

ip rsvp reservation 224.250.250.1 172.16.1.2 UDP 20 30 172.16.3.4 Lo0 **FF** RATE 100 200

The only change in the command was to replace WF with FF. Verify the reservation by examining routers A, B, and C.

```
A#sh ip rsvp request

To           From        Pro    Dport   Sport   Next Hop   I/F   Fi   Serv   BPS    Bytes
224.250.250.1 172.16.1.2 UDP    20      30      172.16.1.2 Lo0   FF   RATE   100K   200K


A#sh ip rsvp reservation

To           From        Pro    Dport   Sport   Next Hop   I/F   Fi   Serv   BPS    Bytes
224.250.250.1 172.16.1.2 UDP    20      30      10.1.2.2   Se0   FF   RATE   100K   200K
```

```
B#sh ip rsvp request

To           From        Pro    Dport   Sport   Next Hop   I/F   Fi   Serv   BPS    Bytes
224.250.250.1 172.16.1.2 UDP    20      30      10.1.2.1   Se0   FF   RATE   100K   200K


Bash ip rsvp reservation

To           From        Pro    Dport   Sport   Next Hop   I/F   Fi   Serv   BPS    Bytes
224.250.250.1 172.16.1.2 UDP    20      30      10.1.3.2   Se1   FF   RATE   100K   200K
```

```
C#show ip rsvp request

To            From    Pro   Dport  Sport  Next Hop   I/F   Fi   Serv   BPS   Bytes
224.250.250.1 172.16.1.2 UDP  20     30     10.1.3.1   Se1   FF   RATE   100K  200K

C#show ip rsvp reservation

To            From    Pro   Dport  Sport  Next Hop   I/F   Fi   Serv   BPS   Bytes
224.250.250.1 172.16.1.2 UDP  20     30     172.16.3.4 Lo0   FF   RATE   100K  200K
```

Notice that three fields have changed. The most obvious is the reservation style which has changed from WF to FF. The from address was 0.0.0.0 with a source port of 0 for the WF style. With the FF style the from address is 172.16.1.2 with a source port of 30. The WF filter style did not care about the source of the traffic but the FF style does. Finally replace the FF style reservation with the SE style reservation and examine the effect.

ip rsvp reservation 224.250.250.1 172.16.1.2 UDP 20 30 172.16.3.4 Lo0 **SE** RATE 100 200.

```
A#sh ip rsvp request

To            From    Pro   Dport  Sport  Next Hop   I/F   Fi   Serv   BPS   Bytes
224.250.250.1 172.16.1.2 UDP  20     30     172.16.1.2 Lo0   SE   RATE   100K  200K

A#sh ip rsvp reservation

To            From    Pro   Dport  Sport  Next Hop   I/F   Fi   Serv   BPS   Bytes
224.250.250.1 172.16.1.2 UDP  20     30     10.1.2.2   Se0   SE   RATE   100K  200K
```

```
B#sh ip rsvp request

To            From    Pro   Dport  Sport  Next Hop   I/F   Fi   Serv   BPS   Bytes
224.250.250.1 172.16.1.2 UDP  20     30     10.1.2.1   Se0   SE   RATE   100K  200K

B#sh ip rsvp reservation

To            From    Pro   Dport  Sport  Next Hop   I/F   Fi   Serv   BPS   Bytes
224.250.250.1 172.16.1.2 UDP  20     30     10.1.3.2   Se1   SE   RATE   100K  200K
```

```
C#show ip rsvp request

To              From     Pro   Dport   Sport   Next Hop    I/F   Fi   Serv   BPS    Bytes
224.250.250.1   172.16.1.2 UDP  20      30      10.1.3.1    Se1   SE   RATE   100K   200K


C#show ip rsvp reservation

To              From     Pro   Dport   Sport   Next Hop    I/F   Fi   Serv   BPS    Bytes
224.250.250.1   172.16.1.2 UDP  20      30      172.16.3.4  Lo0   FF   RATE   100K   200K
```

Notice that the only change is that FF has changed to SE. Before moving on to the scenarios involving multiple senders and receivers, the rest of the rsvp show commands will be presented. All of the `ip rsvp show` commands can be listed by executing

```
B#show ip rsvp ?
installed       RSVP installed reservations
interface       RSVP interface information
neighbor        RSVP neighbor information
request         RSVP Reservations Upstream
reservation     RSVP Reservation Requests from Downstream
sender          RSVP Path State information
```

The show commands listed above will be demonstrated on router B for the previous scenario.

```
B#show ip rsvp installed ?
Loopback Loopback interface
Null Null interface
Serial Serial
<cr>
```

The `show ip rsvp installed` command has the option of showing all interfaces, if <cr> is chosen, or a particular interface as shown below.

```
B#show ip rsvp installed serial1
RSVP: Serial1
BPS    To            From       Protoc  DPort  Sport  Weight  Conversation
100K   224.250.250.1 172.16.1.2 UDP     20     30     4       264
```

The weight and conversion entries are *Weighed Fair Queueing* (WFQ) parameters. If WFQ is not configured on the interface then these parameters will be zero.

```
B#show ip rsvp interface ?
 Loopback Loopback interface
 Null Null interface
 Serial Serial
 <cr>
```

```
B#show ip rsvp interface Serial1

interfac  allocate  i/f max  flow max  per/255   UDP IP  UDP_IP  UDP M/C
Se1       100K      1158K    1158K     22 /255    0   1    0         0
```

The fields for the `show ip rsvp interface` command are

interfac	interface name
allocate	current allocation
i/f max	maximum bandwidth that can be allocated
flow max	maximum flow possible on the interface
per/255	percent of the bandwidth utilized (22/255 = 8.6 percent)
UDP	number of neighbors sending UDP encapsulated RSVP
IP	number of neighbors sending IP encapsulated RSVP
UDP_IP	number of neighbors sending both UDP and IP encapsulated RSVP
UDP M/C	IS UDP configured on this interface? 0 = no 1 = yes

```
B#show ip rsvp neighbor ?
 Loopback Loopback interface
 Null Null interface
 Serial Serial
 <cr>
```

```
B#show ip rsvp neighbor

Interfac   Neighbor    Encapsulation
Se0        10.1.2.1    RSVP
Se1        10.1.3.2    RSVP
```

The `show ip rsvp neighbor` command simply displays the routers current rsvp neighbors.

Now configure and examine scenarios with multiple receivers and multiple senders for the three RSVP reservation styles. The scenarios that will be configured are listed.

1. Multiple WF requests with a single source.

2. Multiple FF requests with a single source.

3. Multiple SE requests with a single source.

4. Multiple WF requests with multiple sources.

5. Multiple FF requests with multiple sources.

6. Multiple SE requests with multiple sources.

For the first three scenarios involving multiple receivers we need to configure two more receivers on router C.

```
Router C

interface Loopback0
ip address 172.16.3.1 255.255.255.0
ip pim dense-mode
ip rsvp bandwidth 1705033 1705033
ip rsvp udp-multicasts 224.0.0.14
ip igmp join-group 224.250.250.1
!
interface Loopback1
ip address 172.16.5.1 255.255.255.0
ip pim dense-mode
ip rsvp bandwidth 1705033 1705033
ip rsvp udp-multicasts 224.0.0.14
ip igmp join-group 224.250.250.1
!
interface Loopback2
ip address 172.16.4.1
ip pim dense-mode
ip rsvp bandwidth 1705033 1705033
ip rsvp udp-multicasts 224.0.0.14
ip igmp join-group 224.250.250.1
!
ip rsvp reservation 224.250.250.1 0.0.0.0 UDP 20 0 172.16.3.2 Lo0 WF RATE 100 200
ip rsvp reservation 224.250.250.1 0.0.0.0 UDP 20 0 172.16.5.2 Lo1 WF RATE 100 200
ip rsvp reservation 224.250.250.1 0.0.0.0 UDP 20 0 172.16.4.2 Lo2 WF RATE 100 200
```

There are now three WF reservations for the multicast group 224.250.250.1 installed on router C.

Figure 10-39
RSVP scenario with
multiple receivers
and a single source

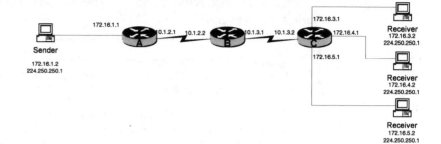

```
C#show ip rsvp reservation

To              From    Pro   Dport  Sport   Next Hop     I/F   Fi   Serv   BPS    Bytes
224.250.250.1   0.0.0.0  UDP   20     0       172.16.3.2   Lo0   WF   RATE   100K   200K
224.250.250.1   0.0.0.0  UDP   20     0       172.16.5.2   Lo1   WF   RATE   100K   200K
224.250.250.1   0.0.0.0  UDP   20     0       172.16.4.2   Lo2   WF   RATE   100K   200K

C#show ip rsvp installed

RSVP: Loopback0
BPS    To             From     Protoc   DPort   Sport
100K   224.250.250.1  0.0.0.0  UDP      20      0
RSVP: Loopback1
BPS    To             From     Protoc   DPort   Sport
100K   224.250.250.1  0.0.0.0  UDP      20      0
RSVP: Loopback2
BPS    To             From     Protoc   DPort   Sport
100K   224.250.250.1  0.0.0.0  UDP      20      0
```

What reservations do you expect to see installed on router B?

```
B#show ip rsvp reservation

To              From    Pro   Dport  Sport   Next Hop   I/F   Fi   Serv   BPS    Bytes
224.250.250.1   0.0.0.0  UDP   20     0       10.1.3.2   Se1   WF   RATE   100K   200K

R4#show ip rsvp installed

RSVP: Serial1
BPS    To             From     Protoc   Dport   Sport   Weight   Conversation
100K   224.250.250.1  0.0.0.0  UDP      20      0       4        264
```

Router B has a reservation that has merged the three WF reservations
from router C.

For the FF case remove the WF reservations and install the FF reservations on router C.

```
no ip rsvp reservation 224.250.250.1 0.0.0.0 UDP 20 0 172.16.3.2 Lo0 WF RATE 100 200
no ip rsvp reservation 224.250.250.1 0.0.0.0 UDP 20 0 172.16.5.2 Lo1 WF RATE 100 200
no ip rsvp reservation 224.250.250.1 0.0.0.0 UDP 20 0 172.16.4.2 Lo2 WF RATE 100 200

ip rsvp reservation 224.250.250.1 0.0.0.0 UDP 20 0 172.16.3.2 Lo0 FF RATE 100 200
ip rsvp reservation 224.250.250.1 0.0.0.0 UDP 20 0 172.16.5.2 Lo1 FF RATE 100 200
ip rsvp reservation 224.250.250.1 0.0.0.0 UDP 20 0 172.16.4.2 Lo2 FF RATE 100 200
```

```
C#show ip rsvp reservation

To            From       Pro   Dport  Sport   Next Hop    I/F   Fi   Serv   BPS    Bytes
224.250.250.1 172.16.1.2 UDP   20     0       172.16.3.2  Lo0   FF   RATE   100K   200K
224.250.250.1 172.16.1.2 UDP   20     0       172.16.5.2  Lo1   FF   RATE   100K   200K
224.250.250.1 172.16.1.2 UDP   20     0       172.16.4.2  Lo2   FF   RATE   100K   200K

C#show ip rsvp installed

RSVP: Loopback0
BPS    To            From         Protoc    Dport    Sport
100K   224.250.250.1 172.16.1.2   UDP       20       0
RSVP: Loopback1
BPS    To            From         Protoc    Dport    Sport
100K   224.250.250.1 172.16.1.2   UDP       20       0
RSVP: Loopback2
BPS    To            From         Protoc    Dport    Sport
100K   224.250.250.1 172.16.1.2   UDP       20       0
```

```
B#show ip rsvp reservation

To            From       Pro   Dport  Sport   Next Hop   I/F   Fi   Serv   BPS    Bytes
224.250.250.1 172.16.1.2 UDP   20     0       10.1.3.2   Se1   FF   RATE   100K   200K

R4#show ip rsvp installed

RSVP: Serial1
BPS    To            From         Protoc    DPort    Sport   Weight   Conversation
100K   224.250.250.1 172.16.1.2   UDP       20       0       4        264
```

As with the WF case, the three FF reservations have been merged into one FF reservation since all reference the same source.

The final single-source multiple-receiver case is the SE style reservation. Configure the SE style on router C using the following commands to verify that the reservations have been installed.

```
no ip rsvp reservation 224.250.250.1 0.0.0.0 UDP 20 0 172.16.3.2 Lo0 FF RATE 100 200
no ip rsvp reservation 224.250.250.1 0.0.0.0 UDP 20 0 172.16.5.2 Lo1 FF RATE 100 200
no ip rsvp reservation 224.250.250.1 0.0.0.0 UDP 20 0 172.16.4.2 Lo2 FF RATE 100 200

ip rsvp reservation 224.250.250.1 0.0.0.0 UDP 20 0 172.16.3.2 Lo0 SE RATE 100 200
ip rsvp reservation 224.250.250.1 0.0.0.0 UDP 20 0 172.16.5.2 Lo1 SE RATE 100 200
ip rsvp reservation 224.250.250.1 0.0.0.0 UDP 20 0 172.16.4.2 Lo2 SE RATE 100 200
```

```
C#show ip rsvp reservation

To            From        Pro   Dport   Sport   Next Hop    I/F    Fi    Serv    BPS     Bytes
224.250.250.1 172.16.1.2  UDP   20      0       172.16.3.2  Lo0    SE    RATE    100K    200K
224.250.250.1 172.16.1.2  UDP   20      0       172.16.5.2  Lo1    SE    RATE    100K    200K
224.250.250.1 172.16.1.2  UDP   20      0       172.16.4.2  Lo2    SE    RATE    100K    200K

C#show ip rsvp installed

RSVP: Loopback0
BPS    To             From        Protoc     DPort     Sport
100K   224.250.250.1  172.16.1.2  UDP        20        0
RSVP: Loopback1
BPS    To             From        Protoc     DPort     Sport
100K   224.250.250.1  172.16.1.2  UDP        20        0
RSVP: Loopback2
BPS    To             From        Protoc     DPort     Sport
100K   224.250.250.1  172.16.1.2  UDP        20        0
```

```
B#show ip rsvp reservation

To            From        Pro   Dport   Sport   Next Hop   I/F    Fi    Serv    BPS     Bytes
224.250.250.1 172.16.1.2  UDP   20      0       10.1.3.2   Se1    SE    RATE    100K    200K

B#sh ip rsvp installed

RSVP: Serial0 has no installed reservations
RSVP: Serial1
BPS    To             From        Protoc     Dport     Sport   Weight   Conversation
100K   224.250.250.1  172.16.1.2  UDP        20        0       4        264
```

Figure 10-40
Multiple sender and
multiple receiver
RSVP scenario

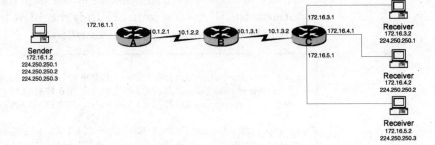

The final three RSVP scenarios involve multiple senders and multiple receivers as shown in Figure 10-40.

The loopback interfaces and reservation requests on router C need to be reconfigured, as do the senders on router A.

```
Router C

interface Loopback0
 ip address 172.16.3.1 255.255.255.0
 ip pim dense-mode
 ip rsvp bandwidth 1705033 1705033
 ip rsvp udp-multicasts 224.0.0.14
 ip igmp join-group 224.250.250.1
!
interface Loopback1
 ip address 172.16.5.1 255.255.255.0
 ip pim dense-mode
 ip rsvp bandwidth 1705033 1705033
 ip rsvp udp-multicasts 224.0.0.14
 ip igmp join-group 224.250.250.2
!
interface Loopback2
 no ip address
 ip pim dense-mode
 ip rsvp bandwidth 1705033 1705033
 ip rsvp udp-multicasts 224.0.0.14
 ip igmp join-group 224.250.250.3

ip rsvp reservation 224.250.250.1 0.0.0.0 UDP 20 0 172.16.3.2 Lo0 WF RATE 100 200
ip rsvp reservation 224.250.250.2 0.0.0.0 UDP 20 0 172.16.4.2 Lo1 WF RATE 100 200
ip rsvp reservation 224.250.250.3 0.0.0.0 UDP 20 0 172.16.5.2 Lo2 WF RATE 100 200


Router A

ip rsvp sender 224.250.250.1 172.16.1.2 UDP 20 30 172.16.1.2 Lo0 50 10
ip rsvp sender 224.250.250.2 172.16.1.2 UDP 20 30 172.16.1.2 Lo0 50 10
ip rsvp sender 224.250.250.3 172.16.1.2 UDP 20 30 172.16.1.2 Lo0 50 10
```

```
A#show ip rsvp sender
```

To	From	Pro	Dport	Sport	Prev Hop	I/F	BPS	Bytes
224.250.250.1	172.16.1.2	UDP	20	30	172.16.1.2	Lo0	50K	10K
224.250.250.2	172.16.1.2	UDP	20	30	172.16.1.2	Lo0	50K	10K
224.250.250.3	172.16.1.2	UDP	20	30	172.16.1.2	Lo0	50K	10K

```
C#show ip rsvp reservation
```

To	From	Pro	DPort	Sport	Next Hop	I/F	Fi	Serv	BPS	Bytes
224.250.250.1	0.0.0.0	UDP	20	0	172.16.3.2	Lo0	WF	RATE	100K	200K
224.250.250.2	0.0.0.0	UDP	20	0	172.16.4.2	Lo1	WF	RATE	100K	200K
224.250.250.3	0.0.0.0	UDP	20	0	172.16.5.2	Lo2	WF	RATE	100K	200K

```
B#show ip rsvp reservation
```

To	From	Pro	DPort	Sport	Next Hop	I/F	Fi	Serv	BPS	Bytes
224.250.250.1	0.0.0.0	UDP	20	0	10.1.3.2	Se1	WF	RATE	100K	200K
224.250.250.2	0.0.0.0	UDP	20	0	10.1.3.2	Se1	WF	RATE	100K	200K
224.250.250.3	0.0.0.0	UDP	20	0	10.1.3.2	Se1	WF	RATE	100K	200K

```
B#sh ip rsvp installed
```

```
RSVP: Serial1
```

BPS	To	From	Protoc	DPort	Sport	Weight	Conversation
100K	224.250.250.3	0.0.0.0	UDP	20	0	4	266
100K	224.250.250.2	0.0.0.0	UDP	20	0	4	265
100K	224.250.250.1	0.0.0.0	UDP	20	0	4	264

```
ip rsvp reservation 224.250.250.1 172.16.1.2 UDP 20 0 172.16.3.2 Lo0 FF RATE 100 200
ip rsvp reservation 224.250.250.2 172.16.1.2 UDP 20 0 172.16.4.2 Lo1 FF RATE 100 200
ip rsvp reservation 224.250.250.3 172.16.1.2 UDP 20 0 172.16.5.2 Lo2 FF RATE 100 200
```

```
C#show ip rsvp reservation
```

To	From	Pro	Dport	Sport	Next Hop	I/F	Fi	Serv	BPS	Bytes
224.250.250.1	172.16.1.2	UDP	20	0	172.16.3.2	Lo0	FF	RATE	100K	200K
224.250.250.2	172.16.1.2	UDP	20	0	172.16.3.2	Lo1	FF	RATE	100K	200K
224.250.250.3	172.16.1.2	UDP	20	0	172.16.3.2	Lo2	FF	RATE	100K	200K

```
C#show ip rsvp installed
```

```
RSVP: Loopback0
```

BPS	To	From	Protoc	Dport	Sport
100K	224.250.250.1	172.16.1.2	UDP	20	0

```
RSVP: Loopback1
```

BPS	To	From	Protoc	Dport	Sport
100K	224.250.250.2	172.16.1.2	UDP	20	0

```
RSVP: Loopback2
```

BPS	To	From	Protoc	DPort	Sport
100K	224.250.250.3	172.16.1.2	UDP	20	0

B#show ip rsvp reservation

To	From	Pro	Dport	Sport	Next Hop	I/F	Fi	Serv	BPS	Bytes
224.250.250.1	172.16.1.2	UDP	20	0	10.1.3.2	Se1	FF	RATE	100K	200K
224.250.250.2	172.16.1.2	UDP	20	0	10.1.3.2	Se1	FF	RATE	100K	200K
224.250.250.3	172.16.1.2	UDP	20	0	10.1.3.2	Se1	FF	RATE	100K	200K

B#show ip rsvp installed

RSVP: Serial1

BPS	To	From	Protoc	Dport	Sport	Weight	Conversation
100K	224.250.250.3	172.16.1.2	UDP	20	0	4	266
100K	224.250.250.2	172.16.1.2	UDP	20	0	4	265
100K	224.250.250.1	172.16.1.2	UDP	20	0	4	264

ip rsvp reservation 224.250.250.1 172.16.1.2 UDP 20 0 172.16.3.2 Lo0 SE RATE 100 200
ip rsvp reservation 224.250.250.2 172.16.1.2 UDP 20 0 172.16.3.2 Lo1 SE RATE 100 200
ip rsvp reservation 224.250.250.3 172.16.1.2 UDP 20 0 172.16.3.2 Lo2 SE RATE 100 200

C#show ip rsvp reservation

To	From	Pro	Dport	Sport	Next Hop	I/F	Fi	Serv	BPS	Bytes
224.250.250.1	172.16.1.2	UDP	20	0	172.16.3.2	Lo0	SE	RATE	100K	200K
224.250.250.2	172.16.1.2	UDP	20	0	172.16.3.2	Lo1	SE	RATE	100K	200K
224.250.250.3	172.16.1.2	UDP	20	0	172.16.3.2	Lo2	SE	RATE	100K	200K

C#show ip rsvp installed

RSVP: Loopback0

BPS	To	From	Protoc	Dport	Sport
100K	224.250.250.1	172.16.1.2	UDP	20	0

RSVP: Loopback1

BPS	To	From	Protoc	Dport	Sport
100K	224.250.250.2	172.16.1.2	UDP	20	0

RSVP: Loopback2

BPS	To	From	Protoc	Dport	Sport
100K	224.250.250.3	172.16.1.2	UDP	20	0

B#show ip rsvp reservation

To	From	Pro	Dport	Sport	Next Hop	I/F	Fi	Serv	BPS	Bytes
224.250.250.1	172.16.1.2	UDP	20	0	10.1.3.2	Se1	SE	RATE	100K	200K
224.250.250.2	172.16.1.2	UDP	20	0	10.1.3.2	Se1	SE	RATE	100K	200K
224.250.250.3	172.16.1.2	UDP	20	0	10.1.3.2	Se1	SE	RATE	100K	200K

B#show ip rsvp installed

RSVP: Serial1

BPS	To	From	Protoc	DPort	Sport	Weight	Conversation
100K	224.250.250.3	172.16.1.2	UDP	20	0	4	266
100K	224.250.250.2	172.16.1.2	UDP	20	0	4	265
100K	224.250.250.1	172.16.1.2	UDP	20	0	4	264

```
                    B#show ip rsvp res
To              From        Pro   Dport   Sport   Next Hop    I/F   Fi   Serv    BPS    Bytes
224.250.250.1   172.16.1.2  UDP   20      0       172.16.3.2  Lo0   SE   RATE    100K   200K
224.250.250.2   172.16.1.2  UDP   20      0       172.16.3.2  Lo1   FF   RATE    100K   200K
224.250.250.3   0.0.0.0     UDP   20      0       172.16.3.2  Lo2   WF   RATE    100K   200K

                    RSVP: Serial0 has no installed reservations
                    RSVP: Serial1
                    BPS     To              From        Protoc   Dport   Sport   Weight   Conversation
                    100K    224.250.250.3   0.0.0.0     UDP      20      0       4        266
                    100K    224.250.250.2   172.16.1.2  UDP      20      0       4        265
                    100K    224.250.250.1   172.16.1.2  UDP      20      0       4        264

                    ip rsvp reservation 224.250.250.1 172.16.1.2 UDP 20 0 172.16.3.2 Lo0 SE RATE 100 200
                    ip rsvp reservation 224.250.250.2 172.16.1.2 UDP 20 0 172.16.3.2 Lo1 FF RATE 100 200
                    ip rsvp reservation 224.250.250.3 0.0.0.0 UDP 20 0 172.16.3.2 Lo2 WF RATE 100 200
```

Debugging RSVP

To verify the operation of RSVP use the following debug commands.

```
B#debug ip rsvp

RSVP debugging is on
B#

RSVP: Sending RESV message for 224.250.250.3
RSVP: send reservation to 10.1.2.1 about 224.250.250.3
RSVP: IP to 10.1.2.1 length=108 checksum=4DA7 (null)
RSVP: send path multicast about 224.250.250.2 on Serial1
RSVP: IP to 224.250.250.2 length=172 checksum=567F (Serial1)
RSVP: RESV message for 224.250.250.2 (Serial1) from 10.1.3.2
RSVP: PATH message for 224.250.250.2(Serial0) from 10.1.2.1
RSVP: send path multicast about 224.250.250.2 on Serial1
RSVP: IP to 224.250.250.2 length=172 checksum=567F (Serial1)
RSVP: Sending RESV message for 224.250.250.1
RSVP: send reservation to 10.1.2.1 about 224.250.250.1
RSVP: IP to 10.1.2.1 length=108 checksum=5393 (null)
RSVP: Sending RESV message for 224.250.250.2
RSVP: send reservation to 10.1.2.1 about 224.250.250.2
RSVP: IP to 10.1.2.1 length=108 checksum=4DA8 (null)
RSVP: send path multicast about 224.250.250.3 on Serial1
RSVP: IP to 224.250.250.3 length=172 checksum=567E (Serial1)
RSVP: PATH message for 224.250.250.3(Serial0) from 10.1.2.1
RSVP: send path multicast about 224.250.250.3 on Serial1
RSVP: IP to 224.250.250.3 length=172 checksum=567E (Serial1)
RSVP: send path multicast about 224.250.250.1 on Serial1
RSVP: IP to 224.250.250.1 length=172 checksum=5680 (Serial1)
```

```
RSVP: PATH message for 224.250.250.1(Serial0) from 10.1.2.1
RSVP: send path multicast about 224.250.250.1 on Serial1
RSVP: IP to 224.250.250.1 length=172 checksum=5680 (Serial1)
RSVP: RESV message for 224.250.250.1 (Serial1) from 10.1.3.2
RSVP: RESV message for 224.250.250.3 (Serial1) from 10.1.3.2


B#debug ip rsvp detail ?
<1–99> Access list
path RSVP packet contents (PATH only)
resv RSVP packet contents (RESV only)
<cr>


B#debug ip rsvp detail path ?
<1–99> Access list
<cr>
```

Detailed debug information can be gathered using the detail form of the RSVP debug command for either Path or RESV debugging.

```
B#debug ip rsvp detail path
RSVP debugging is on
B#
RSVP: IP to 10.1.2.1 length=108 checksum=4DA8 (null)
RSVP: IP to 10.1.2.1 length=108 checksum=5393 (null)
RSVP: message received from 172.16.1.2
RSVP: version:1 flags:0000 type:PATH cksum:0000 ttl:62 reserved:0 length:172
  SESSION              type 1 length 12: E0FAFA03
                       : 11000014
  HOP                  type 1 length 12: 0A010201
                       : 00000000
  TIME_VALUES          type 1 length 8 : 00007530
  SENDER_TEMPLATE      type 1 length 12: AC100102
                       : 0000001E
  SENDER_TSPEC type 2 length 36:
version=0 length in words=7
service id=1 service length=6
parameter id=127 flags=0 parameter length=5
average rate=6250 bytes/sec burst depth=10000 bytes peak rate=193000 bytes/sec
min unit=0 bytes max unit=1514 bytes
  ADSPEC type 2 length 84:
version=0 length in words=19
General Parameters break bit=0 service length=8
IS Hops:1
Minimum Path Bandwidth (bytes/sec):193000
Path Latency (microseconds):0
Path MTU:1500
Guaranteed Service break bit=0 service length=8
Path Delay (microseconds):3000
Path Jitter (microseconds):7772
Path delay since shaping (microseconds):3000
Path Jitter since shaping (microseconds):7772
```

```
                          Controlled Load Service break bit=0 service length=0

                     B#debug ip rsvp detail resv
                     RSVP debugging is on
                     B#
                     RSVP: Sending RESV message for 224.250.250.1
                     RSVP: send reservation to 10.1.2.1 about 224.250.250.1
                     RSVP: IP to 10.1.2.1 length=108 checksum=5393 (null)
                     RSVP: version:1 flags:0000 type:RESV cksum:5393 ttl:255 reserved:0 length:108
                      SESSION type 1 length 12: E0FAFA01
                      : 11000014
                      HOP type 1 length 12: 0A010202
                      : 00000000
                      TIME_VALUES type 1 length 8 : 00007530
                      STYLE type 1 length 8 : 00000012
                      FLOWSPEC type 2 length 48:
                       version = 0 length in words = 10
                       service id = 2 service length = 9
                       tspec parameter id = 127 tspec flags = 0 tspec length = 5
                       average rate = 12500 bytes/sec burst depth = 200000 bytes peak rate = 12
                     500 bytes/sec
                       min unit = 0 bytes max unit = 65535 bytes
                      rspec parameter id=130 rspec flags=0 rspec length=2
                      requested rate=12500 slack=0
                      FILTER_SPEC type 1 length 12: AC100102
                      : 00000000
```

Finally, reservations on a router can be cleared by using the `clear ip rsvp` command.

```
                     B#clear ip rsvp ?
                     reservation Clear RSVP reservations
                     sender Clear RSVP path state information

                     B#clear ip rsvp res ?
                     ' Clear all reservations
                     Hostname or A.B.C.D Destination address

                     B#clear ip rsvp res '
```

APPENDIX A

Cisco Multicast Command Reference

Internet Group Management Protocol

Interface Configuration Commands

---

ip igmp access-group *access-list-number* [*version*]
no ip igmp access-group *access-list-number* [*version*]

---

access-list-number	The IP standard access-list number (1–99).
version	Optional. This changes the IGMP version number. The default is 2.
IOS Version	10.2

EXAMPLE

Configure the ethernet 0 interface on a router so that hosts can only join multicast groups 239.0.0.0 through 239.255.255.255.

```
interface ethernet 0
 ip igmp access-group 1

access-list 1 permit 239.0.0.0 0.255.255.255
```

---

ip igmp helper-address *ip-address*
no ip igmp helper-address *ip-address*

---

ip-address	The IP address where IGMP Host Reports and Leave messages are forwarded.
IOS Version	11.3

```
ip igmp join-group group-address
no ip igmp join-group group-address
```

group-address   The Multicast group IP address. Packets are process-switched.

IOS Version   10.2

EXAMPLE

Configure interface ethernet 0 to join the multicast group 225.250.250.1.

```
interface ethernet 0
ip igmp join-group 225.250.250.1
```

```
ip igmp query-interval seconds
no ip igmp query-interval seconds
```

seconds   The number of seconds between host-query messages. Its value can be between 0 and 65535.

IOS Version   10.2

EXAMPLE

Change the query interface on interface serial 0 to three minutes.

```
interface serial 0
 ip igmp query-interval 180
```

```
ip igmp query-max-response-time seconds
no ip igmp query-max-response-time seconds
```

seconds   The maximum response time that is advertised in IGMP queries.

IOS Version   11.1

EXAMPLE

Configure the maximum response time on interface ethernet 0 to 15 seconds.

```
interface ethernet 0
 ip igmp query-max-response-time 15
```

> **ip igmp query-timeout** *seconds*
> **no ip igmp query-timeout** *seconds*

seconds   The number of seconds a non-querier router will wait before
                taking over as querier if the current querier times out.

IOS Version   11.1

EXAMPLE

Change the query timeout value to 60 seconds on interface serial 1.

```
interface serial
 ip igmp query-interval 30
 ip igmp query-timeout 60
```

> **ip igmp static-group** *group-address*
> **no ip igmp static-group** *group-address*

group-address   The group IP multicast address. Packets are fast-switched.

IOS Version   11.2

EXAMPLE

Configure interface ethernet 0 to join the multicast group 225.250.250.1.

```
interface ethernet 0
ip igmp static-group 225.250.250.1
```

> **ip igmp version** {2 | 1 }
> **no ip igmp version** {2 | 1 }

IOS Version   11.1

EXAMPLE ▪ ▪ ▪ ▪ ▪ ▪ ▪ ▪ ▪

Configure the ethernet 0 interface to use IGMP version 1. If version 1 is configured on an interface, then the commands `ip igmp query-max-response-time` and `ip igmp query-timeout` cannot be used because they are version 2-specific.

```
interface ethernet 0
  ip igmp version 1
```

Cisco Group Management Protocol Commands

Router Commands Command	Description
ip cgmp	Enables CGMP on an interface or subinterface
ip cgmp proxy	Enables CGMP and DVMRP proxy on an interface or subinterface
clear ip cgmp [*interface*]	Clears all CGMP groups
show ip igmp interface [*interface*]	Shows if CGMP is enabled on an interface
debug ip cgmp	Debugs CGMP traffic
Switch Commands Command	**Description**
set cgmp enable	Enables CGMP on the switch
set cgmp disable	Disables CGMP on the switch
show multicast router	Lists the ports on the switch that are router ports
show multicast group	Displays active groups
clear cgmp statistics	Clears the CGMP statistics
debug ip cgmp	Debugs CGMP traffic

Distance Vector Multicast Routing Protocol Commands

Global Configuration

> **ip dvmrp distance** *admin-distance*
> **no ip dvmrp distance** *admin-distance*

admin-distance   The default administrative distance (0—255).

IOS Version   11.2

This command configures the default administrative distance for received DVMRP routes. It should be used so that routes advertised from the unicast routing table that are reflected back through DVMRP cause the original unicast routes to continue to be advertised. The **ip dvmrp accept-filter** command can override this value when specified on an interface.

> **ip dvmrp route-hog-notification** *count*
> **no ip dvmrp route-hog-notification** *count*

count   Number of routes allowed before a syslog message is sent. The default is 10,000 routes.

IOS Version   10.2

This global command places a limit on the number of routes that can be advertised over a DVMRP-enabled interface, including tunnels, during a one-minute interval.

> **ip dvmrp route-limit** *count*
> **no ip dvmrp route-limit** *count*

count   The number of DVMRP routes that can be advertised. The default value is 7000.

IOS Version   11.0

Interface Configuration Commands

---
ip dvmrp accept-filter *access-list-number* [*distance*] **neighbor-list** *access-list-number*
no ip dvmrp accept-filter *access-list-number* [*distance*] **neighbor-list** *access-list-number*

---

access-list-number	The IP standard access list number (0–99). If 0, then all sources are accepted with the value of *distance*.
distance	Optional. The administrative distance of the reported route.
neighbor-list *access-list-number*	Reports are only accepted from neighbors in the list.
IOS Version	10.2

---
ip dvmrp auto-summary

IOS Version   11.2

This interface command is enabled by default. Auto-summarization is when subnets are advertised as a classful network number. To turn off this feature, use the **no** form of the command.

---
ip dvmrp default-information {originate | only}
no ip dvmrp default-information {originate | only}

---

originate	Routes more specific than the default route (0.0.0.0) can be advertised.
only	Only the default route (0.0.0.0) is advertised.
IOS Version	10.2

This interface command is used to advertise the default network 0.0.0.0 to the DVMRP neighbor on the interface. The **originate** option allows more specific routes to be advertised. The **only** keyword prevents other routes from being advertised. Do not use this command to create a default route to the MBONE.

---
ip dvmrp metric *metric* [**list** *access-list*] {[*protocol process-id*] | **dvmrp**]
ip dvmrp metric *metric* **route-map** *map-name*
no ip dvmrp metric *metric* [**list** *access-list*] {[*protocol process-id*] | **dvmrp**]
no ip dvmrp metric *metric* **route-map** *map-name*

---

metric	The metric to be used for the routes in the DVMRP route report. Its value can be between 0 and 32. A value of 0 prevents a route or routes from being advertised. A value of 32 indicates infinity or an unreachable value.
list *access-list*	Optional. A standard IP access list can be used to control which routes are reported.
protocol	Optional. The unicast routing protocol name (rip, igrp, eigrp, ospf, bgp, isis, static, or dvmrp).
process-id	Optional. The unicast routing protocol process ID.
dvmrp	Optional. This allows routes in the DVMRP routing table to be filtered or have their metric adjusted..
route-map *map-name*	This filters the unicast routes that are reported using a route map..
IOS Version:	10.2. Route Map added in 11.1.

---

ip dvmrp metric-offset [in | out] *increment*
no ip dvmrp metric-offset [in | out] *increment*

---

in	Optional. The value of *increment* is added to routes in incoming DVMRP route reports. The default *increment* for **in** is 1.
out	Optional. The value of the *increment* is added to routes in outgoing DVMRP reports. The default *increment* for **out** is 0.
increment	Value added to the routes in a DVMRP route report.
IOS Version	11.0

Use this interface command to adjust the metric of DVMRP routes being received on an interface (in) or reported to a neighbor (out). The default value when applied to incoming routes is 1 and the default value applied to outgoing routes is 0. Be careful, this command adds the same metric to all incoming or outgoing routes.

---

ip dvmrp output-report-delay *delay-time* [*burst*]
no ip dvmrp output-report-delay *delay-time* [*burst*]

---

delay-time	The number of milliseconds between DVMRP route reports.
burst	Optional. The number of packets in a set of route reports. The default value is 2.
IOS Version	11.2

Use this interface command to pace the route reports to a neighbor.

```
ip dvmrp reject-non-pruners
no ip dvmrp reject-non-pruners
```

IOS Version   11.0

This interface command prevents peering with a DVMRP neighbor that does not support pruning and grafting.

```
ip dvmrp summary-address address mask [metric value]
no ip dvmrp summary-address address mask [metric value]
```

address   The summary IP address that is advertised.

mask   The mask for the summary address.

metric *value* Optional. The metric that is advertised for the summary address. The default metric is 1.

IOS Version   11.2

Used on an interface to summarize addresses in a route report.

```
tunnel mode dvmrp
no tunnel mode dvmrp
```

IOS Version   10.2

This configures a Cisco tunnel to encapsulate IP using protocol number 4. This mode can be used when a Cisco connects to a mrouted machine to run DVMRP over a tunnel. This is a popular way to connect to the MBONE. It is required to configure PIM and an IP address on a DVMRP tunnel. This mode is not used to construct a tunnel between a pair of Cisco routers.

```
ip dvmrp unicast-routing.
no ip dvmrp unicast-routing.
```

IOS Version   10.3

Enables the exchange of DVMRP routes between routers.

Protocol Independent Multicast Commands

Global Configuration Commands

> **ip pim accept-rp** {*address* | **auto-rp**} [*access-list-number*]
> **no ip pim accept-rp** {*address* | **auto-rp**} [*access-list-number*]

address	The address of the RP.
auto-rp	Messages are accepted only for RPs that are in the Auto-RP cache.
access-list-number	Optional. Defines the groups that are allowed.
IOS Version	11.1

This command causes the router to accept only Join and Prune messages destined for the specified RP. If an access-list is used, then the group must also be allowed by the list.

> **ip pim bsr-candidate** *interface-type interface-number hash-mask-length* [*priority*]
> **no ip pim bsr-candidate** *interface-type interface-number hash-mask-length*
> [*priority*]

interface-type interface-number:	The address of the specified interface identifies the BSR.
hash-mask-length	The length of the mask (32 bits maximum) that is ANDed with the group address before the hash function is called. All groups with the same seed correspond to the same RP. If the value is 24, then only the first 24 bits of the group address are used. Therefore, one RP can have multiple groups.
priority	Optional. Its value can be from 0 to 255. The BSR candidate with the largest priority is preferred. If BSR candidates have the same priority, the one with the highest IP address is elected as the BSR.
IOS Version	11.3T

This command causes the router to send Bootstrap messages to PIM neighbors.

```
ip pim register-rate-limit pps
no ip pim register-rate-limit pps
```

pps   The packet per second rate limit.

IOS Version   11.3T

Sets a limit on the maximum number of data registers per second sent for each (S,G).

```
ip pim rp-address ip-address [access-list-number] [override]
no ip pim rp-address ip-address [access-list-number] [override]
```

ip-address   The IP address of the RP.

access-list-number   Optional. The standard IP access list number from 1–100. If no access list is used, then the RP can handle all groups. Use an access list to limit the groups that the RP will service.

override   Optional. If there is a conflict between the static RP and one configured using Auto-RP, then the static RP takes precedence.

IOS Version   10.2 **override** keyword–11.2

```
ip pim rp-announce-filter rp-list access-list-number group-list access-list number
no ip pim rp-announce-filter rp-list access-list-number group-list access-list number
```

rp-list *access-list-number*   The standard access list of RP addresses from which Auto-RP announcements are accepted.

group-list *access-list-number*   The standard access list of group addresses that are accepted.

IOS Version   11.1

For example, to configure an RP mapping agent to accept Auto-RP announcements from the RP with address 172.16.1.1 for all multicast groups, use

```
ip pim rp-announce-filter rplist 12 group-list 13
access-list 12 permit 172.16.1.1
access-list 13 permit 224.0.0.0 15.255.255.255
```

> **ip pim rp-candidate** *interface-type interface-number* [**group-list** *access-list-number*]
> **no ip pim rp-candidate** *interface-type interface-number* [**group-list** *access-list-number*]

interface-type interface-number	The address of the specified interface identifies the candidate RP.
group-list *access-list-number*	Optional. The standard IP access list that determines the groups that the candidate RP advertises.
IOS Version	11.3T

To configure a candidate RP that will advertise any multicast group starting with 227, the following command can be used.

```
ip pim rp-candidate serial 1 group-list 51
access-list 51 permit 227.0.0.0 0.255.255.255
```

> **ip pim send-rp-announce** *interface-type interface-number* **scope** *ttl*
> **group-list** *access-list-number*
> **no ip pim send-rp-announce** *interface-type interface-number* **scope** *ttl*
> **group-list** *access-list-number*

interface-type interface-number	The address of the specified interface identifies the RP.
scope	The TTL value of the announcements that limits the distance an RP announcement can travel.
access-list-number	An access list determines the groups that the RP is announcing it can service.
IOS Version	11.1

The router sends RP announcements on all PIM-enabled interfaces for a maximum number of hops specified by the scope parameter. The announcements are sent to the group CISCO-RP-ANNOUNCE (224.0.1.39).

> **ip pim send-rp-discovery scope** *ttl*
> **no ip pim send-rp-discovery scope** *ttl*

scope	The TTL of the discovery messages. Used to limit the scope of the message.
IOS Version	11.1

The router configured as a mapping agent listens for RP announcements to group CISCO-RP-ANNOUNCE (224.0.1.39). The RP mapping agent then sends the RP-to-group mappings to the group CISCO-RP-DISCOVERY (224.0.1.40) and PIM routers get their RP information from the discovery messages.

```
ip pim spt-threshold {kbps | infinity} [group-list access-list-number]
no ip pim spt-threshold {kbps | infinity} [group-list access-list-number]
```

kbps	The traffic rate in kilobits per second.
infinity	The specified groups will use the shared-tree.
group-list *access-list-number*	Optional. This determines which groups to apply the threshold to.
IOS Version	11.1

Interface Configuration Commands

```
ip pim border
no ip pim border
```

IOS Version   11.3T

This command is used to configure a bootstrap border router.

```
ip pim dense-mode
ip pim sparse-mode
ip pim sparse-dense-mode
no ip pim dense-mode
no ip pim sparse-mode
no ip pim sparse-dense-mode
```

IOS Version   Dense and Sparse mode, 10.2 Sparse-dense mode, 11.1

This command enables PIM on an interface.

```
ip pim minimum-vc-rate pps
no ip pim minimum-vc-rate pps
```

pps   This sets the minimum packets per second rate to the value given by *pps*.

IOS Version   11.3

This configures the activity level that determines whether VCs will be considered for deletion. If the number of VCs open already equals the maximum number allowed, then packets for new groups are sent over the static multicast VC.

```
ip pim multipoint-signaling
no ip pim multipoint-signaling
```

IOS Version   11.3

This enables the use of multipoint VCs per multicast group.

```
ip pim nbma-mode
no ip pim nbma-mode
```

Only receivers that have joined a particular multicast group receive packets for that group. Use this with PIM-Sparse mode and configure the hub router to be the RP.

```
ip pim neighbor-filter access-list
no ip pim neighbor-filter access-list
```

access-list   The standard IP access list number.

IOS Version   11.3

This filters PIM control messages based on the given access list. It does not filter Auto-RP announcements and is used with Sparse mode PIM on a non-broadcast multi-access network. Multicast packets will only be sent to neighbors that have joined the group.

```
ip pim query-interval seconds
no ip pim query-interval seconds
```

seconds   1–65535 seconds.

IOS Version   10.2

The following command changes the PIM query interval to 60 seconds.

```
interface Serial 0
 ip pim query-interval 60
```

---

ip pim vc-count *number*
no ip pim vc-count *number*

---

number   The maximum number of VCs that PIM can open. The default value is 200.

IOS Version   11.3

---

ip pim version [1 | 2]
no ip pim version [1 | 2]

IOS Version   11.3T

This sets the PIM version number.

---

ip pim message-interval *seconds*

---

seconds   A value in the range from 1 to 65535.

By default, a PIM-SM router sends periodic Join/Prune messages every 60 seconds.

Show and Debug Commands

---

debug ip pim [*group-name-or-address*]

---

group-name-or-address   Optional. This is the group IP address or configured name.

IOS Version   10.2

This displays PIM packets received and transmitted as well as PIM-related events.

---

debug ip pim auto-rp

IOS Version   11.1

This displays Auto-RP packet activity.

> **debug ip pim atm**

IOS Version   11.3

This displays PIM ATM signaling activity.

Multicast Support Commands

Global Commands

> **ip multicast-routing** [*distributed*]
> **no ip multicast-routing**

distributed   This enables distributed fast-switching,.

IOS Version   10.2. *distributed,* added in 11.2

This enables IP multicast forwarding. If disabled, multicast packets are discarded.

> **ip multicast cache-headers** [*rtp*] [*entries*]
> **no ip multicast cache-headers** [*rtp*] [*entries*]

rtp   RTP headers are cached.

entries   The number of cache entries. The number is interpreted as a power of two.

IOS Version   11.1

This allocates a circular buffer to store IP multicast packet headers received by the router. This command allocates a buffer of approximately 32-kilobytes.

> **ip mroute** *source mask* [*protocol process-number*] [**route-map** *map*]
> *rpf-address* | *interface* [*distance*]
> **no ip mroute** *source mask* [*protocol process-number*] [**route-map** *map*]
> *rpf-address* | *interface* [*distance*]

source mask	The IP address/mask of the multicast source.
protocol	Optional. The unicast routing mode (OSPF, EIGRP, etc.).
process-number	Optional. The process number of the routing protocol that is being used.
rpf-address	The incoming interface for the mroute. If the Reverse Path Forwarding address rpf-address is a PIM neighbor, PIM Joins, Grafts, and Prunes are sent.
interface	The interface type and number for the mroute (ethernet 0 , serial 1, etc.).
distance	Optional. This determines whether a unicast route, a DVMRP route, or a static mroute should be used for the RPF lookup. The lower distances have better preference. If the static mroute has the same distance as the other two RPF sources, the static mroute takes precedence. The default is 0.
IOS Version	11.0

This configures a multicast static route (static mroute).

---

ip sdr cache-timeout *minutes*

---

minutes	The amount of time an SDR cache entry stays active in the cache. A value of 0 indicates the entry never expires. The default value is 24 hours.
IOS Version	11.2

Interface Commands

---

ip multicast ttl-threshold *ttl-value*

---

ttl-value	TTL threshold value.
IOS Version	10.2

The TTL-threshold is applied to all outgoing multicast traffic. If the TTL value of a multicast packet is less than the threshold, the packets are not forwarded. The default value is 0, so all multicast packets are forwarded.

> **ip multicast rate-limit in | out [video] | [whiteboard] [group-list** *access-list*]
> [**source-list** *access-list*] [*kbps*]

in
Only packets at the rate of kbps or slower are accepted on the interface.

out
Only a maximum of kbps are transmitted on the interface.

video
Optional. Rate limiting is performed based on the UDP port number used by video traffic, which is identified by consulting the SDR cache.

whiteboard
Optional. Rate limiting is performed based on the UDP port number used by whiteboard traffic, which is identified by consulting the SDR cache.

group-list *access-list*
Optional. An access list that is used to determine which multicast groups will be constrained by the rate limit.

source-list *access-list*
Optional. An access list that is used to determine which senders will be constrained by the rate limit.

kbps
Rate limit in kilobits per second. Packets sent at a rate greater than *kbps* are discarded. If no value is given, then the default rate is 0 kilobits per second. In this case, no multicast traffic is permitted.

IOS Version   11.0

This command requires that **ip sdr listen** be enabled so port numbers can be obtained from the SDR cache. If SDR is not enabled, then no limiting occurs.

> **ip multicast boundary** *access-list-number*
> **no ip multicast boundary** *access-list-number*

access-list-number   The standard IP access-list (1–99).

IOS Version   11.1

Use the following form of the command on the router attached to the sender or first hop route.

> **ip multicast helper-map broadcast** *multicast-address extended-acl*
> **no ip multicast helper-map broadcast** *multicast-address extended-acl*

broadcast   This specifies the traffic is being converted from broadcast
                       to multicast.

multicast-address   The multicast group address of the traffic that is to be
                       converted to broadcast traffic.

Use the following form of the command on the router attached to the
receiver or last hop router.

---

ip multicast helper-map *group-address IP-broadcast-address extended-acl*
no ip multicast helper-map *group-address IP-broadcast-address extended-acl*

---

group-address   The multicast group address of traffic to be converted to
                       broadcast traffic.

IP-broadcast-address The IP broadcast address to which broadcast traffic is
                       sent.

extended-acl   The IP-extended access list that determines which
                       broadcast packets are to be converted to multicast. Based
                       on the UDP port number.

access-list-number   The IP extended access list that controls which broadcast
                       packets are translated, based on the UDP port number.

IOS Version   11.1

This enables broadcast-to-multicast conversion on the first hop router
and multicast-to-broadcast conversion on the last hop router

---

ip mroute-cache [*distributed*]
no ip mroute-cache [*distributed*]

---

distributed   This enables distributed fast-switching on the interface.

IOS Version   11.0

Multicast packets can either be process-switched or fast-switched on an
interface and this command configures IP multicast fast-switching. The
default setting is when all interfaces are multicast fast-switched.

---

ip sdr listen
no ip sdr listen

IOS Version: 11.1

This command enables the router to accept SDAP packets on the interface and the router joins the multicast group 224.2.127.254. SDR entries are cached on the router and the time that an SDR remains in the cache is configured using the global configuration command.

---

ip multicast use-functional
no ip multicast use-functional

IOS Version   11.1

This enables the use of the MAC address 0xc000.0004.0000 for the transmission and reception of IP Multicast traffic on token ring interfaces.

Clear commands

---

clear ip mroute [*group-name* | *group-address* [*source-address*]] | [*]

IOS Version   10.2.

This deletes entries from the IP multicast routing table

---

clear ip igmp group [*group-name* | *group-address* |*interface-type interface-number*]

---

group-name	Optional. The multicast group name defined either in DNS or by the **ip host** command.
group-address	Optional. The multicast group address.
interface-type *interface-number*	This specifies the interface (Ethernet 0, serial 0, and so on)
IOS Version	10.2

EXAMPLES

To clear a particular group, **clear ip igmp group** 225.250.250.1.
To clear all groups on an interface, **clear ip igmp group** ethernet 0.
To clear all groups, **clear ip igmp group**.

```
clear ip cgmp [interface]
```

IOS Version   11.1

This sends a CGMP Leave message with a group address of 0000.0000.0000 and a unicast address of 0000.0000.0000. This instructs the switches to clear all group entries they have cached. If *interface* is specified, the Leave is sent only on *interface*. Otherwise, it is sent on all CGMP-enabled interfaces.

```
clear ip dvmrp route ˙ | route
```

˙   Deletes all DVMRP routes

route   Deletes a specific DVMRP route.

IOS Version   10.2

Deletes routes from the DVMRP routing table

```
clear ip sdr [group-address | "session-name"]
```

group-address   The address of the group to clear.

session-name   The name of the session to clear.

IOS Version   11.1

Clears an SDR cache entry. If no parameters are given, then the entire SDR cache is cleared.

```
clear ip pim interface [interface] count
```

Clears the multicast packet counters for interface [interface] or clears for all interfaces when [interface] is not specified ([11.2]).

```
clear ip pim auto-rp <rp-address>
```

rp-address   Optional. The address of the RP to clear.

IOS Version   11.2

Clears the Auto-RP cache.

Show Commands

```
show ip pim neighbor [interface]
```

interface   Optional. Interface name and number.

IOS Version   10.2

Displays PIM neighbors.

```
show ip pim vc [group-or-name] [interface]
```

group-or-name   Optional. The IP address of the multicast group or
                   configured name.

interface   Optional. The interface name and number.

IOS Version   11.3

Displays ATM VC status information for multipoint VCs opened by PIM.

```
show ip pim bsr
```

IOS Version   11.3T

Displays *Bootstrap router* (BSR) information.

```
show ip pim rp-hash <group>
```

IOS Version   11.3T

Displays which RP is being selected for the <group>.

```
show ip pim interface [interface-type interface-number] [count]
```

interface-type   Optional. The type and number of the interface (Ethernet
interface-number   0, Serial 1, and so on).

count   Optional. The number of packets that have been sent and received on the interface.

IOS Version   10.2

---

show ip pim rp [*group-name* | *group-address* | **mapping**]

---

group-name   Optional. Shows RPs for the named group.

group-address   Optional. Shows RPs for the group with the entered group address.

mapping   Optional. Displays all group to RP mappings.

IOS Version   10.2

---

show ip mroute [[*group-name* | *group-address*] [*source-address*]] [**summary**]

This displays the IP multicast routing table. When "summary" is specified, a one-line abbreviated display is provided. When "count" is specified, group count, source count, and packet count statistics are provided ([10.2]).

---

show ip mroute [[*group-name* | *group-address*] [*source-address*]] count

---

This displays the packet count per the (S,G) multicast routing table entry. It also includes the average packet size and data rate in kilobits per second ([10.2]).

---

show ip mroute [<*group-name* | *group-address*] **active** [*kbps*]

This command shows you the rate that active sources send to multicast groups. You can display for all groups or specify a single group. [kbps] only displays sources that are sending greater than or equal to itself. The default setting shows all sources sending at a rate greater than or equal to one kilobit per second. If SD is running on the router, the SD session name is displayed ([11.0]).

RSVP Commands

Interface Commands

---

ip rsvp bandwidth *interface-kbps single-flow-kbps*
no ip rsvp bandwidth *interface-kbps single-flow-kbps*

---

interface-kbps	Optional parameter. Its value can be from 1–10,000,000.
single-flow-kbps	Optional parameter. Its value can be 1–10,000,000.

The parameters shown in brackets are optional parameters. The first optional parameter is the total amount of bandwidth that will be reserved on the interface for RSVP flows. The second optional parameter is the amount of bandwidth that can be allocated to a single flow. By default, 75 percent of the bandwidth on an interface can be reserved.

---

ip rsvp neighbors *access-list-number*
no ip rsvp neighbors *access-list-number*

---

access-list-number	Integer from 1 to 199. 1 to 99 for a standard access list. 100 to 199 for an extended access list.

By default, any neighbor can request a reservation on a router interface. If only selected neighbors are to be permitted to request a reservation using RSVP, we would use this interface command for PATH messages:

---

ip rsvp sender *session-ip-address sender-ip-address*
[**tcp**|**udp**|*ip-protocol*] *session-dport sender-sport*
previous-hop-ip-address previous-hop-interface bandwidth burst-size

---

We would use this command for RESV messages:

---

ip rsvp reservation *session-ip-address sender-ip-address*
[**tcp**|**udp**|*ip-protocol*] *session-dport sender-sport*
next-hop-ip-address next-hop-interface
{**ff**|**se**|**wf**} {**rate**|**load**} *bandwidth* burst-size

---

The explanations of the parameters for the two messages are listed below.

session-ip-address	For a unicast session, this is the address of the receiver. For a multicast session, this is the session IP multicast address.
sender-ip-address	The IP address of the sender.
tcp|udp|*ip-protocol*	
session dport	The destination and source port numbers. If one is zero, then it will be session sport; otherwise, both must be zero.
session sport	
previous-hop-ip-address	The address of the sender if the sender is connected to the interface or address of the router interface on the path back to the sender.
previous-hop-interface	The interface type of the previous hop, which can be ethernet, loopback, null, or serial.
next-hop-ip-address	The hostname or address of the receiver, or the address of the router interface on the path back to the receiver.
next-hop-interface	The interface type of the next hop, which can be ethernet, loopback, null, or serial.
ff | se | wf	The reservation style, which can be fixed filter, shared explicit, or wild card.
rate | load	Quality of Service's guaranteed bit rate service or controlled load service.
bandwidth	Optional. The average bit rate (in kbps) to reserve, which can be up to 75 percent of the interface capacity. Its range is from 1 to 10,000,000.
burst-size	Optional. The maximum burst size (in kilobytes of data in the queue). Its range is from 1 to 65,535.

To remove the effect, use the no form of the command.

```
ip rsvp udp-multicast multicast-address
no ip rsvp udp-multicast multicast-address
```

Configures the router to generate UDP-encapsulated RSVP multicasts.

APPENDIX B

Assigned Multicast Addresses

224.0.0.0	Base Address (Reserved)
224.0.0.1	All Systems on This Subnet
224.0.0.2	All Routers on This Subnet
224.0.0.3	Unassigned
224.0.0.4	DVMRP Routers
224.0.0.5	OSPFIGP OSPFIGP All Routers
224.0.0.6	OSPFIGP Designated Routers
224.0.0.7	ST Routers
224.0.0.8	ST Hosts
224.0.0.9	RIP2 Routers
224.0.0.10	IGRP Routers
224.0.0.11	Mobile Agents
224.0.0.12	DHCP Server/Relay Agent
224.0.0.13	All PIM Routers
224.0.0.14	RSVP-ENCAPSULATION
224.0.0.15	All CBT Routers
224.0.0.16	Designated SBM
224.0.0.17	All SBMs
224.0.0.18	VRRP
224.0.0.19–224.0.0.255	Unassigned
224.0.1.0	VMTP Managers Group
224.0.1.1	*Network Time Protocol* (NTP)
224.0.1.2	SGI Dogfight
224.0.1.3	Rwhod
224.0.1.4	VNP
224.0.1.5	Artificial Horizons, Aviator
224.0.1.6	*Name Service Server* (NSS)

224.0.1.7	AUDIONEWS, Audio News Multicast
224.0.1.8	SUN NIS+ Information Service
224.0.1.9	MTP Multicast Transport Protocol
224.0.1.10	IETF−1-LOW-AUDIO
224.0.1.11	IETF−1-AUDIO
224.0.1.12	IETF−1-VIDEO
224.0.1.13	IETF−2-LOW-AUDIO
224.0.1.14	IETF−2-AUDIO
224.0.1.15	IETF−2-VIDEO
224.0.1.16	MUSIC-SERVICE
224.0.1.17	SEANET-TELEMETRY
224.0.1.18	SEANET-IMAGE
224.0.1.19	MLOADD
224.0.1.20	Any Private Experiment
224.0.1.21	DVMRP on MOSPF
224.0.1.22	SVRLOC
224.0.1.23	XINGTV
224.0.1.24	microsoft-ds
224.0.1.25	nbc-pro
224.0.1.26	nbc-pfn
224.0.1.27	lmsc-calren−1
224.0.1.28	lmsc-calren−2
224.0.1.29	lmsc-calren−3
224.0.1.30	lmsc-calren−4]
224.0.1.31	ampr-info
224.0.1.32	mtrace
224.0.1.33	RSVP-encap−1
224.0.1.34	RSVP-encap−2
224.0.1.35	SVRLOC-DA
224.0.1.36	rln-server
224.0.1.37	proshare-mc
224.0.1.38	dantz
224.0.1.39	cisco-rp-announce

224.0.1.40	cisco-rp-discovery
224.0.1.41	gatekeeper
224.0.1.42	iberiagames
224.0.1.43	nwn-discovery
224.0.1.44	nwn-adaptor
224.0.1.45	isma−1
224.0.1.46	isma−2
224.0.1.47	telerate
224.0.1.48	ciena
224.0.1.49	dcap-servers
224.0.1.50	dcap-clients
224.0.1.51	mcntp-directory
224.0.1.52	mbone-vcr-directory
224.0.1.53	heartbeat
224.0.1.54	sun-mc-grp
224.0.1.55	extended-sys
224.0.1.56	pdrncs
224.0.1.57	tns-adv-multi
224.0.1.58	vcals-dmu
224.0.1.59	zuba
224.0.1.60	hp-device-disc
224.0.1.61	tms-production
224.0.1.62	sunscalar
224.0.1.63	mmtp-poll
224.0.1.64	compaq-peer
224.0.1.65	iapp
224.0.1.66	multihasc-com
224.0.1.67	serv-discovery
224.0.1.68	mdhcpdisover
224.0.1.69	MMP-bundle-discovery1
224.0.1.70	MMP-bundle-discovery2
224.0.1.71	XYPOINT DGPS Data Feed
224.0.1.72	GilatSkySurfer

224.0.1.73	SharesLive
224.0.1.74	NorthernData
224.0.1.75	SIP
224.0.1.76	IAPP
224.0.1.77	AGENTVIEW
224.0.1.78	Tibco Multicast1
224.0.1.79	Tibco Multicast2
224.0.1.80	MSP
224.0.1.81	*One-way Trip Time* (OTT)
224.0.1.82	TRACKTICKER
224.0.1.83	dtn-mc
224.0.1.84	jini-announcement
224.0.1.85	jini-request
224.0.1.86	sde-discovery
224.0.1.87	DirecPC-SI
224.0.1.88	B1RMonitor
224.0.1.89	3Com-AMP3 dRMON
224.0.1.90	imFtmSvc
224.0.1.91	NQDS4
224.0.1.92	NQDS5
224.0.1.93	NQDS6
224.0.1.94	NLVL12
224.0.1.95	NTDS1
224.0.1.96	NTDS2
224.0.1.97	NODSA
224.0.1.98	NODSB
224.0.1.99	NODSC
224.0.1.100	NODSD
224.0.1.101	NQDS4R
224.0.1.102	NQDS5R
224.0.1.103	NQDS6R
224.0.1.104	NLVL12R
224.0.1.105	NTDS1R

224.0.1.106	NTDS2R
224.0.1.107	NODSAR
224.0.1.108	NODSBR
224.0.1.109	NODSCR
224.0.1.110	NODSDR
224.0.1.111	MRM
224.0.1.112	TVE-FILE
224.0.1.113	TVE-ANNOUNCE
224.0.1.114	Mac Srv Loc
224.0.1.115	Simple Multicast
224.0.1.116	SpectraLinkGW
224.0.1.117	dieboldmcast
224.0.1.118	Tivoli Systems
224.0.1.119	pq-lic-mcast
224.0.1.120	HYPERFEED
224.0.1.121	Pipesplatform
224.0.1.121–224.0.1.255	Unassigned
224.0.2.1	"rwho" Group (BSD) (Unofficial)
224.0.2.2	SUN RPC PMAPPROC_CALLIT
224.0.2.064–224.0.2.95	SIAC MDD Service
224.0.2.096–224.0.2.127	CoolCast
224.0.2.128–224.0.2.191	WOZ-Garage
224.0.2.192–224.0.2.255	SIAC MDD Market Service
224.0.3.000–224.0.3.255	RFE Generic Service
224.0.4.000–224.0.4.255	RFE Individual Conferences
224.0.5.000–224.0.5.127	CDPD Groups
224.0.5.128–224.0.5.191	SIAC Market Service
224.0.5.192–224.0.5.255	Unassigned
224.0.6.000–224.0.6.127	Cornell ISIS Project
224.0.6.128–224.0.6.255	Unassigned
224.0.7.000–224.0.7.255	Where-Are-You
224.0.8.000–224.0.8.255	INTV
224.0.9.000–224.0.9.255	Internet Railroad

224.0.10.000–224.0.10.255	DLSw Groups
224.0.11.000–224.0.11.255	NCC.NET Audio
224.0.12.000–224.0.12.63	Microsoft and MSNBC
224.0.13.000–224.0.13.255	UUNET PIPEX Net News
224.0.14.000–224.0.14.255	NLANR
224.0.15.000–224.0.15.255	Hewlett Packard
224.0.16.000–224.0.16.255	XingNet
224.0.17.000–224.0.17.31	Mercantile and Commodity Exchange
224.0.18.000–224.0.18.255	Dow Jones
224.0.19.000–224.0.19.63	Walt Disney Company
224.0.19.064–224.0.19.95	Cal Multicast
224.0.19.096–224.0.19.127	SIAC Market Service
224.0.19.128–224.0.19.191	IIG Multicast
224.0.19.192–224.0.19.207	Metropol
224.0.19.208–224.0.19.239	Xenoscience, Inc.
224.0.20.000–224.0.20.63	MS-IP/TV
224.0.20.064–224.0.20.127	Reliable Network Solutions
224.0.20.128–224.0.20.143	TRACKTICKER Group
224.0.252.000–224.0.252.255	Domain-Scoped Group
224.0.253.000–224.0.253.255	Report Group
224.0.254.000–224.0.254.255	Query Group
224.0.255.000–224.0.255.255	Border Routers
224.1.0.0–224.1.255.255	ST Multicast Groups
224.2.0.0–224.2.127.253	Multimedia Conference Calls
224.2.127.254	SAPv1 Announcements
224.2.127.254	SAPv0 Announcements
224.2.128.0–224.2.255.255	SAP Dynamic Assignments
224.252.0.0–224.255.255.255	DIS Transient Groups
225.0.0.0–225.255.255.255	MALLOC (Temp, Renew 12/99)
232.0.0.0–232.255.255.255	VMTP Transient Groups
239.000.000.000–239.255.255.255	Administratively Scoped
239.000.000.000–239.63.255.255	Reserved
239.064.000.000–239.127.255.255	Reserved

239.128.000.000–239.191.255.255	Reserved
239.192.000.000–239.251.255.255	Organization, Local Scope
239.252.000.000–239.252.255.255	Site, Local Scope (Reserved)
239.253.000.000–239.253.255.255	Site, Local Scope (Reserved)
239.254.000.000–239.254.255.255	Site, Local Scope (Reserved)
239.255.000.000–239.255.255.255	Site, Local Scope

APPENDIX C

References

2502

"Limitations of Internet Protocol Suite for Distributed Simulation the Large Multicast Environment."

M. Pullen, M. Myjak, C. Bouwens

2490

"A Simulation Model for IP Multicast with RSVP."

M. Pullen, R. Malghan, L. Lavu, G. Duan, J. Ma, H. Nah

2432

"Terminology for IP Multicast Benchmarking."

K. Dubray

2417

"Definitions of Managed Objects for Multicast over UNI 3.0/3.1-Based
ATM Networks."

C. Chung, M. Greene

2382

"A Framework for Integrated Services and RSVP over ATM."

E. Crawley, L. Berger, S. Berson, F. Baker, M. Borden, J. Krawczyk

2380

"RSVP over ATM Implementation Requirements."

L. Berger

2379

"RSVP over ATM Implementation Guidelines."

L. Berger

2375

"IPv6 Multicast Address Assignments."

R. Hinden, S. Deering

2366

"Definitions of Managed Objects for Multicast over UNI 3.0/3.1-Based
ATM Networks."

C. Chung, M. Greene

2365

"Administratively Scoped IP Multicast."

D. Meyer

2362

"Protocol Independent Multicast-Sparse Mode (PIM-SM): Protocol
Specification."

D. Estrin, D. Farinacci, A. Helmy, D. Thaler, S. Deering, M. Handley,
V. Jacobson, C. Liu, P. Sharma, L. Wei

2357

"IETF Criteria for Evaluating Reliable Multicast Transport and Application Protocols."

A. Mankin, A. Romanow, S. Bradner, V. Paxson

2337

"Intra-LIS IP Multicast Among Routers over ATM Using Sparse-Mode PIM."

D. Farinacci, D. Meyer, Y. Rekhter

2210

"The Use of RSVP with IETF Integrated Services."

J. Wroclawski

2209

"Resource ReSerVation Protocol (RSVP)—Version 1 Message Processing Rules."

R. Braden, L. Zhang

2208

"Resource ReSerVation Protocol (RSVP)—Version 1 Applicability Statement Some Guidelines on Deployment."

A. Mankin, Ed., F. Baker, B. Braden, S. Bradner, M. O'Dell, A. Romanow, A. Weinrib, L. Zhang

2207

"RSVP Extensions for IPSEC Data Flows."

L. Berger, T. O'Malley

2206

"RSVP Management Information Base Using SMIv2."

F. Baker, J. Krawczyk, A. Sastry

2205

"Resource ReSerVation Protocol (RSVP)—Version 1 Functional Specification."

R. Braden, Ed., L. Zhang, S. Berson, S. Herzog, S. Jamin

2201

"Core Based Trees (CBT) Multicast Routing Architecture."

2189

"Core Based Trees (CBT Version 2) Multicast Routing."
A. Ballardie

2149

"Multicast Server Architectures for MARS-Based ATM Multicasting."
R. Talpade, M. Ammar

2117

"Protocol Independent Multicast Sparse-Mode (PIM-SM): Protocol
   Specification."
D. Estrin, D. Farinacci, A. Helmy, D. Thaler, S. Deering, M. Handley,
   V. Jacobson, C. Liu, P. Sharma, L. Wei

2102

"Multicast Support for Nimrod: Requirements and Solution
   Approaches."
R. Ramanathan

2090

"TFTP Multicast Option."
A. Emberson

2022

"Support for Multicast over UNI 3.0/3.1-Based ATM Networks."
G. Armitage

1949

"Scalable Multicast Key Distribution."
A. Ballardie

1768

"Host Group Extensions for CLNP Multicasting."
D. Marlow

1584

"Multicast Extensions to OSPF."

J. Moy

1469

"IP Multicast over Token-Ring Local Area Networks."

T. Pusateri

1458

"Requirements for Multicast Protocols."

R. Braudes, S. Zabele

1301

"Multicast Transport Protocol."

S. Armstrong, A. Freier, K. Marzullo

1112

"Host Extensions for IP Multicasting."

S. E. Deering

1075

"Distance Vector Multicast Routing Protocol."

D. Waitzman, C. Partridge, S. E. Deering

1054

"Host Extensions for IP Multicasting."

S. E. Deering

988

"Host Extensions for IP Multicasting."

S. E. Deering

966

"Host Groups: A Multicast Extension to the Internet Protocol."

S. E. Deering, D. R. Cheriton

Multicast Internet Drafts

1. http://search.ietf.org/internet-drafts/draft-whetten-rmtp-
   ii-00.txt

   Title: "The RMTP-II Protocol."

   Abstract:

The *Reliable Multicast Transport Protocol II* (RMTP-II) is a reliable
multicast protocol designed to reliably and efficiently send data
from a few senders to large groups of simultaneous recipients. It
is designed primarily for use over controlled network topologies.
It works over both symmetric networks, as well as over asymmetrical network topologies such as those provided by satellite, cable
modem, or *Asymmetrical Digital Subscriber Line* (ADSL) carriers.

2. http://search.ietf.org/internet-drafts/draft-handley-aap-00.txt

   Title: "Multicast Address Allocation Protocol (AAP)."

   Abstract:

The document defines a multicast *Address Allocation Protocol* (AAP)
that forms a part of a larger multicast address allocation architecture currently being defined. AAP addresses the specific issue of
intra-domain multicast address allocation between multicast
address allocation servers.

3. http://search.ietf.org/internet-drafts/draft-ohta-static-
   multicast-01.txt

   Title: "Static Multicast."

   Abstract:

The current IP Multicast model appears to achieve a level of simplicity by extending the IP unicast addressing model (historically
the classful A, B, and C net numbers) from the mask and longest
match schemes of CIDR with a new classful address space, class D.
The routing systems have also been built in a deceptively simple
way in one of three manners—either broadcast and prune
(DVMRP and Dense Mode PIM), destination list-based tree com-
putation (MOSPF), or single centered trees (current sparse-mode
PIM and CBT). The multicast service creates the illusion of a
spectrum that one can "tune in to," such as an application writer.
Due to this view, many have seen the multicast pilot service, the
Mbone, as a worldwide Ethernet, where simple distributed algorithms can be used to allocate "wavelengths" and advertise them

through "broadcast" on a channel (the session directory) associated with a spectrum.

4. `http://search.ietf.org/internet-drafts/draft-finlayson-mafp-02.txt`

Title: "The Multicast Attribute Framing Protocol."

Abstract:

The Internet has recently seen the emergence of applications that involve the ongoing transmission, or "pushing," of structured data from a server to one or more client nodes. Most current applications send this data using unicast communications—usually over TCP connections. However, similar applications can also be implemented using Multicast-based protocols. Multicast not only improves the scalability of this particular class of application, but it also makes possible an additional class of application in which the participants can act as peers—sending data, as well as receiving data.

5. `http://search.ietf.org/internet-drafts/draft-handley-malloc-arch-00.txt`

Title: "The Internet Multicast Address Allocation Architecture."

Abstract:

This document proposes a multicast address allocation architecture for the Internet. The architecture is three-layered, comprising a client-server protocol, an intra-domain protocol, and an inter-domain protocol.

6. `http://search.ietf.org/internet-drafts/draft-ietf-ipsec-intragkm-00.txt`

Title: "Intra-Domain Group Key Management Protocol."

Abstract:

This document describes a protocol for intra-domain group key management for IP Multicast security based on the framework of [HCD98]. In order to support multicast groups, the domain is divided into a number of administratively-scoped "areas." A host-member of a multicast group is defined to reside within one (and only one) of these areas. The purpose of placing host-members in areas is to achieve flexible and efficient key management, particularly in the face of the problem of changes (joining, leaving, and ejections) in the membership of a multicast group. A separate administratively-scoped area control-group is defined for each (data) multicast group—for the express purpose of key management and other control-message delivery.

7. http://search.ietf.org/internet-drafts/draft-canetti-secure-multicast-taxonomy-00.txt

Title: "A Taxonomy of Multicast Security Issues (Temporary Version)."

Abstract:

With the growth and commercialization of the Internet, the need for secure IP Multicast is growing. In this draft, we present a taxonomy of multicast security issues. We first sketch some multicast group parameters that are relevant to security and outline the basic security issues concerning multicast in general, with emphasis on IP Multicast. Next, we suggest two "benchmark" scenarios for secure multicast solutions. Last, we review some previous works.

8. http://search.ietf.org/internet-drafts/draft-briscoe-ama-00.txt

Title: "End to End Aggregation of Multicast Addresses."

Abstract:

This paper presents an approach for solving the inherent problem with multicast routing scalability—by cooperation between end-systems and the network. We introduce an extremely efficient and elegant way to name arbitrarily sized, inter-meshed aggregations of multicast addresses. This is done in such a way that it is easy to calculate how to change the name to encompass many more related names. We describe how these aggregate names could be used anywhere in place of the set of addresses to which they refer—not by resolving them into multiple operations, but by a single bulk action throughout the routing tree, and in session descriptions potentially including those for reservations. Initial aggregation in end-systems might only reduce the problem by an order of magnitude, but it is believed that this will provide sufficient structure for routers to be able to recognize further aggregation potential. To improve the chances of router aggregation, address set allocation schemes must fulfill certain criteria that are laid down in this paper.

9. http://search.ietf.org/internet-drafts/draft-crowcroft-rmfp-02.txt

Title: "RMFP: A Reliable Multicast Framing Protocol."

Abstract:

There has been considerable interest in reliable multicast, and a number of reliable multicast transport applications and systems have been built in the past years, including [PGM], [RMDP], [RMTP], and [SRM]. A survey of most of the current, reliable multicast protocols is available in [Diot97].

10. http://search.ietf.org/internet-drafts/draft-honton-sdp-02.txt

Title: "Simple Server Discovery Protocol."

Abstract:

The Simple Server Discovery Protocol enables clients to use a multicast address to discover the unicast interface of a cooperating server for a desired service port and optionally authenticate the identity of the client and/or server.

11. http://search.ietf.org/internet-drafts/draft-ietf-manet-aodv-02.txt

Title: "Ad Hoc On Demand Distance Vector (AODV) Routing."

Abstract:

The *Ad Hoc On-Demand Distance Vector* (AODV) routing protocol is intended for use by mobile nodes in an ad hoc network characterized by frequent changes in link connectivity to each other caused by relative movement. It offers quick adaptation to dynamic link conditions, low processing and memory overhead, low network utilization, and establishment of both unicast and multicast routes between sources and destinations which are loop-free at all times. It makes use of destination sequence numbers, which are a novel means of ensuring loop freedom—even in the face of anomalous delivery of routing control messages—and solving classical problems associated with distance vector protocols, including the problem of "counting to infinity."

12. http://search.ietf.org/internet-drafts/draft-kim-jtc1-sc6-ects-04.txt

Title: "Enhanced Communications Transport Service Definition."

Abstract:

This memo is the final Committee Draft of the Enhanced Transport Service Definition under development within ISO/IEC JTC1/SC6/WG7 since the last several years, in order to provide the upper-layer applications with enhanced transport services over the current OSI transport service. Major enhancements include multicast services and enhanced QoS.

13. `http://search.ietf.org/internet-drafts/draft-saito-ip1394-mcap-ext-00.txt`

Title: "An Extension of MCAP for Data Transmission on IEEE1394 Isochronous Channel."

Abstract:

IEEE1394 bus is a link layer network with isochronous transfer mode capability. Therefore, it is quite natural that the following demands appear:

1. Transmit specific IP flow through a certain isochronous channel of IEEE1394 bus.

2. Transmit specific AV flow (such as MPEG2-TS with CIP header [61883]) through a certain isochronous channel of IEEE1394 bus (and control these flows by IP applications).

To achieve these goals, this draft proposes the protocol with following features:

1. Notifying the relation between channel ID and IP flow

2. Notifying the bandwidth of the isochronous channel

3. Notifying the direction of the IP flow transmitted through the channel

4. Notify the attribute of the flow. This protocol is defined as the extension of *Multicast Channel Allocation Protocol* (MCAP).

14. `http://search.ietf.org/internet-drafts/draft-sola-ocbt-static-multicast-00.txt`

Title: "Modifications to OCBT for Static Multicast."

Abstract:

OCBT is a CBT-based multicast protocol that enables multiple cores for a multicast group. The goal in OCBT is to set up and maintain a unique, bi-directional multicast tree connecting members with cores—and also cores among themselves. This tree is used to deliver multicast traffic to members of the multicast group. To accomplish that objective, members, non-member senders, and routers with members and cores must know the IP unicast address of cores and the IP Multicast address for the multicast group. This is a key issue in tree-based multicast protocols using centers, cores, or rendezvous points—and their main source of lack of scalability. In OCBT, this key issue is open.

15. `http://search.ietf.org/internet-drafts/draft-ietf-pim-simplekmp-00.txt`

Title: "Simple Key Management Protocol for PIM."

Abstract:

This document describes a simple key management approach for the PIM multicast routing protocol, observing the key arrangement for PIM defined in [Wei98] for PIM Version 2.

16. `http://search.ietf.org/internet-drafts/draft-banerjea-qosmic-00.txt`

Title: "Designing QoSMIC: A Quality of Service Sensitive Multicast Internet."

Abstract:

We present QoSMIC, a multicast protocol for the Internet that supports QoS-sensitive routing and minimizes the importance of *a priori* configuration decisions (such as core selection). The protocol is resource-efficient, robust, flexible, and scalable. In addition, our protocol is provably loop-free.

17. `http://search.ietf.org/internet-drafts/draft-ietf-mospf-prunes-00.txt`

Title: "MOSPF Prunes."

Abstract:

MOSPF is a link-state multicast routing protocol based on OSPF. Inside a single OSPF area, the delivery of multicast datagrams is restricted to group members only by propagating the location of group members through group-membership-LSAs. However, group membership is not propagated across area and/or AS boundaries, relying instead on so-called wild card multicast receivers. This means that in some cases, multicast datagrams are transmitted further than necessary—wasting link and processor resources in the process.

18. `http://search.ietf.org/internet-drafts/draft-yamanouchi-radius-ext-00.txt`

Title: "RADIUS Extension for Multicast Router Authentication."

Abstract:

This memo describes an extension of RADIUS authentication protocol (RFC2138) and RADIUS accounting protocol (RFC2139) to provide authentication service for multicast receivers and senders to the ingress and egress routers—and to keep track of the receiving and sending clients for multicast data feed service management. New services and attributes are added to the RADIUS definitions, while the authentication transaction mechanisms are preserved. The authentication server authenticates the multicast receiver/sender by using the CHAP-based mechanism. The account server logs the start and stop points of multicast route usage. This extension is intended to be used in conjunction with the IGMP extension for multicast receiver and sender authentication.

19. `http://search.ietf.org/internet-drafts/draft-ietf-idmr-multicast-routmib-07.txt`

Title: "IP Multicast Routing MIB."

Abstract:

This memo defines an experimental portion of the *Management Information Base* (MIB) for use with network management protocols in the Internet community. In particular, it describes managed objects used for managing IP Multicast Routing [16], independent of the specific multicast routing protocol [17-21] in use. Managed objects specific to particular multicast routing protocols are specified elsewhere.

20. `http://search.ietf.org/internet-drafts/draft-ietf-svrloc-wasrv-01.txt`

Title: "Wide Area Network Service Location."

Abstract:

We propose extensions to the *Service Location Protocol* (SLP), which allow for registration and discovery of services scattered across the wide area network. We make use of scalable wide area multicast to enable agents within an administrative domain to learn about services within other domains. We also describe a new agent, the *Brokering Agent* (BA), which is responsible for providing information about a particular set of services types.

21. `http://search.ietf.org/internet-drafts/draft-borgonovo-qos-ds-00.txt`

Title: "End-to-end QoS Provisioning Mechanism for Differentiated Services."

Abstract:

This document presents an end-to-end mechanism to guarantee bandwidth and delay into the Differentiated Services mechanism to constant rate traffic, such as voice and video. The mechanism requires network routers to be able to serve packets according to three classes of priority. The needed call admission control is performed by an end-to-end signaling procedure that implicitly looks for the required bandwidth and seizes it, if available. Short delays are guaranteed by the regular structure of constant rate traffic. No entities other than source and destination are involved, and multicast operation comes at no further cost, which makes the mechanism fully scalable and integratable into the existing Internet.

22. `http://search.ietf.org/internet-drafts/draft-ietf-pim-ipv6-01.txt`

Title: "Protocol Independent Multicast Routing in the Internet Protocol Version 6 (IPv6)."

Abstract:

This document outlines recommendations in the use of Protocol Independent Multicast routing protocol to support Internet Protocol Version 6. It describes the changes needed in order to handle the differences between IPv6 and IPv4 and conform to the logic introduced by other routing protocols enabled for IPv6.

23. `http://search.ietf.org/internet-drafts/draft-ietf-rsvp-routing-02.txt`

Title: "RSRR: A Routing Interface for RSVP."

Abstract:

This memo describes Version 2 of RSRR, a routing interface for RSVP. By using this interface, RSVP may obtain forwarding information from routers and use it to place reservation state within the network. Version 1 of this interface was designed primarily for RSVP interaction with IPv4 multicast routing protocols. Version 2 adds support for IPv4 unicast as well as IPv6 unicast and multicast routing. A backwards compatibility mechanism is provided.

24. `http://search.ietf.org/internet-drafts/draft-ietf-idmr-traceroute-ipm-04.txt`

Title: "A 'Traceroute' Facility for IP Multicast."

Abstract:

This draft describes the IGMP multicast traceroute facility. As the deployment of IP Multicast has spread, it has become clear that a method for tracing the route that a multicast IP packet takes from a source to a particular receiver is absolutely required. Unlike unicast traceroute, multicast traceroute requires a special packet type and implementation on the part of routers. This specification describes the required functionality.

25. `http://search.ietf.org/internet-drafts/draft-ietf-ipngwg-scoped-routing-00.txt`

Title: "Routing of Scoped Addresses in the Internet Protocol Version 6 (IPv6)."

Abstract:

This document outlines a mechanism for generating routing tables that include scoped IPv6 addresses. It defines a set of rules for routers to implement in order to forward scoped unicast and multicast addresses, regardless of the routing protocol. It should be noted that these rules will apply to all scoped addresses.

26. `http://search.ietf.org/internet-drafts/draft-irtf-smug-sec-mcast-arch-00.txt`

Title: "An Architecture for Secure Internet Multicast."

Abstract:

This document proposes an architecture for secure IP Multicast. It identifies the basic components and their functionalities, and specifies how these components interact with each other and with the surrounding systems.

27. `http://search.ietf.org/internet-drafts/draft-ietf-manet-odmrp-00.txt`

Title: "On-Demand Multicast Routing Protocol (ODMRP) for Ad-Hoc Networks."

Abstract:

On-Demand Multicast Routing Protocol (ODMRP) is a multicast routing protocol designed for ad hoc networks with mobile hosts. ODMRP is a mesh-based, rather than a conventional tree-based, multicast scheme and uses a Forwarding Group concept (only a subset of nodes forwards the multicast packets via scoped flooding). It applies on-demand procedures to dynamically set up routes and maintain multicast group membership.

28. `http://search.ietf.org/internet-drafts/draft-wallner-key-arch-01.txt`

Title: "Key Management for Multicast: Issues and Architectures."

Abstract:

This report contains a discussion of the difficult problem of key management for multicast communication sessions. It focuses on two main areas of concern with respect to key management, which are initializing the multicast group with a common net key and rekeying the multicast group. A rekey may be necessary upon the compromise of a user or for other reasons (e.g., periodic rekey). In particular, this report identifies a technique which enables for secure compromise recovery, while also being robust against collusion of excluded users. This is one important feature of multicast key management which has not been addressed in detail by most other multicast key management proposals [1, 2, 4]. The benefits of this proposed technique are that it minimizes the number of transmissions required to rekey the multicast group, and it imposes minimal storage requirements on the multicast group.

This document describes extension to the CBT protocol to maintain a multicast tree with user-specified QoS properties. Specifically, it describes enhancements in the member join/leave and state update/refresh procedures to facilitate the deployment of additive (e.g., end-to-end delay bound), multiplicative (e.g., packet loss ratio along a path) and concave (e.g., minimum bandwidth available) QoS.

30. http://search.ietf.org/internet-drafts/draft-cai-ssdp-v1-00.txt

Title: "Simple Service Discovery Protocol/1.0."

Abstract:

The *Simple Service Discovery Protocol* (SSDP) provides a mechanism where by network clients, with little or no static configuration, can discover desired network services. SSDP uses HTTP over multicast and unicast UDP to provide two functions: OPTIONS and ANNOUNCE. OPTIONS is used to determine whether a desired network service exists on the network. ANNOUNCE is used by network services to announce their existence.

31. http://search.ietf.org/internet-drafts/draft-sola-pim-static-multicast-00.txt

Title: "Modifications to PIM-SM for Static Multicast."

Abstract:

The *Protocol Independent Multicast—Sparse Mode* (PIM-SM) is currently defined as an intra-domain multicast protocol. Although in PIM-SM more than one *Candidate Rendezvous Point* (C-RP) may exist, only one can be active at a given time, and this will be the one to which receivers will send Join messages or sources will send Register messages. The method used in PIM-SM to make public the set of C-RPs for a multicast group is to flood all over the domain packets with the list of C-RPs using the so-called Bootstrap method. This approach may scale in domains with few routers but does not scale if the protocol would have to be applied to provide multicast throughout the whole internet.

32. http://search.ietf.org/internet-drafts/draft-ietf-idmr-cbt-br-spec-02.txt

Title: "Core Based Tree (CBT) Multicast Border Router Specification."

Abstract:

This draft specifies the behavior of a CBT multicast *border router* (BR). This specification assumes the use of CBTv3—the latest CBT protocol version [3].

33. http://search.ietf.org/internet-drafts/draft-ietf-mboned-mzap-03.txt

Title: "Multicast-Scope Zone Announcement Protocol (MZAP)."

Abstract:

This document defines a protocol, the *Multicast-Scope Zone Announcement Protocol* (MZAP), for discovering the multicast administrative scope zones that are relevant at a particular location. MZAP also provides mechanisms whereby two common misconfigurations of administrative scope zones can be discovered.

34. http://search.ietf.org/internet-drafts/draft-ietf-manet-amris-spec-00.txt

Title: "Ad Hoc Multicast Routing Protocol Utilizing Increasing Id-Numbers."

Abstract:

This document introduces a new multicast routing protocol for use over ad hoc networks. The protocol is called AMRIS, short for Ad Hoc Multicast Routing protocol utilizing Increasing id-numberS. The conceptual idea behind AMRIS is to assign every node in a multicast session with an id-number. A delivery tree rooted at a particular node called Sid joins up the nodes participating in the multicast session. The relationship between the id-numbers (and the node that owns it) and Sid is that the id-numbers increase in numerical value as they radiate from the root of the delivery tree. The significance of the Sid is that it has the smallest id-number within that multicast session. Utilizing the id-numbers, nodes are able to adapt rapidly to changes in link connectivity. Recovery messages due to link breakages are confined to the region where it occurred.

35. http://search.ietf.org/internet-drafts/draft-rfced-exp-rupp-04.txt

Title: "A Protocol for the Transmission of Net News Articles over IP Multicast."

Abstract:

Multicast News Transfer Protocol (MCNTP) provides a way to use the IP Multicast infrastructure to transmit NetNews articles between news servers. Doing so will reduce the bandwidth that is actually needed for transmission of articles which is mostly done via NNTP. This does not affect how news reading clients communicate with servers.

36. http://search.ietf.org/internet-drafts/draft-ietf-mboned-mdh-01.txt

Title: "Multicast Debugging Handbook."

Abstract:

This document serves as a handbook for the debugging of multicast connectivity problems. In addition to reviewing commonly encountered problems, the draft summarizes publicly distributable multicast diagnostic tools, and provides examples of their use, along with pointers to source and binary distributions.

37. http://search.ietf.org/internet-drafts/draft-ietf-mboned-mrm-use-00.txt

Title: "Justification for and use of the Multicast Routing Monitor (MRM) Protocol."

Abstract:

This document motivates the need for the *Multicast Routing Monitor* (MRM) [MRM] protocol by describing the niche that exists for a router-based multicast management protocol. Using the "sufficient and necessary" argument, we suggest that existing protocols and techniques lack important management functionality. This document briefly describes the methodology used by

MRM, justifies the existence of MRM, and describes some of the scenarios in which MRM will be of value.

38. `http://search.ietf.org/internet-drafts/draft-nagami-csr-fanpv2-dcmode-00.txt`

Title: "Flow Attribute Notification Protocol Version 2 (FANPv2) Distributed Control Mode."

Abstract:

This memo describes the specification *of Flow Attribute Notification Protocol Version 2* (FANPv2) *distributed control mode* (DC-mode). The FANPv2 is a protocol used by *Cell Switch Routers* (CSRs) to communicate mapping information between a specific packet flow and a virtual connection that conveys the packet flow. In the DC-mode, the control message exchange for a packet flow between each pair of neighboring CSRs is initiated independently from the message exchange for the same flow between any other pair of CSRs. The DC-mode is applicable to the control of both unicast and multicast cut-through paths.

39. `http://search.ietf.org/internet-drafts/draft-ietf-ipngwg-bsd-api-new-06.txt`

Title: "Basic Socket Interface Extensions for IPv6."

Abstract:

The de facto standard *application program interface* (API) for TCP/IP applications is the "sockets" interface. Although this API was developed for UNIX in the early 1980s, it has also been implemented on a wide variety of non-UNIX systems. TCP/IP applications written using the sockets API have in the past enjoyed a high degree of portability and we would like the same portability with IPv6 applications. But changes are required to the sockets API to support IPv6 and this memo describes these changes. These include a new socket address structure to carry IPv6 addresses, new address conversion functions, and some new socket options. These extensions are designed to provide access to the basic IPv6 features required by TCP and UDP applications, including multicasting, while introducing a minimum of change into the system and providing complete compatibility for existing IPv4 applications. Additional extensions for advanced IPv6 features (raw sockets and access to the IPv6 extension headers) are defined in another document [4].

References

319

40. http://search.ietf.org/internet-drafts/draft-kermode-madcap-nest-opt-00.txt

Title: "MADCAP Multicast Scope Nesting State Option."

Abstract:

This document defines a new option to the *Multicast Address Dynamic Client Allocation Protocol* (MADCAP) to support nested scoping. The new option's purpose is to enable clients to learn which scopes nest inside each other, and hence may be used for expanding scope searches or hierarchical multicast transport.

41. http://search.ietf.org/internet-drafts/draft-anker-congress-01.txt

Title: "IMSS: IP Multicast Shortcut Service."

Abstract:

This memo describes an *IP Multicast Shortcut Service* (IMSS) over a large ATM cloud. The service enables cut-through routing between routers serving different *Logical IP Subnets* (LISs). The presented solution is complementary to MARS [2], adopted as the IETF standard solution for IP Multicast over ATM.

42. http://search.ietf.org/internet-drafts/draft-ietf-idmr-membership-reports-02.txt

Title: "Domain Wide Multicast Group Membership Reports."

Abstract:

When running a multi-level multicast routing protocol, upper levels need to know about group memberships in lower levels in a protocol-independent fashion. Domain Wide Multicast Group Membership Reports enable this information to be learned in a fashion similar to IGMP[Fenn97] at the domain level.

43. http://search.ietf.org/internet-drafts/draft-bormann-mnnp-nndp-00.txt

Title: "Network News Distribution Protocol: Architecture and Design Guidelines."

Abstract:

This document describes an architecture and a set of protocols for distributing NetNews [RFC0977, RFC1036] via IP Multicast enabled networks. The architecture is designed to be useful in the global Internet. In particular, it enables multiple news servers to cooperate on multicasting each new article only once. To facilitate scalability to tens of thousands of news servers, it also provides for receive-only multicast participants (that continue to send articles via conventional NNTP).

44. `http://search.ietf.org/internet-drafts/draft-hanna-marp-00.txt`

Title: "Multicast Address Request Protocol (MARP)."

Abstract:

The *Multicast Address Request Protocol* (MARP) serves as a front end to the Multicast Address Allocation Architecture. Any host that wishes to allocate a multicast address may contact a Multicast Address Allocation Server and use MARP to request an address allocation for a specific interval, scope, etc. Later, the host may request an extension of the address allocation or de-allocate the address if it is no longer needed.

45. `http://search.ietf.org/internet-drafts/draft-yamamoto-ipv6-over-p2p-atm-01.txt`

Title: "IPv6 over Point-to-Point ATM Link."

Abstract:

This memo defines a communication mechanism to exchange both IPv6 unicast and multicast packets over an ATM network used as a point-to-point link.

46. `http://search.ietf.org/internet-drafts/draft-ietf-lsma-requirements-02.txt`

Title: "Taxonomy of Communication Requirements for Large-Scale Multicast Applications."

Abstract:

The intention of this draft is to define a classification system for the communication requirements of any *large-scale multicast application* (LSMA). It is very unlikely one protocol can achieve a compromise between the diverse requirements of all the parties involved in any LSMA. It is therefore necessary to understand the worst-case scenarios in order to minimize the range of protocols needed. Dynamic protocol adaptation is likely to be necessary which will require logic to map particular combinations of requirements to particular mechanisms. Standardizing the way that applications define their requirements is a necessary step towards this. Classification is a first step towards standardization.

47. http://search.ietf.org/internet-drafts/draft-ietf-idmr-igmp-mrdisc-01.txt

Title: "IGMP Multicast Router Discovery."

Abstract:

Companies have been proposing "IGMP snooping" type schemes for layer 2 bridging devices. A method for discovery multicast capable routers is necessary for these schemes. An IGMP query message is inadequate for discovering multicast routers as one querier is elected. In order to "discover" multicast routers, we introduce two new types of IGMP messages: Multicast Router Advertisement and Multicast Router Solicitation. These two messages can be used by any device which listens to IGMP to discovery multicast routers. Multicast Router Solicitation messages may be used by any network device (e.g. layer 2 switch) to solicit discovery messages from multicast routers.

48. http://search.ietf.org/internet-drafts/draft-fenner-igmp-proxy-00.txt

Title: "IGMP-based Multicast Forwarding ('IGMP Proxying')."

Abstract:

In certain topologies, it is not necessary to run a multicast routing protocol. It is sufficient to learn group membership information and simply forward based upon that information. This draft describes a mechanism for forwarding based solely upon IGMP membership information.

49. http://search.ietf.org/internet-drafts/draft-thaler-multicast-interop-03.txt

Title: "Interoperability Rules for Multicast Routing Protocols."

Abstract:

The rules described in this document will enable efficient interoperation among multiple independent multicast routing domains. Specific instantiations of these rules are given for the DVMRP, MOSPF, PIM-DM, PIM-SM, and CBT multicast routing protocols, as well as for IGMP-only links. Future versions of these protocols, and any other multicast routing protocols, may describe their interoperability procedure by stating how the rules described herein apply to them.

50. `http://search.ietf.org/internet-drafts/draft-ietf-malloc-malloc-mib-00.txt`

Title: "Multicast Address Allocation MIB."

Abstract:

This memo defines an experimental portion of the *Management Information Base* (MIB) for use with network management protocols in the Internet community. In particular, it describes managed objects used for managing multicast address allocation. Other MIBs may be defined for specific allocation protocols.

51. `http://search.ietf.org/internet-drafts/draft-bradner-multicast-problem-00.txt`

Title: "Internet Protocol Multicast Problem Statement."

Abstract:

This document outlines the evolving requirements for Multicast functionality within next generation Internet Protocol networks, and is the product of an ad hoc Internet2 working group meeting held August 25–27, 1997 hosted by Cisco Systems, Inc. This document is offered to the IP community for its consideration and comments.

52. `http://search.ietf.org/internet-drafts/draft-ietf-mospf-mospf-01.txt`

Title: "Multicast Extensions to OSPF."

Abstract:

This memo documents the MOSPF protocol. MOSPF, which stands for the Multicast extensions to OSPF, is an enhancement to the OSPF protocol enabling the routing of IP Multicast datagrams. The extensions have been implemented so that a multicast routing capability can be introduced piecemeal into an OSPF Version 2 routing domain. Some of the OSPF Version 2 routers may run the multicast extensions, while others may continue to be restricted to the forwarding of regular IP traffic (unicasts).

53. `http://search.ietf.org/internet-drafts/draft-ietf-idmr-pim-mib-05.txt`

Title: "Protocol Independent Multicast MIB."

Abstract:

This memo defines an experimental portion of the *Management Information Base* (MIB) for use with network management protocols in the Internet community. In particular, it describes managed objects used for managing the *Protocol Independent Multicast* (PIM) protocol [16,17,18,19]. This MIB module is applicable to IP Multicast routers which implement PIM.

54. http://search.ietf.org/internet-drafts/draft-farinacci-msdp-00.txt

Title: "Multicast Source Discovery Protocol (MSDP)."

Abstract:

This proposal describes a mechanism to connect multiple PIM-SM domains together. Each PIM-SM domain uses its own independent RP(s) and does not have to depend on RPs in other domains.

55. http://search.ietf.org/internet-drafts/draft-ooms-mpls-multicast-01.txt

Title: "Framework for IP Multicast in MPLS."

Abstract:

This document offers a framework for IP Multicast deployment in an MPLS environment. Issues arising when MPLS techniques are applied to IP Multicast are overviewed. The pros and cons of existing IP multicast routing protocols in the context of MPLS are described and the relation to the different trigger methods and LDP modes are discussed. The consequences of various layer 2 (L2) technologies are listed. Both point-to-point and multi-access networks are considered.

56. http://search.ietf.org/internet-drafts/draft-ietf-ipngwg-6over4-02.txt

Title: "Transmission of IPv6 over IPv4 Domains without Explicit Tunnels."

Abstract:

This memo specifies the frame format for transmission of IPv6 [IPV6] packets and the method of forming IPv6 link-local addresses over IPv4 domains. It also specifies the content of the Source/Target Link-layer Address option used in the Router Solicitation, Router Advertisement, Neighbor Solicitation, and Neighbor Advertisement and Redirect messages, when those messages are transmitted on an IPv4 multicast network.

57. http://search.ietf.org/internet-drafts/draft-ietf-idmr-igmp-mib-07.txt

Title: "Internet Group Management Protocol MIB."

Abstract:

This memo defines an experimental portion of the *Management Information Base* (MIB) for use with network management protocols in the Internet community. In particular, it describes managed objects used for managing the *Internet Group Management Protocol* (IGMP). All of this MIB module is applicable to IP Multicast routers [17,18,19,20,21]; a subset is applicable to hosts implementing IGMPv1 [16] or IGMPv2 [22].

58. `http://search.ietf.org/internet-drafts/draft-ietf-mboned-mix-00.txt`

Title: "Multicast-Friendly Internet Exchange (MIX)."

Abstract:

This document describes an architecture for a *Multicast-friendly Internet eXchange* (MIX), and the actual implementation at the NASA Ames Research Center *Federal Internet eXchange* (FIX-West, or FIX). The MIX has three objectives: native IP Multicast routing, scalable interdomain policy-based route exchange, and to enable a variety of IGP protocols and topologies for intra-domain use. In support of these objectives, the MIX architecture defines the following components: a peer-peer routing protocol, a method for multicast forwarding, a method for exchanging information about active sources, and a medium which provides native multicast. This document describes the protocols and configurations necessary to provide a current, working multicast-friendly internet exchange, or MIX.

59. `http://search.ietf.org/internet-drafts/draft-thaler-dvmrp-mib-09.txt`

Title: "Distance-Vector Multicast Routing Protocol MIB."

Abstract:

This memo defines an experimental portion of the *Management Information Base* (MIB) for use with network management protocols in the Internet community. In particular, it describes managed objects used for managing the *Distance-Vector Multicast Routing Protocol* (DVMRP) protocol [5, 6]. This MIB module is applicable to IP Multicast routers which implement DVMRP.

60. `http://search.ietf.org/internet-drafts/draft-ietf-ipcdn-igmp-proxy-mib-00.txt`

Title: "Cable Device IGMP Proxy MIB for DOCSIS-Compliant Cable Modems."

Abstract:

This memo defines an experimental portion of the *Management Information Base* (MIB) for use with network management protocols in the Internet community. In particular, it defines a basic set of managed objects for SNMP-based management of conditional access to IP Multicast groups by DOCSIS-compliant cable modems.

61. `http://search.ietf.org/internet-drafts/draft-ietf-idmr-gum-04.txt`

Title: "Border Gateway Multicast Protocol (BGMP): Protocol Specification."

Abstract:

This document describes BGMP, a protocol for inter-domain multicast routing. BGMP builds shared trees for active multicast groups, and enables receiver domains to build source-specific, inter-domain, distribution branches where needed. Building upon concepts from CBT and PIM-SM, BGMP requires that each multicast group be associated with a single root (in BGMP it is referred to as the root domain). BGMP assumes that at any point in time, different ranges of the class D space are associated (e.g., with MASC [MASC]) with different domains. Each of these domains then becomes the root of the shared domain-trees for all groups in its range.

62. `http://search.ietf.org/internet-drafts/draft-finlayson-umtp-03.txt`

Title: "The UDP Multicast Tunneling Protocol."

Abstract:

Many Internet hosts—such as PCs—while capable of running multicast applications, cannot access the MBone because 1) the router(s) that connect them to the Internet do not yet support IP Multicast routing, and 2) their operating systems cannot support a tunneled implementation of IP Multicast routing.

63. `http://search.ietf.org/internet-drafts/draft-acharya-ipsofacto-mpls-mcast-00.txt`

Title: "IP Multicast Support in MPLS Networks."

Abstract:

Multicast support in a MPLS network has yet to be defined. This document discusses both dense-mode and sparse-mode IP Multicast within the context of a MPLS network. Unlike unicast routing, dense-mode multicast routing trees are established in a data-driven manner and it is not possible to topologically aggregate such trees, which are rooted at different sources. In sparse-mode multicast, source-specific trees may coexist with a core/shared tree, and it is not possible to assign a common label to traffic from different sources on a branch of the shared tree. This leads us to suggest a per-source traffic-driven label allocation scheme for supporting all three types of multicast (dense mode, shared tree, source tree) routing trees in a MPLS network.

64. `http://search.ietf.org/internet-drafts/draft-ietf-malloc-api-04.txt`

Title: "An Abstract API for Multicast Address Allocation."

Abstract:

This document describes the "abstract service interface" for the dynamic multicast address allocation service, as seen by applications. While it does not describe a concrete API (i.e., for a specific programming language), it describes—in abstract terms—the semantics of this service, including the guarantees that it makes to applications.

65. `http://search.ietf.org/internet-drafts/draft-bakre-mcast-atm-00.txt`

Title: "IP Multicast over ATM Networks with Cut-Through Forwarding."

Abstract:

This document proposes a scheme for IP Multicasting in ATM networks, which can achieve cut-through forwarding for inter LIS multicast traffic using ATM protocols.

66. `http://search.ietf.org/internet-drafts/draft-ietf-dhc-multopt-03.txt`

Title: "Multicast Address Allocation Configuration Options."

Abstract:

This document describes DHCP options that may be used to provide access to Multicast Address Allocation servers, such as MDHCP servers.

67. `http://search.ietf.org/internet-drafts/draft-ietf-malloc-madcap-04.txt`

Title: "Multicast Address Dynamic Client Allocation Protocol (MADCAP)."

Abstract:

This document defines a protocol, *Multicast Address Dynamic Client Allocation Protocol* (MADCAP), that enables hosts to request multicast addresses from multicast address allocation servers.

68. http://search.ietf.org/internet-drafts/draft-talwar-rsvp-kr-01.txt

Title: "RSVP Killer Reservations."

Abstract:

This document describes the Killer Reservation Problem encountered when merging RSVP reservation requests. These requests get merged as they travel up the multicast distribution tree, losing information about individual requests. A request, which would have succeeded on its own, may suffer denial of service when the "merged request" fails admission control. This is the problem for which we present different solutions.

69. http://search.ietf.org/internet-drafts/draft-rfced-exp-yung-00.txt

Title: "TFTP Multicast Option."

Abstract:

The Trivial File Transfer Protocol [1] is a simple, lock-step, file transfer protocol which enables a client to get or put a file onto a remote host.

70. http://search.ietf.org/internet-drafts/draft-ietf-aft-mcast-fw-traversal-01.txt

Title: "SOCKS V5 UDP and Multicast Extensions to Facilitate Multicast Firewall Traversal."

Abstract:

This proposal creates a mechanism for managing the ingress or egress of IP Multicast through a firewall. It does this by defining extensions to the existing SOCKS V5 protocol [RFC-1928], which provides a framework for doing user-level, authenticated firewall traversal of unicast TCP and UDP traffic. However, because the current UDP support in SOCKS V5 has scalability problems as well as other deficiencies—and these need to be addressed before multicast support can be achieved—the extensions are defined in two parts: Base-level UDP extensions, and Multicast UDP extensions.

71. `http://search.ietf.org/internet-drafts/draft-irtf-smug-gsadef-00.txt`

Title: "Group Security Association (GSA) Definition for IP Multicast."

Abstract:

This document provides a definition of the *Group Security Association* (GSA) for IP Multicast, derived from the *Security Association* (SA) definition for unicast. The document describes the motivations of a GSA and other issues related to the GSA usage in the context of the existing IPsec implementations.

72. `http://search.ietf.org/internet-drafts/draft-ietf-idmr-dvmrp-v3-08.txt`

Title: "Distance Vector Multicast Routing Protocol."

Abstract:

DVMRP is an Internet routing protocol that provides an efficient mechanism for connection-less datagram delivery to a group of hosts across an internetwork. It is a distributed protocol that dynamically generates IP Multicast delivery trees using a technique called *Reverse Path Multicasting* (RPM) [Deer90]. This document is an update to Version 1 of the protocol specified in RFC 1075 [Wait88].

73. `http://search.ietf.org/internet-drafts/draft-ooms-mpls-pimsm-00.txt`

Title: "MPLS for PIM-SM."

Abstract:

This document describes the issues which rise when PIM-SM ([ESTR]) is chosen as the protocol for IP Multicast deployment in an MPLS environment. The relevant characteristics of PIM-SM are further explored and a trigger for the establishment of LSPs for multicast trees is proposed.

74. `http://search.ietf.org/internet-drafts/draft-pansiot-logical-addressing-00.txt`

Title: "Logical Addressing and Routing for Multicasting (LAR)."

Abstract:

This document describes an architecture based on two levels of addressing. A logical addressing level is used to identify logical objects independently of their current IP address, such as multicast groups or mobile hosts. This schema is then used to define in a unified way mechanisms for inter-domain multicasting and mobility.

75. http://search.ietf.org/internet-drafts/draft-balenson-groupkeymgmt-oft-00.txt

Title: "Key Management for Large Dynamic Groups: One-Way Function Trees and Amortized Initialization."

Abstract:

We present a scalable method for establishing group session keys for secure large, dynamic groups such as multicast sessions. Our method is based on a novel application of *One-Way Function Trees* (OFTs). The number of keys stored by group members, the number of keys broadcast to the group when new members are added or evicted, and the computational efforts of group members, are logarithmic in the number of group members. The method provides perfect forward and backward security: evicted members cannot read future messages, even with collusion by arbitrarily many evicted members, and newly admitted group members cannot read previous messages.

76. http://search.ietf.org/internet-drafts/draft-seif-ion-mcm-01.txt

Title: "Multicast Manager (MCM): A Multipoint-to-Multipoint Multicasting Protocol for ATM."

Abstract:

This document describes MCM, a protocol for controlling a shared ATM multicast tree supporting Mutipoint-to-Multipoint communication. The protocol guarantees that there is no cell interleaving at any group receiver. No cell buffering inside the network is required, and all cell forwarding is performed at the ATM layer.

77. http://search.ietf.org/internet-drafts/draft-ietf-idmr-igmp-v3-01.txt

Title: "Internet Group Management Protocol, Version 3."

Abstract:

This document specifies Version 3 of the Internet Group Management Protocol, IGMPv3. IGMP is the protocol used by IP systems to report their IP Multicast group memberships to neighboring multicast routers. Version 3 of IGMP adds support for "source filtering," that is, the ability for a system to report interest in receiving packets *only* from specific source addresses, or from *all but* specific source addresses, sent to a particular multicast address. That information may be used by multicast routing protocols to avoid delivering multicast packets from specific sources to networks where there are no interested receivers.

78. http://search.ietf.org/internet-drafts/draft-miller-mftp-spec-03.txt

Title: "StarBurst Multicast File Transfer Protocol (MFTP) Specification."

Abstract:

The *Multicast File Transfer Protocol* (MFTP) is a protocol that operates above UDP in the application layer to provide a reliable means for transferring files from a sender to up to thousands (potentially millions with network "aggregators" or relays) of multiple receivers simultaneously over a multicast group in a multicast IP enabled network. The protocol consists of two parts; an administrative protocol to set up and tear down groups and sessions, and a data transfer protocol used to send the actual file reliably and simultaneously to the multiple recipients residing in the group.

79. http://search.ietf.org/internet-drafts/draft-lim-ip-reliable-multicast-01.txt

Title: "IP Extension for Reliable Multicast."

Abstract:

This memo presents IP extension for recovering multicast packets from congestion. Dropped packets can be recovered far faster by IP routers with extension of this memo than by group member end-hosts. Because necessary interactions are limited among adjacent routers, this scheme substantially reduces overall signaling overhead among group members for packet recovery.

80. http://search.ietf.org/internet-drafts/draft-ietf-ipsec-gkmframework-01.txt

Title: "A Framework for Group Key Management for Multicast Security."

Abstract:

This document provides a framework for group key management for multicast security, motivated by three main considerations, namely the multicast application, scalability and trust-relationships among entities. It introduces two planes corresponding to the network entities and functions important to multicasting and to security. The key management plane consists of two hierarchy-levels in the form of a single "trunk region" (inter-region) and one or more "leaf regions" (intra-region). The advantages of the framework among others is that it is scalable, it has reduced complexity and enables the independence in regions of group key management.

81. http://search.ietf.org/internet-drafts/draft-ietf-mboned-sadp-01.txt

Title: "Scoped Address Discovery Protocol (SADP)."

Abstract:

This document defines an application-layer protocol, the *Scoped Address Discovery Protocol* (SADP), for discovering the scoped multicast address(es) associated with a session at particular scopes within a hierarchically nested set of multicast scopes. SADP is designed to work within the context of *Multicast Address Allocation Architecture* [MAAA]. It is intended that SADP will provide the necessary general services for reliable multicast and searching applications to use expanding-scope searches in lieu of the well-known, but less efficient expanding-ring search.

82. http://search.ietf.org/internet-drafts/draft-ishikawa-igmp-auth-01.txt

Title: "IGMP Extension for Authentication of IP Multicast Senders and Receivers."

Abstract:

The security enhancement is one of the most important enhancements to IP Multicast. IP Multicast requires many security functions that include user authentication of IP Multicast, encryption of IP Multicast datagrams and key management protocols for IP Multicast. Among them, the user authentication function for IP Multicast is considered one of the most important security functions for IP Multicast. This document describes the extension to IGMP, version 2 (IGMPv2) [1] for the authentication of IP Multicast senders and receivers, which prevents an unauthorized user from sending and receiving IP Multicast datagrams.

83. `http://search.ietf.org/internet-drafts/draft-thaler-multipath-`
`02.txt`

Title: "Multipath Issues in Unicast and Multicast."

Abstract:

Various routing protocols, including OSPF [1] and ISIS, explicitly allow "Equal-Cost Multipath" routing. Some router implementations also allow equal-cost multipath usage with RIP and other routing protocols. Using equal-cost multipath means that if multiple equal-cost routes to the same destination exist, they can be discovered and used to provide load balancing among redundant paths.

84. `http://search.ietf.org/internet-drafts/draft-speakman-pgm-spec-`
`02.txt`

Title: "PGM Reliable Transport Protocol Specification."

Abstract:

Pragmatic General Multicast (PGM) is a reliable multicast transport protocol for applications that require ordered, duplicate-free, multicast data delivery from multiple sources to multiple receivers. PGM guarantees that a receiver in the group either receives all data packets from transmissions and retransmissions, or is able to detect unrecoverable data packet loss. PGM is specifically intended as a workable solution for multicast applications with basic reliability requirements. Its central design goal is simplicity of operation with due regard for scalability and network efficiency.

85. `http://search.ietf.org/internet-drafts/draft-ietf-pim-v2-dm-`
`01.txt`

Title: "Protocol Independent Multicast Version 2 Dense Mode Specification."

Abstract:

This specification defines a multicast routing algorithm efficient for multicast groups that are densely distributed across a network. This protocol does not have a topology discovery mechanism often used by a unicast routing protocol. It employs the same packet formats sparse-mode PIM [PIMSM] uses. This protocol is called dense-mode PIM. The foundation of this design was largely built on Deering's early work on IP Multicast routing [Deering 91].

86. http://search.ietf.org/internet-drafts/draft-viswanathan-remote_boot-mtftp-00.txt

Title: "Multicast TFTP in the Intel PXE Remote Boot Environment."

Abstract:

This document defines a protocol, *Multicast Trivial File Transfer Protocol* (MTFTP), which enables several clients to simultaneously receive a file multicast by a TFTP server as implemented in Intel's Universal Network Boot (PXE [1]) which is part of Intel's Wired for Management Initiative [2].

87. http://search.ietf.org/internet-drafts/draft-bormann-mtp-so-01.txt

Title: "MTP/SO: Self-Organizing Multicast."

Abstract:

Multiparty cooperative applications have recently received much attention, as has the multicasting of datagrams in the internet. The internet datagram multicasting mechanism is not reliable, often requiring a higher level protocol to achieve the level of reliability required for an application.

88. http://search.ietf.org/internet-drafts/draft-ietf-ip1394-mcap-00.txt

Title: "Multicast Channel Allocation Protocol (MCAP) for IEEE 1394."

Abstract:

This document specifies how IP-capable Serial Bus devices may allocate IEEE 1394 channel number(s) for use in the multicast transmission of IP datagrams. It defines the necessary methods, data structures and codes for that purpose.

89. http://search.ietf.org/internet-drafts/draft-kadansky-tram-00.txt

Title: "Tree-based Reliable Multicast (TRAM)."

Abstract:

This paper describes TRAM, a scalable reliable multicast transport protocol. TRAM is designed to support bulk data transfer from a single sender to many receivers. A dynamically formed repair tree provides local error recovery enabling the multicast group to support a large number of receivers. TRAM provides flow control, congestion control, and other adaptive techniques necessary to operate efficiently with other protocols. Several bulk data applications have been implemented with TRAM. TRAM has been tested and simulated in a number of network environments.

90. `http://search.ietf.org/internet-drafts/draft-ietf-idmr-bgp-mcast-attr-00.txt`

Title: "BGP Attributes for Multicast Tree Construction."

Abstract:

The Multiprotocol Extensions for BGP-4 [MBGP] enable Network Layer Reachability Information to contain prefixes used for multicast forwarding. This document defines extensions to BGP-4 [BGP-4] which can be used to annotate such prefixes with information that can be used by multicast routing protocols when constructing trees.

91. `http://search.ietf.org/internet-drafts/draft-allan-ion-mars-proxy-00.txt`

Title: "MARS Proxy."

Abstract:

The *Point-to-Point Protocol* (PPP) [1] has been proposed as an access vehicle for public ATM networks. Support for multicast in this environment via either RAS replication, or a adding MARS client side by side with PPP is problematic on several fronts.

92. `http://search.ietf.org/internet-drafts/draft-ietf-mmusic-sip-12.txt`

Title: "SIP: Session Initiation Protocol."

Abstract:

The *Session Initiation Protocol* (SIP) is an application-layer control (signaling) protocol for creating, modifying and terminating sessions with one or more participants. These sessions include Internet multimedia conferences, Internet telephone calls and multimedia distribution. Members in a session can communicate via multicast or via a mesh of unicast relations, or a combination of these.

93. `http://search.ietf.org/internet-drafts/draft-ietf-ipvbi-nabts-01.txt`

Title: "The Transmission of IP Over the Vertical Blanking Interval of a Television Signal."

Abstract:

This is an Internet-Draft, which describes a method for broadcasting multicast IP data using the vertical blanking interval of television signals. It includes a description for compressing multicast IP headers on unidirectional networks, a framing protocol identical to SLIP, a forward error correction scheme, and the NABTS byte structures.

94. http://search.ietf.org/internet-drafts/draft-ietf-ipngwg-mld-01.txt

Title: "Multicast Listener Discovery (MLD) for IPv6."

Abstract:

This document specifies the protocol used by an IPv6 router to discover the presence of multicast listeners (that is, nodes wishing to receive multicast packets) on its directly attached links, and to discover specifically which multicast addresses are of interest to those neighboring nodes. This protocol is referred to as Multicast Listener Discovery, or MLD.

95. http://search.ietf.org/internet-drafts/draft-farinacci-multicast-label-part-00.txt

Title: "Partitioning Label Space among Multicast Routers on a Common Subnet."

Abstract:

There are three major functions that must be performed to achieve multicast Label Switching:

1. Label Allocation, which requires each multicast *Label Switching Router* (LSR) to have a label value range that it uses.

2. Label Binding, using the labels allocated, a LSR must assign them to multicast routes.

3. Label Binding Distribution, after binding label values to routes, they must be distributed to other LSRs so they all forward on a common and consistent distribution tree.

96. http://search.ietf.org/internet-drafts/draft-talpade-manet-amroute-00.txt

Title: "AMRoute: Ad Hoc Multicast Routing Protocol."

Abstract:

The *Adhoc Multicast Routing Protocol* (AMRoute) enables for robust IP Multicast in mobile adhoc networks by exploiting user-multicast trees and dynamic cores. It creates a bi-directional shared-tree for data distribution using only the group senders and receivers as tree nodes. Unicast tunnels are used as the tree links to connect neighbors on the "user-multicast tree." Thus, AMRoute does not need to be supported by network nodes that are not interested/ capable of multicast, and cost is incurred only by group senders and receivers. AMRoute makes certain nodes "core nodes" to initiate the signaling component of AMRoute, such as detection of group members and tree setup. Core nodes differ significantly from those in CBT and PIM-SM, since they are not a central point for data distribution and can move dynamically among member nodes. Since AMRoute is not dependent on any specific unicast routing protocol, it can operate seamlessly over separate domains with different unicast protocols.

97. http://search.ietf.org/internet-drafts/draft-ietf-mboned-mcast-firewall-02.txt

Title: "IP Multicast and Firewalls."

Abstract:

Many organizations use a firewall computer that acts as a security gateway between the public Internet and their private, internal "intranet." In this document, we discuss the issues surrounding the traversal of IP multicast traffic across a firewall, and describe possible ways in which a firewall can implement and control this traversal. We also explain why some firewall mechanisms—such as SOCKS—that were designed specifically for unicast traffic, are less appropriate for multicast.

98. http://search.ietf.org/internet-drafts/draft-ietf-malloc-masc-01.txt

Title: "The Multicast Address Set Claim (MASC) Protocol."

Abstract:

This document describes the *Multicast Address-Set Claim* (MASC) protocol which can be used for inter-domain multicast address set allocation. MASC is used by a node (typically a router) to claim and allocate one or more address prefixes to that node's domain. While a domain does not necessarily need to allocate an address set for hosts in that domain to be able to allocate group addresses, allocating an address set to the domain does ensure that inter-domain distribution trees will be locally-rooted, and that traffic will be sent outside the domain only when and where external receivers exist.

99. `http://search.ietf.org/internet-drafts/draft-ietf-rap-rsvp-identity-03.txt`

Title: "Identity Representation for RSVP."

Abstract:

This document describes the representation of identity information in POLICY_DATA object [POL-EXT] for supporting policy based admission control in RSVP. The goal of identity representation is to enable a process on a system to securely identify the owner and the application of the communicating process (e.g., user id) and convey this information in RSVP messages (PATH or RESV) in a secure manner. We describe the encoding of identities as RSVP policy element. We describe the processing rules to generate identity policy elements for multicast merged flows. Subsequently, we describe representations of user identities for Kerberos and Public Key based user authentication mechanisms. In summary we describe the use of this identity information in an operational setting.

100. `http://search.ietf.org/internet-drafts/draft-quinn-multicast-apps-00.txt`

Title: "IP Multicast Applications: Challenges and Solutions."

Abstract:

This document highlights the challenges of creating multicast applications, and describes the solutions available or under development. It provides a taxonomy of multicast applications in terms of their requirements, and discusses some existing multicast-based protocols. Many of the solutions—especially in the areas of reliable multicast data delivery, congestion control, and security—have not yet emerged from the research realms. We describe the general state of on-going research in these areas, highlighting the strategies under investigation.

101. `http://search.ietf.org/internet-drafts/draft-salgarelli-issll-mis-00.txt`

Title: "Supporting IP Multicast Integrated Services in ATM Networks."

Abstract:

This memo presents an integrated, server-based mechanism for the efficient support of the *IP Integrated Services* (IIS) model in ATM networks, namely the *Multicast Integration Server* (MIS) architecture. Instead of viewing IP-ATM multicast address resolution and QoS support separately, the approach in this memo is to consider such issues in an integrated manner. In particular, the MIS architecture defines how a layer-3 setup protocol as RSVP can be mapped to and integrated with a layer-2 multicast address resolution protocol as EARTH—EAsy Multicast Routing THrough ATM clouds. With the use of EARTH, several ATM point-to-multipoint connections with different QoS parameters can be associated to a single IP Multicast address. An RSVP server (RSVP-S) within the MIS is used to distribute RSVP messages inside the ATM cloud and to set the corresponding QoS state in the address resolution table of EARTH (setup protocol mapping). In addition, this memo defines a quantized heterogeneity model which supports, together with the MIS, advanced IIS features as QoS heterogeneity and dynamic QoS changes in IP-ATM networks.

102. http://search.ietf.org/internet-drafts/draft-farinacci-multicast-tagsw-01.txt

Title: "Multicast Tag Binding and Distribution Using PIM."

Abstract:

This document describes a method for advertising labels for multicast flows. It strives to use downstream label assignment to be consistent with unicast label distribution. This proposal is media-type independent. Therefore, it works for multi-access/multicast capable LANs, point-to-point links, and NBMA networks.

103. http://search.ietf.org/internet-drafts/draft-ietf-avt-rtpsample-02.txt

Title: "Sampling of the Group Membership in RTP."

Abstract:

In large multicast groups, the size of the group membership table maintained by *Real Time Transport Protocol* (RTP) participants may become unwieldy, particularly for embedded devices with limited memory and processing power. This document discusses mechanisms for sampling of this group membership table in order to reduce the memory requirements. Several mechanisms are proposed, and the performance of each is considered.

104. http://search.ietf.org/internet-drafts/draft-liao-lrmp-00.txt

Title: "Light-Weight Reliable Multicast Protocol Specification."

Abstract:

This document describes LRMP, the Light-weight Reliable Multicast Protocol. LRMP provides a minimum set of functions for end-to-end reliable network transport suitable for bulk data transfer to multiple receivers. LRMP is designed to work in heterogeneous network environments and support multiple data senders. A totally distributed control scheme is used for error recovery so that no prior configuration and no router support are required. LRMP also includes a selective feedback mechanism enabling to monitor the quality of service at receivers. In LRMP, flow and congestion control is performed based on NACK packets and congestion indication from receivers. Forward error correction is supported as an independent optional module.

105. `http://search.ietf.org/internet-drafts/draft-ietf-mboned-mcast-apps-00.txt`

Title: "IP Multicast Applications: Challenges and Solutions."

Abstract:

This document describes the challenges involved with designing and implementing multicast applications. It is an introductory guide for application developers that highlights the unique considerations of multicast applications as compared to unicast applications.

106. `http://search.ietf.org/internet-drafts/draft-perlman-simple-multicast-02.txt`

Abstract:

This paper describes a design for multicast that is simple to understand and low enough overhead for routers that a single scheme can work both within and between domains. It also eliminates the need for coordinated multicast address allocation across the Internet. It is not very different from the tree-based schemes CBT, PIM-SM, and BGMP. Essentially all of the mechanisms to support this have already been implemented in the other designs. The contribution of this protocol is in what is NOT required to be implemented.

107. `http://search.ietf.org/internet-drafts/draft-ietf-idmr-pim-arch-05.txt`

Abstract:

Traditional multicast routing mechanisms (e.g., DVMRP and MOSPF [1][2]) were intended for use within regions where groups are widely represented or bandwidth is universally plentiful. When group members, and senders to those group members, are distributed sparsely across a wide area, these schemes are not efficient; data packets or membership report information are periodically sent over many links that do not lead to receivers or senders, respectively. This characteristic led the Internet community to investigate multicast routing architectures that efficiently establish distribution trees across wide-area internets, where many groups are sparsely represented and where bandwidth is not uniformly plentiful due to the distances and multiple administrations traversed. Efficiency is evaluated in terms of the state, control message processing, and data packet processing required across the entire network in order to deliver data packets to the members of the group.

RSVP Internet Drafts

1. http://search.ietf.org/internet-drafts/draft-lindell-rsvp-procrules-00.txt

Title: "Resource ReSerVation Protocol (RSVP)—Version 1 Message Processing Rules."

Abstract:

This memo contains an algorithmic description of the rules used by an RSVP implementation for processing messages. It is intended to clarify the version 1 RSVP protocol specification [RFC 2205]. These rules are decomposed into pieces which are contained inside of an abstract processing architecture.

2. http://search.ietf.org/internet-drafts/draft-lee-insignia-00.txt

Title: "INSIGNIA."

Abstract:

This document specifies INSIGNIA, an in-band signaling system for supporting *quality of service* (QOS) in mobile ad hoc networks. The term "in-band signaling" refers to the fact that control information is carried along with data in IP packets. We argue that in-band signaling is more suitable than explicit out-of-band approaches (e.g., RSVP) when supporting end-to-end quality of service in highly dynamic environments such as mobile ad hoc networks where network topology, node connectivity and end-to-end quality of service are strongly time-varying. INSIGNIA is designed to support the delivery of adaptive real-time services and includes fast session/flow/microflow reservation, restoration and adaptation algorithms between source/destination pairs. In this memo we discuss how INSIGNIA fits into our broader vision of a wireless flow management model for mobile ad hoc networks and how it interfaces to the proposed MANET Working Group routing algorithms and IMEP specification.

3. http://search.ietf.org/internet-drafts/draft-ietf-rsvp-diagnostic-msgs-06.txt

Title: "RSVP Diagnostic Messages."

Abstract:

This document specifies the RSVP diagnostic facility, which enables a user to collect information about the RSVP state along the path. This specification describes the functionality, diagnostic message formats, and processing rules.

4. http://search.ietf.org/internet-drafts/draft-smith-sbm-config-00.txt

Title: "Definitions of Managed Parameters for RSVP and SBM Network Nodes."

Abstract:

This memo includes a list of manageable parameters for RSVP and SBM implementations. These are in addition to those already described in RFC 2206 and RFC 2213. Specifically, it describes parameters for control of the base signaling protocols themselves, as well as a basic set of parameters for control of policy decisions by a Local Policy Module. These are not intended to be exhaustive lists, but they have been identified as useful for practical implementations.

5. http://search.ietf.org/internet-drafts/draft-fhns-rsvp-support-in-mipv6-00.txt

Title: "RSVP Support for Mobile IP Version 6 in Wireless Environments."

Abstract:

This draft describes a specific problem encountered when using RSVP (Resource Reservation Protocol) over optimized routes in MIPv6 (Mobile IP Version 6). The address translation in the MIP's binding cache creates a mismatch between the flow-id of the packets sent from correspondent node to mobile node and the flow-id signaled by RSVP.

6. `http://search.ietf.org/internet-drafts/draft-greis-aggregation-with-pbac-00.txt`

Title: "Aggregation of Internet Integrated Services State Using Parameter-Based Admission Control."

Abstract:

Aggregation has been proposed as one possible solution to the scalability problem of the Internet Integrated Services. The current suggestions for aggregation are based on measurement-based admission control, which enables for the omission of RSVP soft state in the interior routers of an aggregating domain.

7. `http://search.ietf.org/internet-drafts/draft-pan-rsvp-timer-00.txt`

Title: "Staged Refresh Timers for RSVP."

Abstract:

The current resource *Reservation Protocol* (RSVP) design has no reliability mechanism for the delivery of control messages. Instead, RSVP relies on periodic refresh between routers to maintain reservation states. This approach has several problems in a congested network. End systems send Path and Resv messages to set up RSVP connections. If the first Path or Resv message from an end system is accidentally lost in the network, a copy of the message will not be retransmitted until the end of a refresh interval, causing a delay of 30 seconds or more until a reservation is established. If a congested link causes a tear-down message (PathTear or ResvTear) to be dropped, the corresponding reservation will not be removed from the routers until the RSVP cleanup timer expires.

8. `http://search.ietf.org/internet-drafts/draft-guerin-expl-path-rsvp-01.txt`

Title: "Setting Up Reservations on Explicit Paths Using RSVP."

Abstract:

This document presents motivations for extensions to RSVP in order to enable setting up of reservations on explicit routes. The advantages of providing this support are discussed in the context of MPLS and QoS routing. An approach to providing these extensions by means of opaque routing objects in RSVP messages is presented.

9. http://search.ietf.org/internet-drafts/draft-ietf-rsvp-md5-08.txt

Title: "RSVP Cryptographic Authentication."

Abstract:

This document describes the format and use of RSVP's INTEGRITY object to provide hop-by-hop integrity and authentication of RSVP messages.

10. http://search.ietf.org/internet-drafts/draft-ietf-rap-cops-rsvp-04.txt

Title: "COPS usage for RSVP."

Abstract:

This document describes usage directives for supporting COPS policy services in RSVP environments.

11. http://search.ietf.org/internet-drafts/draft-ietf-rsvp-routing-02.txt

Title: "RSRR: A Routing Interface for RSVP."

Abstract:

This memo describes Version 2 of RSRR, a routing interface for RSVP. By using this interface, RSVP may obtain forwarding information from routers and use it to place reservation state within the network. Version 1 of this interface was designed primarily for RSVP interaction with IPv4 multicast routing protocols. Version 2 adds support for IPv4 unicast as well as IPv6 unicast and multicast routing. A backwards compatibility mechanism is provided.

12. http://search.ietf.org/internet-drafts/draft-berson-rsvp-aggregation-00.txt

Title: "Aggregation of Internet Integrated Services State."

Abstract:

The *Internet Integrated Services* (IIS) architecture [2] has a fundamental scaling problem in that per flow state is maintained at all routers and end-systems supporting a flow. This draft examines the use of aggregation as a technique to reduce the amount of state needed to provide IIS, and describes the modifications to RSVP to support aggregation. In our approach, routers at the edge of a region doing aggregation keep detailed IIS state, while in the interior of this region, routers keep a greatly reduced amount of state. Packets will be tagged at the edge with scheduling information that will be used in place of the detailed IIS state. The aggregation scheme described will enable large scale deployment of IIS without overloading routers with state and associated processing.

13. `http://search.ietf.org/internet-drafts/draft-balabanian-intserv-mpeg4-dmif-00.txt`

Title: "The Use of MPEG-4/DMIF and RSVP with Integrated Services."

Abstract:

This draft proposal explains how the ISO/IEC MPEG DMIF (Delivery Multimedia Integration Framework) can be used to carry MPEG-4 streams according to required media specific QoSs using RSVP with Integrated Services.

14. `http://search.ietf.org/internet-drafts/draft-bernet-dclass-00.txt`

Title: "Usage and Format of the DCLASS Object with RSVP Signaling."

Abstract:

RSVP signaling may be used to enhance the manageability of application traffic's QoS in a differentiated service (diff-serv) network [intdiff]. In this model, certain network elements within or at the edges of the diff-serv network may use RSVP messages to effect admission control or to apply QoS policy. One mechanism by which network elements may apply QoS policy is by causing a DCLASS object to be returned to a sending host in an RSVP RESV message. The DCLASS object indicates the diff-serv DSCP that the sender should include when submitting packets on the admitted flow, to the diff-serv network. This draft describes the usage and format of the DCLASS object.

15. `http://search.ietf.org/internet-drafts/draft-ietf-rap-signaled-priority-03.txt`

Title: "Signaled Preemption Priority Policy Element."

Abstract:

This document describes a preemption priority policy element for use by signaled policy based admission protocols (such as [RSVP] and [COPS]).

16. `http://search.ietf.org/internet-drafts/draft-schmid-rsvp-fl-01.txt`

Title: "RSVP Extensions for IPv6 Flow Label Support."

Abstract:

This document is an addendum to Version 1 of RSVP (Resource ReSerVation Protocol) as defined in the proposed standard [RFC2205]. The flow label, one of the new header fields of the IPv6 protocol, enables improvements to resource reservation protocols on IPv6 capable networks. Utilization of the flow label simplifies packet classification and optimizes packet processing in routers along the transport path.

17. `http://search.ietf.org/internet-drafts/draft-ietf-mpls-rsvp-lsp-tunnel-01.txt`

Title: Extensions to RSVP for LSP Tunnels

Abstract:

This document describes the use of RSVP, including all the necessary extensions, to establish label-switched paths (LSPs) in MPLS. Since the flow along an LSP is completely identified by the label applied at the ingress node of the path, these paths may be treated as tunnels. A key application of LSP tunnels is traffic engineering with MPLS as specified in [3].

18. `http://search.ietf.org/internet-drafts/draft-ietf-rap-rsvp-ext-04.txt`

Title: "RSVP Extensions for Policy Control."

Abstract:

This memo presents a set of extensions for supporting generic policy based admission control in RSVP. It should be perceived as an extension to the RSVP functional specifications [RSVP].

19. `http://search.ietf.org/internet-drafts/draft-ietf-diffserv-rsvp-02.txt`

Title: "Interoperation of RSVP/Int-Serv and Diff-Serv Networks."

Abstract:

Differentiated Services (diff-serv) and *RSVP/Integrated Services* (RSVP/int-serv) provide complementary approaches to the problem of providing QoS for Internet end systems. These approaches must be able to coexist and effectively interoperate. This document outlines one important model for such interoperation, in which diff-serv is used by transit networks in the core of the Internet while hosts and edge networks use RSVP/int-serv. It also contains a brief discussion of some alternative models for inter-operation.

20. `http://search.ietf.org/internet-drafts/draft-guerin-aggreg-rsvp-00.txt`

Title: "Aggregating RSVP-Based QoS Requests."

Abstract:

This document describes issues and approaches related to aggregation of QoS requests, when RSVP [BZB+97] is the protocol used to convey such requests. Aggregation is an important component to provide scalable QoS solutions, especially in the core of the backbone where the sheer number of flows mandates some form of aggregation. However, aggregation needs to be provided without impacting the ability to provide end-to-end QoS guarantees to individual flows. In this document, we review some of the main goals of aggregation and describe possible solutions, that do not preclude support for end-to-end QoS guarantees. Those solutions are targeted at unicast flows as we expect them to represent a large fraction of the flows requesting reservation, and hence to be the main contributors to potential scalability problems with RSVP.

21. `http://search.ietf.org/internet-drafts/draft-moore-qualsvc-00.txt`

Title: "Specification of the Qualitative Service Type."

Abstract:

This draft describes the use of RSVP [RFC2205] with applications that do not have resource requirements that may not be readily quantifiable (qualitative applications). We introduce the \146qualitative\106 service-type. This service-type can be used in conjunction with RSVP signaling to manage the allocation of network resources to traffic originating from qualitative applications. This mode of RSVP usage is particularly applicable to networks that combine differentiated service (diff-serv) QoS mechanisms with RSVP signaling [intdiff].

22. `http://search.ietf.org/internet-drafts/draft-loa-mpls-cap-set-00.txt`

Title: "MPLS Capability Set."

Abstract:

Several protocols might be used for Label Distribution in an MPLS network, e.g. Label Distribution Protocol (LDP), including the part of LDP described in Constraint-Based LSP Setup using LDP, the BGP-4 and RSVP.

23. http://search.ietf.org/internet-drafts/draft-zhang-qos-ospf-01.txt

Title: "Quality of Service Extensions to OSPF or Quality Of Service Path First Routing (QOSPF)."

Abstract:

This document describes a series of extensions for OSPF[1] and MOSPF[2] that can be used to provide *Quality of Service* (QoS) routing in conjunction with a resource reservation protocol such as RSVP[4] or other mechanisms that can notify routing of the QoS needs of a data flow. Advertisements indicating the resources available and the resources used are advertised to the OSPF routing domain and paths are computed based on topology information, link resource information, and the resource requirements of a particular data flow.

24. http://search.ietf.org/internet-drafts/draft-ietf-rsvp-tunnel-02.txt

Title: "RSVP Operation Over IP Tunnels."

Abstract:

This document describes an approach for providing RSVP protocol services over IP tunnels. We briefly describe the problem, the characteristics of possible solutions, and the design goals of our approach. We then pre-sent the details of an implementation which meets our design goals.

25. http://search.ietf.org/internet-drafts/draft-bernet-intdiff-00.txt

Title: "A Framework for End-to-End QoS Combining RSVP/Intserv and Differentiated Services."

Abstract:

In the past several years, work on QoS enabled networks led to the development of the *Integrated Services* (Intserv) architecture [12] and the RSVP signaling protocol [1]. RSVP addresses the needs of applications that require QoS, promising per-flow service. As the RSVP/Intserv (from here on abbreviated to intserv) work has proceeded, we have recognized barriers to the deployment of intserv. The reliance of intserv on per-flow state and per-flow processing is an impediment to its deployment in the Internet at large, and in particular in large carrier networks. Additionally, RSVP signaling is supposed to originate from hosts, which as of yet are not RSVP enabled in large numbers.

26. http://search.ietf.org/internet-drafts/draft-katsube-csr-arch-00.txt

Title: "Cell Switch Router—Architecture and Protocol Overview"

Abstract:

This memorandum describes an internetworking architecture of *Cell Switch Router* (CSR) and related control protocol overview. Cell Switch Router is an ATM-based label switching router that can provide ATM cut-through paths for packet flows with various levels of granularity while retaining current router-based internetworking architecture. The proposed architecture is able to provide the cut-through path in response to the creation of IP forwarding entry (topology-driven), the arrival of data packets (traffic-driven), and the reception of control packets such as RSVP (request-driven). One important feature that is provided by the proposed architecture is interoperability with the emerging ATM network platform, specified by the ATM Forum and/or ITU-T, which provides PVC (Permanent Virtual Channel), VP (Virtual Path), or SVC (Switched Virtual Channel) services.

27. http://search.ietf.org/internet-drafts/draft-calhoun-diameter-res-mgmt-03.txt

Title: "DIAMETER Resource Management Extensions."

Abstract:

DIAMETER is a policy protocol used between a client and a server for authentication, authorization and accounting of various services. Examples of such services are for dial-up users (ROAMOPS), RSVP Admission Policies (RAP), FAX Over IP (FAXIP), Voice over IP (IP Tel), Integrated services, etc.

28. http://search.ietf.org/internet-drafts/draft-talwar-rsvp-kr-01.txt

Title: "RSVP Killer Reservations."

Abstract:

This document describes the Killer Reservation Problem encountered when merging RSVP reservation requests. These requests get merged as they travel up the multicast distribution tree, losing information about individual requests. A request, which would have succeeded on its own, may suffer denial of service when the "merged request" fails admission control. This is the problem for which we present different solutions.

29. http://search.ietf.org/internet-drafts/draft-putzolu-heuristic-00.txt

Title: "Heuristics for Utilizing ISSL Mechanisms for A/V Streams Over Low Bandwidth Links in the Absence of Announcement Protocols."

Abstract:

The ISSLOW subgroup of the ISSL working group has defined a set of mechanisms for providing integrated services over low bandwidth links [1]. These mechanisms rely on an announcement protocol (typically RSVP [2]) to determine which streams require other than best-effort service and to determine what level and type of service to provide for such streams. It is anticipated that at least some of the mechanisms defined by the ISSLOW subgroup, specifically Compressed RTP [3] (CRTP) [4] and Multi-Channel Multi-Link PPP (MCML) [5], will be available well before RSVP has been widely deployed.

30. http://search.ietf.org/internet-drafts/draft-wu-mpls-diff-ext-01.txt

Title: "MPLS Support of Differentiated Services by ATM LSRs and Frame Relay LSRs."

Abstract:

This document proposes updates to the current MPLS LDP and MPLS RSVP messages for LSP establishment in order to support *Differentiated Services* (Diff-Serv) over ATM LSRs and Frame Relay LSRs.

31. http://search.ietf.org/internet-drafts/draft-calhoun-diameter-qos-00.txt

Title: "DIAMETER QOS Extension."

Abstract:

This document describes a simple client/server model for supporting QOS policies. A router that supports RSVP or one of the proposed differentiated service schemes will require a policy database and a means to access it. This document describes the extensions to a protocol based originally on RADIUS [1] called

DIAMETER[2]. This document does not describe the policy database or policy enforcement.

32. `http://search.ietf.org/internet-drafts/draft-ferguson-delay-drop-02.txt`

Title: "Simple Differential Services: IP TOS and Precedence, Delay Indication, and Drop Preference."

Abstract:

Recent opinions and sentiments expressed in the *Internet Service Provider* (ISP) community, as well as the Internet community at-large, have voiced concern over the applicability and scalability of RSVP and the Integrated Service model in the global Internet infrastructure. Convincing arguments have been made for a differential services model which offers packet delivery services better than traditional best effort, especially in the face of congestion, yet not as resource intensive as RSVP. As a result, the *differentiated Service* (diffserv) working group in the IETF has been examining methods to provide simpler, less resource intensive methods of offering differentiated services. This draft provides a practical method to use bit values expressed in the IP *Type or Service* (TOS) and IP precedence subfields of the TOS byte in the IP packet header for delay indication and packet drop preference, respectively.

33. `http://search.ietf.org/internet-drafts/draft-ietf-issll-is802-framework-05.txt`

Title: "A Framework for Providing Integrated Services Over Shared and Switched IEEE 802 LAN Technologies."

Abstract:

This memo describes a framework for supporting IETF Integrated Services on shared and switched LAN infrastructure. It includes background material on the capabilities of IEEE 802 like networks with regard to parameters that affect Integrated Services such as access latency, delay variation and queuing support in LAN switches. It discusses aspects of IETF's Integrated Services model that cannot easily be accommodated in different LAN environments. It outlines a functional model for supporting the *Resource Reservation Protocol* (RSVP) in such LAN environments. Details of extensions to RSVP for use over LANs are described in an accompanying memo [14]. Mappings of the various Integrated Services onto IEEE 802 LANs are described in another memo [13].

34. http://search.ietf.org/internet-drafts/draft-bernet-appid-00.txt

Title: "Application and Sub Application Identity Policy Element for Use with RSVP."

Abstract:

RSVP [RFC 2205] signaling messages typically include policy data objects, which in turn contain policy elements. Policy elements may describe user and/or application information, which may be used by RSVP aware network elements to apply appropriate policy decisions to a traffic flow. This informational draft details the usage of policy elements that provide application information.

35. http://search.ietf.org/internet-drafts/draft-baker-rsvp-aggregation-00.txt

Title: "Aggregation of RSVP for IP4 and IP6 Reservations."

Abstract:

A key problem in the design of RSVP version 1 is, as noted in its applicability statement, that it lacks facilities for aggregation of individual reserved sessions into a common class. The use of such aggregation is recommended in the paper by Clark, Shenker, and Zhang in SIGCOMM '92, and required for scalability.

36. http://search.ietf.org/internet-drafts/draft-lindell-rsvp-scrapi-02.txt

Title: "SCRAPI—A Simple 'Bare Bones' API for RSVP."

Abstract:

This document describes SCRAPI, a simple "bare bones" API for RSVP. The goal of this API is to produce an interface which simplifies the augmentation of applications with RSVP support.

37. http://search.ietf.org/internet-drafts/draft-ietf-mpls-rsvp-00.txt

Title: "Use of Label Switching With RSVP."

Abstract:

Multiprotocol Label Switching (MPLS) enables labels to be bound to various granularities of forwarding information, including application flows. In this document we present a specification for allocating and binding labels to RSVP flows, and to distributing the appropriate binding information using RSVP messages.

38. `http://search.ietf.org/internet-drafts/draft-swallow-mpls-rsvp-trafeng-00.txt`

Title: "Extensions to RSVP for Traffic Engineering."

Abstract:

This document describes the use of RSVP, including all the necessary extensions, to support traffic engineering with MPLS as specified in [6].

39. `http://search.ietf.org/internet-drafts/draft-ietf-rap-rsvp-identity-03.txt`

Title: "Identity Representation for RSVP."

Abstract:

This document describes the representation of identity information in POLICY_DATA object [POL-EXT] for supporting policy based admission control in RSVP. The goal of identity representation is to enable a process on a system to securely identify the owner and the application of the communicating process (e.g. user id) and convey this information in RSVP messages (PATH or RESV) in a secure manner. We describe the encoding of identities as RSVP policy element. We describe the processing rules to generate identity policy elements for multicast merged flows. Subsequently, we describe representations of user identities for Kerberos and Public Key based user authentication mechanisms. In summary we describe the use of this identity information in an operational setting.

40. `http://search.ietf.org/internet-drafts/draft-davie-mpls-explicit-routes-00.txt`

Title: "Explicit Route Support in MPLS."

Abstract:

We define an "explicit route" as a route which is explicitly specified as a sequence of hops rather than being determined solely by conventional routing algorithms on a hop by hop basis. Using the explicit route object proposed for use in RSVP [1] and the ability to bind MPLS labels to RSVP flows [2] we describe how explicit routes may be set up in an MPLS environment. The resulting label switched paths may have associated resource reservations, or may be purely best effort.

41. http://search.ietf.org/internet-drafts/draft-salgarelli-issll-
mis-00.txt

Title: "Supporting IP Multicast Integrated Services in ATM Networks."

Abstract:

This memo presents an integrated, server-based mechanism for the efficient support of the *IP Integrated Services* (IIS) model in ATM networks, namely the *Multicast Integration Server* (MIS) architecture. Instead of viewing IP-ATM multicast address resolution and QoS support separately, the approach in this memo is to consider such issues in an integrated manner. In particular, the MIS architecture defines how a layer-3 setup protocol as RSVP can be mapped to and integrated with a layer-2 multicast address resolution protocol as EARTH—EAsy Multicast Routing THrough ATM clouds. With the use of EARTH, several ATM point-to-multipoint connections with different QoS parameters can be associated to a single IP Multicast address. An *RSVP server* (RSVP-S) within the MIS is used to distribute RSVP messages inside the ATM cloud and to set the corresponding QoS state in the address resolution table of EARTH (setup protocol mapping). In addition, this memo defines a quantized heterogeneity model which supports, together with the MIS, advanced IIS features as QoS heterogeneity and dynamic QoS changes in IP-ATM networks.

Cisco Systems Application Notes

http://www.cisco.com/warp/customer/732/multicast/literature.shtml
Protocol Independent Multicast (PIM)
IP Multicast Load Splitting Across Equal Cost Paths

Protocol Independent Multicast (PIM)
Why Auto-RP and How to Deploy It Painlessly

Protocol Independent Multicast (PIM)
IP Multicast Uses ATM Multipoint VCs

Protocol Independent Multicast (PIM)
A Sample Configuration for Multicasting over ISDN

Other Multicast Topics
Definition of RPF

Other Multicast Topics
Multicasting Over GRE Tunnels

Other Multicast Topics
Helper-Map for Broadcast to Multicast Conversion and Vice Versa

Cisco Systems Multicast Training

Fundamentals of IP Multicasting
`ftp://ftp-end.cisco.com/ipmulticast/training/Module1.pdf`

Multicasting at layer 2
`ftp://ftp-end.cisco.com/ipmulticast/training/Module2.pdf`

PIM Dense Mode
`ftp://ftp-end.cisco.com/ipmulticast/training/Module3.pdf`

Basic Multicast Debugging
`ftp://ftp-end.cisco.com/ipmulticast/training/Module4.pdf`

PIM Sparse Mode
`ftp://ftp-end.cisco.com/ipmulticast/training/Module5.pdf`

DVMRP
`ftp://ftp-end.cisco.com/ipmulticast/training/Module6.pdf`

Interconnecting PIM and DVMRP Multicast Networks
`ftp://ftp-eng.cisco.com/ipmulticast/training/Module7.pdf`

Advanced Multicast Topics
`ftp://ftp-eng.cisco.com/ipmulticast/training/Module8.pdf`

CGMP
`ftp://ftp-eng.cisco.com/ipmulticast/training/Module9.pdf`

Starburst Communications
`http://www.starburst.com/patches/mcastres.htm#Routing`

INDEX

A

address family assignment
PIM-DM, 141, **144**
PIM-SM, 166, **168**
address resolution, IP to Ethernet address
resolution, 5—7, **5, 6**
address resolution protocol (ARP), **6**
addressing, 2, 3
content addressable memory (CAM)
CGMP, 72—73, 78—79
Ethernet multicast addressing, 40—42, **41**
Ethernet, 5—7
token ring multicast addressing, 43—44
administrative distance
DVMRP, 118
PIM-DVMRP networks, 198—199
advertisement of routes
DVMRP, 101, 118
PIM-DVMRP networks, 204, 205
AppleTalk, 3, 192
Ask-Neighbors packet tracing, DVMRP,
112—114, **113**
Assert message
PIM-DM, 135—138, **136, 137, 138**, 141, **143**
PIM-SM, 159—163, **161, 162**, 166, **169**
assignment of IP addresses, 18—19
asynchronous serial links, 2
asynchronous transfer mode (ATM), 2,
221—222
autonomous systems (AS), RIP, 88, **88**
Auto-RP, PIM-SM, 152, 176—177, 179,
184—186, **186**

auto-summarization
DVMRP, 119—120
PIM-DVMRP networks, 205

B

bandwidth
rate limiting, IP multicast, 214—215
RSVP, 224
blocks of IP addresses, 18
Bootstrap message, PIM-SM, 170—174
bootstrap router (BSR), PIM-SM, 169—174,
170, 174, 177—179, 187—188, **189**
border gateway protocol (BGP), DVMRP, 84
border router, PIM-DVMRP networks,
202, **202**
boundaries, multicast, 208—210, **209, 210**
broadcast, 7, **7,** 9
broadcast/multicast conversion,
211—212, **211**
PIM-DM, 122
broadcast/multicast conversion,
211—212, **211**

C

Cisco Group Management Protocol
(CGMP), 10, 67—81, 84
command summary, 80
content addressable memory (CAM),
72—73, 78—79

357

W

X

ABOUT THE AUTHOR

William R. Parkhurst Ph.D., CCIE #2969, is a Senior Network Architect with Sprint-Paranet. He is a member of the network design team for Sprint's World Headquarters Campus, which will contain the largest ATM-to-the-desktop network in existence. While a Professor at Wichita State University, he developed and led the first Cisco CCIE Preparation Laboratory.